GORBACHEV'S FAILURE IN LITHUANIA

Gorbachev's Failure in Lithuania

ALFRED ERICH SENN

St. Martin's Press
New York

ISBN 0-312-12457-0

Library of Congress Cataloging-in-Publication Data

Senn, Alfred Erich.
    Gorbachev's failure in Lithuania / Alfred Erich Senn.
        p. cm.
    Includes bibliographical references and index.
    ISBN 0-312-12457-0
    1. Lithuania—Relations—Soviet Union. 2. Soviet Union-
-Relations—Lithuania. 3. Soviet Union—Politics and
government—1985-1991. 4. Soviet Union—Relations—United States.
5. United States—Relations—Soviet Union. 6. Lithuania-
-History—1945-1991. I. Title
DK505.69.S65S46 1995
947'.50854—dc20   94-35578
                                                          CIP

First Edition: June 1995
10 9 8 7 6 5 4 3 2 1

CONTENTS

*To Marie and Kaye Andrus, and to the memory of our parents,
Alfred and Mary Senn and Vincas and Ludviga Alksninis*

INTRODUCTION:
UNCHARTED PATHS

Mikhail Sergeevich Gorbachev steered the Soviet Union (the USSR) onto new and uncharted paths of reform. These paths eventually led off the end of the earth, and the state disintegrated beneath him. What should Gorbachev have expected when he opened his Pandora's box of reform initiatives? Was the Soviet order unreformable? a doomed *ancien regime?* or was Gorbachev a great reformer who in fact laid the foundation for a new order we have yet to appreciate—a Moses, so to speak, to be succeeded eventually by a Joshua?

Analysts will long debate Gorbachev's role in the collapse of the Soviet order, but they will probably agree that Lithuania occupied an important place among his problems and especially his failures. Some analysts, to be sure, might prefer to consider how the Soviet Union had survived for so long: "The question that the surge of nationalist activity properly poses is not why it is happening at all, but why it did not happen until now."[1] Nevertheless, all must agree that Gorbachev could not crack his Lithuanian nut.

Other republics, other actors, may claim to have delivered the coup de grâce, but as Hedrick Smith has put it, "The most insistent and menacing challenge to the unity and integrity of the Soviet state came...from tiny Lithuania." According to Egor Ligachev, a conservative Soviet politician, the situation in Lithuania went from critical, to threatening, to catastrophic and eventually became "the catalyst for the centrifugal, destructive processes that brought into question the existence of the USSR." Valery Legostaev, an aide to Ligachev, complained that in 1988 the Baltic, especially Riga and Vilnius, became "an incubator" for "anti-Communism and nationalism in the entire country."[2]

This study examines the interplay between Vilnius and Moscow in the decisive period of Gorbachev's time in power, from 1988 to the August coup in Moscow in 1991. After the collapse of the Soviet Union, Gorbachev at first could not speak about Lithuania without using exclamation marks: "Oh how many meetings we had with the Balts!" he told *Nezavisimaia gazeta* in December 1991. In a television interview with Larry King on November 6, 1993, on the other hand, he omitted Vilnius in answering a question as to whether he had ever used his "military in a violent manner." In January 1993, in an interview published in the German *Der Spiegel*, he had declared that his conscience was clear regarding Lithuania. On the King show, he expressed the hope that history, which he called "a capricious lady," would "judge me fairly," but he would probably prefer that Lithuania not be the test case.

Gorbachev's policies clashed with the newly emerging national consciousness in Lithuania on at least two levels: center against province, and center against a rebelling nationality. Gorbachev declared that he wanted to dismantle the centralized Soviet administrative system, but as he tried to build a new political structure, he looked askance at local power centers and especially those identifiable with a minority nationality. What could he have expected in the multi-national Soviet state? Therein lay the root of his ultimate failure: When his reforms stimulated change in Lithuania, he objected and joined the forces in the republic opposed to his reforms. The events in Lithuania then led directly to the August coup in Moscow.

Gorbachev's Lithuanian debacle also posed problems for American foreign policy. President George Bush had established what he considered a special personal relationship with Gorbachev. He counted on Gorbachev to lead the Soviet state into a new international order, and the Lithuanian problem became what he called a "thorn in the side" of Soviet-American relations. In the words of one commentator, American "officials had been on an exhilarating ride.... Then, with Lithuania, they hit a wall."[3] The "Lithuanian question" became a touchstone of the Bush Administration's pro-Gorbachev policies, and to a great extent Gorbachev's failure in Lithuania also meant the failure of the Bush administration's policies toward the Soviet Union.

THE SORCERER'S APPRENTICE

After Mikhail Gorbachev came to power in the Soviet Union in 1985, he invoked and released forces that soon escaped his control. He understood the old order and how to work within it, but he attacked and began to change it. While alienating entrenched interests, he failed to establish his authority over the new forces. The resulting turmoil led to the collapse of the Soviet system.

The Soviet system had rested on a set of seemingly strong pillars: the Communist Party of the Soviet Union (CPSU), which maintained a monopoly on the society's decision-making powers; a bureaucracy that controlled the economic resources and production of the society; a censorship that prevented people from complaining too much and demanded their assurances that everything was fine; and repressive forces, including the KGB (Committee for State Security, the political police), that enforced the will of the CPSU.

In this system ultimate power lay outside the constitutional order, in the hands of the Communist Party and specifically in its leadership. Article 6 of the Soviet constitution recognized the subordinate status of government by giving the party special status as the *fons et origo* of authority in the society;[1] at every level, in every institution or enterprise, a party cell was supposed to monitor the organization's work and report back to higher authorities. Ultimate authority in the Soviet system belonged to the party leadership: the Central Committee, or CC, named by a party congress; the Politburo, the political bureau, chosen by the Central Committee; and the general secretary, the post Gorbachev assumed when he took power in 1985.

By the early 1980s, under the leadership of party secretary Leonid Brezhnev, this system had lost the dynamism of which it had once boasted. In contrast to the impressive, albeit exaggerated, growth figures of earlier generations, it had fallen into a condition of "stagnation"; it had become a system of control rather than of progress and growth. It still maintained a powerful military and bestowed favors on its privileged leadership, but its "stagnation" limited the Soviet Union's potential for keeping up with the dynamic changes taking place in the western world of the 1980s.

At first Gorbachev, like his predecessors, tried cosmetic measures, but then he launched fundamental reforms. He changed the structure of the party administration; he challenged the bureaucracy's management record; he loosened censorship to encourage substantive criticism of both party and bureaucracy; he blunted the bite of the KGB; and he toyed with the thought of moving the center of power from the party to the government. To promote his program of stimulating new economic growth and technological development, he offered a series of slogans: "perestroika" (reform or restructuring), together with its corollaries of "glasnost" (openness), "democratization," and the "state ruled by law."

The system, however, resisted change—as his advisor Aleksandr Iakovlev later explained, "It was clear from the very outset that without a profound economic reform the country had no future. However, in practice, the potential of organized resistance by the economic and state apparatus was not realistically taken into account."[5] As Gorbachev looked for support against the entrenched interests he wanted to uproot, nationality became a powerful rallying point and organizing weapon for local change.

The Soviet Union was a multinational state made up of fifteen "union republics" and a number of lesser national administrative units; Russians constituted only about half its population. Soviet spokespersons trumpeted that the Soviet order had definitively resolved the nationalities question, that the nationalities lived together in an internationalist spirit that should yet show the way to the rest of the world. Weighed down by party, bureaucracy, censorship, and the repressive forces of the state, the nationalities, at least before 1986, seemed quiescent under Moscow's forceful controls, and many observers, both Russian and foreign, believed that the nationalities question no longer had any significance.

The nationalities of the Soviet Union, however, unexpectedly responded to Gorbachev's calls. New leaders arose to translate the empty slogans of self-rule and "sovereignty" into separatist tendencies of varying degrees of intensity. Although the conservatives in the Soviet regime had always feared that nationalist passions lay only shallowly buried under their propaganda blanket, the explosions of national feeling took almost everyone by surprise.

Western observers watched Gorbachev's activity with fascination. They understood his policies in different ways, but they recognized the risks that he was taking. George Kennan spoke of "a movement from the party monopoly of power to an elected governmental apparatus," and Marshall Shulman discerned "the crumbling of the Establishment—that is to say, the

Party." A year later Peter Reddaway noted "the emergence of various forms of anti-Communism." Regarding the Soviet system's economic development, what Kennan called "the movement from a command economy...to an economy based on market principles," Shulman described as "the collapse of the economy," while Reddaway spoke of "the onset in 1988 of economic chaos."

Looking at the nationalities question, westerners saw disintegration. Kennan noted "the movement from the highly centralized nature of the Soviet Empire...to something else that none of us can foresee or describe," and he warned of the danger "that some of these republics might behave as if they were entirely liberated." Shulman emphasized "the crumbling of the Soviet empire and the critical weakening of the Soviet Union as a centralized and unitary state," and Reddaway wrote of the "transformation of the hitherto suppressed nationalism of several republics into revolutionary, anti-imperial struggles for self-determination."

There were, to be sure, some observers who saw Gorbachev as controlling the process. Jerry Hough, for example, wrote in the fall of 1990, "In fact, the real story of the past year has been the further consolidation of Gorbachev's position, major progress toward radical economic reform, and, recently, early signs that the most volatile national hot spots are settling down." Nevertheless, most western observers tended to see Gorbachev as not just loosening the traditional reins of power in the Soviet system but also losing control of them.[6]

Ultimately Gorbachev's fatal flaw lay in his unwillingness to abandon the control apparatus that he himself had weakened. He tried to keep power in his own hands, and he insisted that he alone held the key to the future at a time when he lacked the determination to enforce his will in any consistent way against a cacophonous chorus of protestors.

Inherent in Gorbachev's unwillingness to abandon his control apparatus was his failure to countenance a "loyal opposition," which many western commentators saw as essential for the development of a "liberal democracy."[7] Gorbachev liked to place himself "in the middle," with someone more radical on one side of him and someone more conservative on the other, and when it came to actually dealing with opposing views, he played one off against the other. When facing his conservative opposition, he tended to try to change the institutional battlefield; when facing his radical opposition—the Lithuanians included—he tended to assert his authority or, *in extremis*, to move back closer to the conservatives. In any case, as time went by, he appeared more and more uncertain and inconsistent, while also more authoritarian, and he contributed little if anything to the development of institutions that might have helped him to control the situation.

THE MOUSE THAT ROARED

Lithuanians constituted only about 1 percent of the population of the Soviet Union, and therefore the questions must immediately arise of why and how Lithuania came to play its leading role in the collapse of the Soviet system. This study does not address why it was the Lithuanians and not others—doing so requires a comparative study that would examine the weaknesses and strengths of disruptive forces in all parts of the Soviet Union. Instead, this study focuses on the narrower how and why the Lithuanians acted as they did—and, of course, how and why Gorbachev could not control them.

When the era of Gorbachev's reforms began, the Lithuanians were barely visible on the horizon. Indeed, a few years earlier one western observer had predicted that the three Baltic republics were "on the road, not to assimilation, but to physical extinction." They had no role in the early twists and turns of perestroika. A KGB report dated March 21, 1988, pictured more ferment in Latvia or Ukraine than in Lithuania.[8] Even in the winter and spring 1988, with national conflict raging in the Caucasus and new currents arising in Estonia, Lithuania remained quiet. By the fall of 1988, however, the Lithuanians had surged to the foreground.

The general theories offered by western writers on the development of national revolt in the Soviet Union appear too vague to be useful. For one, western commentators tended, and still tend, to treat the three Baltic republics as a unit, and they do not look into the peculiarities of each. The Lithuanians, for example, constituted a greater percentage of their republic's population—in 1989, 79.6 percent—than the Latvians or the Estonians did in theirs. In turn, Russians—9.4 percent—represented a far lower percentage of the population in Lithuania than in Latvia or Estonia. These simple statistical considerations also meant that a greater percentage of the effective leadership in Lithuania would come from the titular nationality than would be the case in Latvia or Estonia.

Western analyses, moreover, contradict each other. Since the Lithuanians, like the Latvians and Estonians, enjoyed a higher standard of living than people in most other parts of the Soviet Union, for example, perhaps they should not have revolted; but then again, perhaps that is why they did. Alexander Motyl has pointed to cultural homogeneity and nationalist ideals in the Baltic, but according to his self-confessed "questionable mathematics," the Lithuanians had a lower ratio of "nationalist dissent" than the Crimean Tatars, the Estonians, and the Latvians. Graham Smith has noted that the Lithuanians had the requisite "organization with mass mobilization potential"—they created it in the summer of 1988—that could lead an "autonomous ethnoregional movement," but so did others. Arguments that national movements were seeking goods and power explain little; Donald Horowitz has suggested that "group calculations of costs and benefits may make the situation more murky than it may seem."[9]

Many commentators have emphasized the fact that of the peoples in the Soviet Union, only the Estonians, Latvians, and Lithuanians still had living memory of independence. John Armstrong distinguished them as "state nations." Situated as the "Baltic tier of the Middle Soviet Empire," they therefore constituted a distinctive aspect of the Soviet nationalities question,[10] but why should the Lithuanians have acted any differently from the Latvians and Estonians, starting slowly and then forging ahead of the other two?

Insofar as theories treat the Lithuanians and other nationalities as monolithic units, they will not explain the dynamics that drove the Lithuanian activists in 1988 and after. Lithuanian politics in fact evolved in kaleidoscopic fashion. Smith and Motyl argued that under Brezhnev, considerable power and authority devolved to the local party hierarchy in the republics. As Motyl put it, "What do republic elites do when they are allotted the space, authority, and resources to implement decentralization? Naturally, in such optimal circumstances, they pursue their own interests, even to the detriment of all-Union ones." Smith spoke of the "benign neglect of republic political and administrative life." Liah Greenfeld has spoken of "vanity" or a "desire for status" as a powerful force in "nationalism."[11] But the party leaders in Lithuania were not the leaders of the new national movement: Destabilized by the changes in Moscow, they lost their bearings, and a new political spectrum quickly formed, including elements previously excluded from considerations of power. New political leadership emerged, and political competition drove the national movement onto distinctive paths.

The historical consciousness of the Lithuanians undoubtedly played a major role in their behavior. Incorporated into the Soviet Union in 1940 and subjected to wholesale deportations both before and after World War II, the Lithuanians had maintained an underlying cynicism toward the Soviet system even as they had seemed to be contributing to it. They recited the official mantras, they intoned the obligatory dithyrambs, they proclaimed their loyalty, and they even joined the Communist Party. Yet under the surface there remained an animus toward the system, fed by memories that were perhaps weakened by time but nevertheless still very much alive in the late 1980s.

Of particular note were the Stalinist deportations of the 1940s and early 1950s. Beginning during the "first occupation" of 1940–1941, Stalin's agents attempted to destroy the intellectual forces of Lithuania by deporting political and intellectual leaders to Siberia. When Soviet troops returned at the end of World War II, they encountered armed resistance, and they responded with more deportations. In all, the Soviet authorities deported some 200,000 persons; even after the return of most of the survivors in the late 1950s and 1960s, the action left deep, smoldering resentments in Lithuanian society.

In addition, the Lithuanians were the major Catholic group in the Soviet Union. Outside of Lithuania there were only a handful of Catholic churches in the USSR, but in Lithuania over 600 still functioned in the 1980s. As an institution that could function legally in the officially atheistic Soviet Union, the Catholic Church worked under the watchful eye of the authorities, but it constituted a legal rallying point for those who refused to conform. Many Lithuanians could not separate their national consciousness from their religious traditions.

The Lithuanians' contacts with their kin who had emigrated to the West helped keep alive the traditions and memories of the nation. In the 1960s, when the Soviet authorities in Lithuania sought contacts with the émigrés, conservative émigré leaders responded negatively, fearing that the siren songs of the homeland would seduce the naive and gullible abroad. Although the official Soviet posturing could not admit it, these contacts involved an equal potential for seducing the people of Lithuania. Communicating with émigrés contributed to keeping alive—and idealizing—the memories of the past, of the years of independence. Given the opportunity, these memories exploded into public view with a vehemence that probably surprised even the people who had nurtured them.[12]

In what might be called a "primordial explosion," the Lithuanians in 1988 gave voice to their memories and their national consciousness. Almost immediately, however, they began to argue among themselves. Thoughts of reform within the larger Soviet system clashed with smoldering resentments about the past. An infinitely graduated political spectrum developed between the two extremes of reform and secession (or, in a sense, revolution)—there were hardly enough supporters of the old order to merit a place in the spectrum. Conflict with Moscow, Gorbachev's decisions to resort to threats, violence, and force drove the inner dynamic of the Lithuanian national consciousness toward secession.

Although Gorbachev and Aleksandr Iakovlev repeatedly denied the charges of their critics that perestroika had brought national strife to the Soviet Union, perestroika in fact opened the way for the development of local national movements such as that in Lithuania. Thoughts of political and economic decentralization fused with ethnic territorial identity to produce explosive "ethnoregional" movements. Graham Smith wrote, "Thus the most remarkable feature of the new Soviet politics was the speed by which ethnoregional movements emerged to become a central focus of union republic political life."[13] The national movement that swept Lithuania grew from seeds watered by perestroika.

Both Iakovlev and Gorbachev eventually admitted that the explosion of the nationalities question had surprised them: "As a matter of self-criticism," Iakovlev told Hedrick Smith in 1990, "one has to admit that we underestimated the forces of nationalism and separatism that were hidden deep within our system."[14] In repeated interviews after his fall from power, Gorbachev admitted that he had not expected such trouble with the nationalities. At the same time, he seemed incapable of understanding to what degree he had stimulated the actions of the Lithuanians.

Some persons with whom I have discussed this book, to be sure, have disputed its title: Gorbachev meant well, Lithuania is now independent, and *va*, there it is, you cannot speak of failure. One participant in the CPSU Central Committee plenum in February 1990 argued that if Gorbachev had then come out in support of the Lithuanians, the August Putsch of 1991 would have come much earlier. The key to the emergence of the Lithuanian state, he insisted, lay in Gorbachev's unwillingness to use force in Lithuania. Many Americans, moreover, still picture Gorbachev as a "Johnny Gorbelseed,"—planting the seeds of democracy and nurturing the tender shoots—while some Russians might argue that Gorbachev was too good to the Lithuanians.

Whatever his intentions, Gorbachev's practice was a failure, confirming the view of those critics who "knew that he was more tactician than strategist."[15] As a tactic, he liked to assure the Lithuanians of his sympathy, but his outbursts at that February plenum made clear his determination to keep the Soviet Union together. For whatever reason, he entrusted his Lithuanian policy to the conservatives, who were then the architects of the August Putsch. He encouraged ethnic conflict within Lithuania. The blockade, however, did not work, and the "whiff of grapeshot" in January 1991 did not work—one indeed could argue that the January action would have failed even if it had "succeeded." By then "perestroika" resembled the new clothes of Hans Christian Andersen's king. The Lithuanians owed much to the Gorbachev of 1985–1988 for their own success in establishing an independent state, but they owe many of their present problems to the Gorbachev of 1988–1991.

THE MONKEY'S PAW

At first glance the United States government might have welcomed the Lithuanians' initiative. For almost fifty years it had refused to recognize the incorporation of Lithuania into the Soviet Union.[16] When, however, Lithuanians leaders looked to Washington for support against "the evil empire," no help was forthcoming; the U.S. government assigned Lithuania a low priority in its list of Soviet problems.

In "The Monkey's Paw," W. W. Jacobs' classic short story about the costs of wish fulfillment, an English couple ask a talisman for money, which they receive at the cost of their son's death; they then wish for his return; but when someone or something began pounding at their door, they use their third wish to avoid confronting his body. The U.S. government at first thought that all its wishes were coming true as it watched Gorbachev, but then it seemed to regret not having a wish in reserve to exorcise the spirits that came pounding at the door.

Over the years American policy toward the Baltic had in fact not been so consistent as it presented itself. During World War II, while allied with the Soviet Union against Nazi Germany, U.S. State Department officials had chided the Lithuanians for their stern anti-Communist attitudes.[17] After World War II, on the other hand, the U.S. government welcomed

Lithuanian resistance to Soviet rule, and a National Intelligence Estimate of 1958 suggested:

> A marked increase in East-West tensions...would probably encourage more determined attempts at active resistance.... A decrease of East-West tensions would be likely to discourage any sort of active resistance and to increase fatalistic acquiescence to Soviet rule. If accompanied by a liberalization of security precautions and thought control, it might, however, facilitate the spread and development of nationalist sentiment.[18]

It was not the job of such an "estimate" to define what the U.S. government should do in the latter case, but, given the failure of its experts to understand the national question in the USSR, the American government entered the new world of the late 1980s totally unprepared for the prospect of growing nationalist sentiment in the Soviet Union as a response to liberalization in Moscow.

The official policy of the United States had asserted that despite the Soviet occupation, a Lithuanian state—like the Latvian and Estonian states—continued to exist even though it had no recognized government. In the absence of such a government, the United States continued to deal with the duly appointed representatives of that state, the old diplomatic service. As time and age took their toll among the diplomatic corps, the *doyen* of the émigé Lithuanian diplomatic corps, its oldest member in terms of service, could appoint replacements. In the late 1980s, the accredited Lithuanian diplomat in Washington, Stasys Lozoraitis, had the highly provisional title of chargé d'affaires ad interim, representing the Lithuanian Republic of the 1930s, not the government of the Lithuanian Soviet Socialist Republic.

Over the years, the United States had modified its practice in dealing with these diplomats and with the question of Lithuania's "sovereignty." After having encouraged armed resistance to Soviet rule in the late 1940s, the U.S. government long insisted that Lithuania could not be included in any American program dealing with the Soviet Union. Eventually the Americans reduced the restrictions on travel into the Baltic, until by the end of the 1980s the only rule seemed to be that the chief of the American mission in Moscow could not make an official visit to any of the Baltic republics of the Soviet Union.

In the 1980s, on the other hand, the administration of President Ronald Reagan made heavy use of its Baltic card. During its first term in office, the administration recognized June 14, the anniversary of mass deportations in 1941, as a special day of observance of Baltic suffering at the hands of the Soviets. In 1985 Reagan tied support of the Lithuanians to images of freedom in America: "The United States has refused to recognize the forcible incorporation of Lithuania into the Soviet Union...we know that as long as freedom is denied to others, it is not truly secure here."[19] At a conference in Vienna in November 1986, the U.S. representative linked the issue of Baltic independence with the spirit of the Helsinki agreements of 1975.[20] In 1987 Reagan proclaimed, "The United States staunchly defends the right of Lithuania, Latvia and Estonia to exist as independent countries. We will continue to use every opportunity to impress upon the Soviet Union our support for the Baltic nations' right to national independence."[21] In October 1987, the United States raised the issue of Baltic national self-determination in a committee of the United Nations.[22] Each time the Americans used that Baltic card, the Soviets protested.[23]

Lithuanian nationalist émigrés, in turn, praised the administration, but in the 1980s, especially after Gorbachev's visit to the United States in December 1987, the situation changed. The Reagan administration displayed more sympathy for the Soviet leader, and the American public took Gorbachev to their hearts, a phenomenon flippantly called "Gorbomania." The Baltic peoples now became a burden, a problem that policymakers wished they could set aside. The émigrés found themselves swimming against the tide of American public opinion, and not understanding why, they tried shouting more loudly.[24]

In the later 1980s, facing reform in Moscow and turbulence in Lithuania, U.S. government agencies dealt with the Baltic republics in varying ways. The State Department, respecting the policy of "nonrecognition," officially maintained a Baltic desk, independent of its section for Soviet affairs, but it staffed the desk with junior officers. Those junior officers, however, were more ready to accept an idealistic cause than their seniors were, and the Baltic desk could on occasion send tremors through Foggy Bottom.

The Central Intelligence Agency (CIA), on the other hand, buried Lithuania, together with the other smaller republics of the Soviet Union, in SOVA (the Office of Soviet Analysis). In 1984 the agency's chief for Domestic Affairs of the Soviet Union told members of Congress that the minority nationalities of the Soviet Union would not be a factor "in this century."[25] In 1988 the agency had no desk officers following the Baltic who spoke any of the three languages there—Russian was the language for original research. The U.S. government looked at the Baltic through a Russian prism, keeping its focus on Moscow.

The American government welcomed Gorbachev's words of change and his friendly overtures, and it feared that trouble in places like Lithuania could force him to revert to the old patterns of behavior, if it did not in fact bring about his downfall. The State Department kept reaffirming the policy of "nonrecognition," but the White House obviously preferred that the Lithuanians not "rock the boat." For all the lip service paid to Baltic sovereignty, the U.S. government gave its highest priority to maintaining good relations with Gorbachev and the Soviet government.

The Soviet leadership, for its part, built the twists of American policy into its own politics and policies. Gorbachev warned that if he fell, the West would lose its only friend. Given the United States' past encouragement of national feeling in the Baltic republics, conservatives in Moscow argued that western "anti-Soviet organizations" and "foreign centers of ideological diversion" were playing a role in the developments in Lithuania and that therefore Gorbachev was playing into the hands of western anti-Communist crusaders.

Haunted by the possible question of the future "Who lost Gorbachev?" Washington found itself in an awkward position. Having proclaimed its policy of "nonrecognition" of the Soviet incorporation of Lithuania as a "moral" policy, it did not want to admit that foreign policy was in fact driven by political considerations. Therefore it protested its love of the Baltic peoples even as it encouraged Gorbachev. To be sure, Gorbachev limited his actions in Lithuania out of concern about possible American reactions, but when the Lithuanians pounded on the door, Washington refused to answer, fearing that Gorbachev's ghost might also be there.

I had the good fortune to live much of this history while it was happening.[26] In the fall of 1988 I sat in meetings of the Sajudis Initiative Group; in January 1991 I experienced the tension of the "January events." In the summer of 1990 I decided to write a book about the ongoing confrontation between Gorbachev and the Lithuanians, and I began to collect materials and to interview prominent figures in the story. After the collapse of the

Soviet Union, new documentation became available, and I could turn the work into a historical study, giving it a broader perspective than had been possible in the heat of action.

In the course of time I accrued enormous intellectual debts. First of all I would like to express my gratitude to Alfonsas Eidintas, now the Lithuanian ambassador to the United States, who for a full decade has encouraged and helped me in countless ways in my study of contemporary Lithuania. But for him, I would not have been involved in the events of 1988 and after, and I would not have written this book.

Many other people—colleagues, friends, principals in this story—have found materials for me, have criticized the text and have pointed out new roads of inquiry to me. I am especially indebted to Liutas Mockunas, Robert Otto, Anne Jablonski, and David McDonald. The "Senn Scholars," Lithuanians who worked with me at the University of Wisconsin, did their best to educate me: Violeta Motulaite, Vytautas Žalys, Vytautas Radžvilas, Egidijus Aleksandravičius, Rimvydas Valatka, and Raimundas Lopata. Silvija Velavičiene of the Mažvydas Library in Vilnius has provided me with indispensable bibliographical assistance; Edis Bevan has given invaluable aid to all studying the Baltic through his prodigious efforts in moderating the internet discussion group Balt-L. My thanks to these people and to the others who have helped me, including the numerous figures mentioned in these pages who granted me interviews. In the summer of 1992 the Kennan Institute for Contemporary Russian Culture provided me with the opportunity to study my subject in Washington, and I have enjoyed the hospitality of the Summer Research Institute at the University of Illinois several times.

Needless to say, the views and conclusions expressed in this work are my responsibility; I just hope that all those who helped me will feel that their efforts were worthwhile.

I want to dedicate this book to Marie and Kaye Andrus and to the memory of our parents, Alfred and Mary Senn and Vincas and Ludviga Alksninis. The story told here is as much a part of their lives as it is of mine.

AES
Madison, Wisconsin
December 24, 1994

1

INSIDE PERESTROIKA

Mikhail Sergeevich Gorbachev's confrontation with Lithuania followed upon his struggle for power and reform in Moscow in the middle and later 1980s. Some Lithuanians later argued that their revolution would have taken place regardless of what happened in Moscow, but there were few public signs of a new national consciousness in Lithuania until after Gorbachev had begun loosening controls in the Soviet capital. Since the principals of the Moscow drama—Gorbachev, Aleksandr Iakovlev, Egor Ligachev, Vadim Medvedev, and others—also played roles on the smaller Lithuanian stage, it is necessary to look first at the politics within the leadership of the Communist Party of the Soviet Union (CPSU), in order to follow the subsequent events in Lithuania.

Gorbachev inherited a centralized structure that radiated out from the Politburo of the Central Committee (CC) of the CPSU. Although the Soviet constitution made no mention of the Politburo, this agency, which Egor Ligachev called "the highest political organ of the country,"[1] directed the country's affairs. Gorbachev's struggles began here, and when he met with opposition in the central organs of the party, his efforts to find new sources of support in the broader society constituted nothing less than a revolution from above that shook the system.

In March 1985, when Gorbachev took the post of General Secretary (gensek) of the CPSU, the Soviet system was already experimenting with cautious, conservative economic reform, subsumed under the slogan *uskorenie*, or "acceleration." There had been stirrings of reform in the time of Leonid Brezhnev, but these had revolved around all-Union considerations exploiting labor, capital, and natural resources more efficiently, usually by attempting to make people work harder. "Bureaucratic pluralism," as some skeptics called it,[2] had not pursued systemic change.

The impulse for reform arose from problems of economic development and growth. Although the political structure seemed stable and firm, the future lay hidden in heavy shadows of concern about the economy. The Soviet system was already lagging behind in the "scientific-technical revolution" that was driving western economies, and in ten or twenty years the political and military strength of the Soviet state, indeed its international standing, could be threatened. Economic reform was imperative. One might theorize that if not Gorbachev, some other reformer would have had to tinker with the system, but Gorbachev was the man who tried to reform it.

The new era began in 1982 when Iury Andropov succeeded Leonid Brezhnev as the head of the Soviet system. Andropov, during his years as head of the KGB, had participated in study groups considering reform. He agreed that "stagnation was not in the workplace but in the ruling political nucleus of the country,"[3] and he suggested new, unorthodox steps, even a leap into the unknown. "If one speaks openly," he told a party Central Committee plenum in June 1983, "we have not adequately studied the society in which we live and work, we have not fully uncovered its logic, especially in economics. Therefore we are forced now to act so to speak empirically, using the irrational method of trial and error."[4]

Andropov started slowly but firmly. Many Soviet citizens welcomed his efforts, and according to Ligachev, "The Andropov year remained in national memory as a time of introducing order in the interests of the common people."[5] He attacked the corruption that had taken root under his predecessor, and he insisted that the key to improving the social order lay both in getting the people to work better and in finding better leaders, that is, moving personnel around. After his death in February 1984, his successor, K. U. Chernenko repeated: "If you want to live better, you have to work better," but he slowed down the process of reassigning party leaders. It remained for Gorbachev to advance more radical thoughts of reform.

Gorbachev's star had risen sharply under Andropov, but as the "young" man in the Kremlin leadership, he had not been ready to challenge Chernenko in February 1984. His time came when Chernenko died in March 1985. Some Politburo members still hesitated to vote for him, but after Andrei Gromyko spoke out strongly in his favor, the Central

Committee of the party, despite some lingering reservations, unanimously elected Gorbachev the new gensek of the CPSU.[6]

Ensconced in power, Mikhail Gorbachev represented a new era, a new generation, and a new broom. When he joined the Politburo in the late 1970s, he was the youngest member (b. 1931) of a gerontocracy that in 1982 averaged over seventy years of age. He was the first post-Stalinist leader who had not served in World War II. Some observers have argued that Gorbachev embodied the natural passing of generations, some saw him as just following in the path forged by Andropov, but all agreed that he was a man endowed with considerable energy, political talent, and personal charm.

Later his critics found great gaps in his training and preparation for the post of gensek. He came from the provincial party leadership, having headed the party organization in Stavropol; some called him part of the party's "dacha" aristocracy, referring to the fact that many party leaders had country homes, or *dachas*, in his district. As the Politburo's specialist for agricultural questions, he had little or no experience in general party affairs, in urban, industrial problems, and in military questions; most important, he had not worked in any non-Russian area of the USSR. "In March 1985 the new gensek was all in all a political incognito for the country and the party, and hardly anyone could truly claim to know his political face," a party worker later complained.[7]

Gorbachev, of course, evaluated his background differently. He came from the "provincial partocracy," to be sure, but so did Egor Ligachev, the standard-bearer of the party conservatives in the later 1980s.[8] Gorbachev's district in the North Caucasus, moreover, had housed "a host of nationalities," and he therefore claimed to have a special understanding of the "big international family" in this "union and fraternity of free nations in a free country."[9] He had worked closely with Andropov, and he had no doubts about his qualifications.

As gensek, Gorbachev began to campaign on two fronts: to effect new policies and to bring new faces into party and government. As one observer suggested, "The dialectic of the Soviet system demands that the new general secretary must free himself both from his political opponents because they could thwart his ambitions and also from those who helped him into power because they could constrain his freedom of action."[10] For Gorbachev this meant establishing his mastery of the Politburo, and when he found resistance in the party too strongly entrenched, he looked for support outside of the traditional framework of Soviet politics. The fateful question would be whether he could organize and institutionalize such support.

Gorbachev faced no serious challenges in effecting the formal transition of power between generations. He quickly removed key old guard figures of the Brezhnev era, now called "the era of stagnation," and brought new, younger people into the party secretariat and into the Politburo; he replaced Viktor Grishin as head of the Moscow party organization with an energetic newcomer from Sverdlovsk, Boris Yeltsin. By 1990 only two veterans of the Brezhnev era—Gorbachev and his ally Eduard Shevardnadze—remained among the Politburo elite, which now averaged just sixty years of age. The lower ranks of the *nomenklatura*, as the ruling caste of the Soviet system was known, showed less startling change, but new faces were generally rising to power.

Securing freedom of action in his program of reform proved to be more problematic. Party leaders installed by Andropov generally agreed on the desirability of reforming the Soviet system, of improving its operation, but they disagreed on how to put these thoughts into practice. Many in the party soon complained that Gorbachev was going too far too fast. The party must not yield its "guiding role" in society, they argued, and it must proceed with caution. Facing resistance from not only the remnants of the Brezhnev regime but also from the Andropov generation and even from people he himself had brought power, Gorbachev kept looking for new sources of support.

At the Twenty-seventh Party Congress in February 1986, he declared that he would not allow the "apparatus" to block reform, and the congress voted a majority of new faces into the party Central Committee. Gorbachev brought new blood to the party secretariat by adding his own people—Vadim Medvedev, Aleksandr Iakovlev, and Anatoly Dobrynin. He called for glasnost, or openness, in party affairs, and he demanded that the party "rejuvenate" itself. In March 1986 he invited the "initiative of the masses" in pushing for reform.[11]

By pursuing both party and general economic reform at the same time, Gorbachev took a great risk. Some of his supporters referred back to the economic policies of the 1920s, when the Soviet system had tolerated limited capitalism, but in introducing the New Economic Policy in 1921, V. I. Lenin had tightened party discipline and the government's control of the "commanding heights" of the economy. Gorbachev experimented with loosening central control of the economy at the same time as he was restructuring and weakening the party apparatus.

When Gorbachev called on the party to strengthen its position in society by becoming more responsive to the "will of the people," he understood that he was "invoking powerful forces," but he believed that he could rely on the support of the Soviet population. As Hedrick Smith put it, "[Gorbachev] was daring to trust the people."[12] He miscalculated, however, in evaluating the popular will as well as in judging the reliability of his own appointees.

The party showed more resistance to reform than the society did, and the two fronts became disjointed. The Lithuanian party leader Algirdas Brazauskas later argued, "Democratic changes in the party must proceed more quickly than changes in the society as a whole. Otherwise the party inevitably lags behind the political processes in the society."[13] As the process unfolded, the resistance within the party left Gorbachev trying to ride two diverging horses at the same time.

The explosion at the Chernobyl atomic energy plant in April 1986 forced Gorbachev to take a fresh look at the Soviet system. The party leadership, which itself lacked information, at first suppressed news about the catastrophe, thereby hindering relief operations. This painful experience, "like a slow but powerful chain reaction," changed public attitudes and behavior: "The catastrophe in relaying the news seemed just as great as the nuclear catastrophe itself."[14] For Gorbachev the disaster offered lessons not only on problems of public information but also on problems of inner-party and inner-system information; the experience discredited old practices and stimulated new thoughts of reform.

By the fall of 1986 Gorbachev's administration was openly criticizing the record of central economic planning, and Gorbachev took a major stride toward social reconciliation by releasing political exiles and prisoners of the Brezhnev era, the most notable example being the return of Andrei Sakharov from his seven-year exile in the city of Gorky. (The process also permitted some Lithuanian exiles to return home.) Reform, on the other hand, was arousing such tension within the party that a planned Central Committee meeting was postponed several times before finally convening at the end of January 1987.

The CC Plenum of January 1987 marked the beginning of Gorbachev's movement outside the party, adding political restructuring of the Soviet system to economic reform. Although he had succeeded in renewing the membership of the Central Committee at the Twenty-seventh Party Congress the year before, Gorbachev realized that he could not count on winning a majority of the group in support of his various thoughts of reform; he had to look elsewhere. As Aleksandr Iakovlev later explained, "It was not until sometime in 1987 that I realized that what was needed was a fundamental systemic change rather than piecemeal solution."[15]

At the CC plenum, Gorbachev demanded that the party "reestablish the relationship between democracy and socialism,"[16] and he proposed holding a party "conference" in the summer of 1988. (A party conference would be a form of special congress in which he hoped that the delegates would be more responsive to thoughts of reform than the entrenched party bureaucrats were.) He closed the meeting with an appeal for the support of the citizenry of the USSR. To many observers he seemed to be moving from one victory to another: "Once again his adversaries proved that they did not have a strategy, but the struggle would still be long and full of traps."[17] On the other hand, his continual search for new sources of political energy testified to his frustration in trying to build a constituency.

Although most observers now saw a split between "conservatives" and "liberals" within the party leadership, conservative spokespersons preferred to speak of a split between the "practicals," such as Egor Ligachev or Prime Minister Nikolai Ryzhkov, and the "academics," such as Vadim Medvedev, former rector of the Academy of Social Sciences, or Aleksandr Iakovlev, a party worker who had most recently served as USSR ambassador to Canada. The "practicals" claimed to be the true heirs of Andropov's cautious reforms, and they insisted on the need for law and order in the reform process. The "academics," intellectuals who seemed stronger in "ideological and international" matters, called for more daring reforms.[18]

The relationship between Ligachev and Iakovlev personified this tension. Ligachev had come from Tomsk in 1983, with Gorbachev's endorsement, to join Andropov's administration and take charge of party organization and cadres. He supervised the process of renewing the party hierarchy and in December 1983 became a Central Committee secretary. When Gorbachev became gensek, Ligachev entered the Politburo and became the second secretary of the party, from which post he also oversaw the party's ideological work. He endorsed the idea of restructuring the party apparatus but argued that the Soviet system was basically sound and that the first consideration should be to keep the party's leadership role intact. He particularly objected to what he called the "striptease" of publicly discussing inner-party affairs and problems.

Iakovlev, who as head of propaganda was nominally under Ligachev, became a candidate member (nonvoting) of the Politburo in January 1987 and thereby a counterweight to the cautious views of the second secretary in questions of ideology. The conservatives resented this maneuver by Gorbachev; in the words of an assistant of Ligachev's, "On the whole the rise of this sort of dual authority on the ideological level meant nothing less than a new twist in unleashing the political struggle in the party." The tension between the two men became "a struggle for the press, for the subordination of the mass media to the influence of one or another group in the Politburo."[19]

The press became their battleground. Ligachev, the standard-bearer of the conservative camp, insisted that the press must honor the established truths of Soviet society, while Iakovlev encouraged greater and greater daring in challenging the ideas and even the institutions of the Soviet order. Both men agreed that this was a struggle of principles rather than individuals, and after Iakovlev had eventually won control of the mass media, Ligachev called this a key step in Moscow's loss of control in the Baltic.[20]

Of the two, Iakovlev was the more forceful and resourceful, and in many ways he was more forceful even than Gorbachev. Where Gorbachev at times would have "preferred a softer line," Iakovlev proposed more aggressive action and even seemed to be leading Gorbachev. As an American reporter later put it, "Yakovlev [Iakovlev] had always betrayed a certain intellectual condescension toward Gorbachev, but he also appreciated his political gifts, his complexity." According to Iakovlev, he had urged Gorbachev, in 1985, to split the party in two, reformers and conservatives, but even he was surprised by the course of events. As he later explained, glasnost "revolutionized and politicized society," but "hardly anyone expected that in some cases glasnost would come to resemble a brawl in a bazaar."[21]

When asked how he had outmaneuvered Ligachev, Iakovlev spoke of having pursued "a policy of faits accomplis." In the face of repeated "eruptions against glasnost," he had "acted independently, skirted them, taken them by surprise." He took his battles outside the regular channels of party politics, avoiding the constrictions of working with the Politburo. His cultural policies consisted in abolishing the prohibitions and restrictions of the past, in letting things happen, and he channeled his efforts through two publications in particular, the weekly newspaper *Moskovskie novosti* (Moscow News) and the journal *Ogonek*.[22]

Gorbachev placed himself between Iakovlev and the conservatives. When the gensek spoke to the leaders of the Soviet mass media in February 1987, he had both Iakovlev and Ligachev beside him as he urged criticism with moderation, saying "We cannot exhume in one day all the problems that have lain unresolved for ages."[23] As Iakovlev's influence grew, however, Gorbachev became more demanding himself. By raising Iakovlev to the rank of full member of the Politburo in June 1987, Gorbachev made a new commitment; working with Iakovlev meant taking decision-making powers away from other members of the Politburo and weakening the Secretariat, Ligachev's domain, where the conservatives still predominated.

Through the summer and into the fall of 1987, the public confrontation between reformers and conservatives intensified; both sides expressed dissatisfaction with the course and pace of events. "What came out of the offices of the Kremlin and of the Old Square [the party headquarters] continued to leave an aura of staleness in its wake," declared one reformer.[24] Conservative Russians began to enunciate a new form of Russian nationalism, distinct from Communist traditions, but in many ways cooperating with conservative Communists.

Repercussions of these debates were already seeping into the Baltic. In June 1987 Latvian demonstrators marked the anniversary of the deportations of 1941. In August demonstrators in all three Baltic capitals—Vilnius, Tallinn, and Riga—challenged Moscow by marking the anniversary of the Nazi-Soviet pact of 1939 that had led to their incorporation into the USSR.

Rumors concerning the tension among the leadership flooded Moscow, and when Gorbachev disappeared for over seven weeks in August and September, some people thought he had come to a bad end. When he reappeared, however, he announced that he had written a book, his tome *Perestroika*. He seemed to be back in charge, but in October the politicking within the Politburo burst into the open at a Central Committee plenum when Yeltsin, the secretary of the Moscow city organization, bitterly criticized Ligachev.

The party leadership closed ranks behind Ligachev, reprimanding Yeltsin and removing him from his post as head of the Moscow organization. But in contrast to past experience of purges in the Soviet system,

Yeltsin carried his case to the public, becoming a popular hero. The idea that an internal party personnel decision should become the stuff of public discussion distressed party conservatives, and in turn the Yeltsin affair contributed significantly to politicizing the masses. At the same time, the affair represented a defeat for Gorbachev, who had sacrificed a popular supporter to appease the conservatives.[25]

In January 1988 Gorbachev sharply altered the functioning of the party's central organs by restricting the powers of the Secretariat, removing its control of party appointments, and eliminating its ability to take a distinct position on general party questions.[26] Conservatives later looked at this as a major step in Gorbachev's campaign to separate party and governmental institutions; in April 1987 Iakovlev had already given a token of such intentions when he symbolically chose to make a major public speech in a building belonging to the Academy of Sciences rather than in a party building. The weakening of the Secretariat strengthened Gorbachev's hand, although he publicly denied that there were any "antagonisms" within the Politburo—there were only "temporary interests."[27]

Gorbachev immediately renewed his appeal for public support and issued a new set of slogans, speaking of a socialist state "ruled by law" and a socialist pluralism of opinions.[28] He spoke of building a new public order, based on a process of democratization of the society and a limitation of the functions of the party, but in so doing he stimulated previously excluded, even persecuted forces. He soon found himself presiding over the clash between these new forces that he could not control and the old guard that he had already alienated.[29]

The process of perestroika and glasnost reached a crisis and a turning point in March and April 1988. Ethnic conflicts had erupted, and one observer called this the moment of Gorbachev's "greatest uncertainty since taking power."[30] The first sign of trouble with the nationalities of the USSR had come in December 1986, when Kazakhs in Alma-Ata (now Almaty) protested Moscow's replacement of the local party chief. In the summer of 1987 Crimean Tatars demonstrated in Red Square, demanding the right to return to their homeland. Then in the winter of 1987–1988 ethnic conflict reached a new stage when Armenians and Azerbaidzhanis clashed with each other over the region of Nagorno-Karabakh. Some advisors urged decisive, quick action, but Gorbachev hesitated.[31]

At the Central Committee's plenum in February 1988, he announced a future plenum to consider "the national question," but he had no immediate answer. For years the Soviet leadership had claimed to have "solved" the "national question," and therefore it could not respond quickly to a question that it had believed did not exist. Iakovlev later warned, "National relations are an extremely delicate, an acutely sensitive problem. They require tactfulness, the highest possible competence, and real intelligence."[32] Gorbachev's camp continually proclaimed its intention of solving the national question, but as sparks began to ignite the nationalist kindling, Gorbachev did little.

The conservative opposition now struck. On March 13, 1988, with Gorbachev on his way to Belgrade and Iakovlev in Ulan-Bator, the Moscow newspaper *Sovetskaia Rossiia* published a vehement denunciation of the "liberal socialism" and "cosmopolitanism" that were leading the Soviet Union astray. Entitled "I Cannot Deny My Principles," and signed by a Leningrad teacher, Nina Andreeva, the piece criticized the changes going on in society as an abandonment of historic principles and values. On March 15, with Gorbachev and Iakovlev still absent, Ligachev suggested to leading newspaper editors that they consider this "interesting article" carefully.

While the Politburo remained ominously silent, newspapers throughout the country dutifully reprinted Andreeva's essay, and many readers considered this a "program" piece, a sign of a change in policy. Upon his return from Yugoslavia on March 18, Gorbachev, while publicly quiet, launched a counteroffensive within party ranks, and the following week a marathon session of the Politburo resulted in a denunciation of Andreeva's essay. Iakovlev drew up the Politburo's response, which appeared in the party newspaper *Pravda* on April 5, more than three weeks after Nina Andreeva's "manifesto of the antiperestroika forces." On April 6 *Sovetskaia Rossiia* reprinted the Politburo's statement.[33] Perestroika still lived.

The controversy around the Andreeva letter nevertheless illustrated that the basic decision-making political organ was still the Politburo. The constitutional organs of government were not involved in the discussion. Although Gorbachev was looking for support outside the traditional party structure, he was not yet ready to abandon that structure. He had not yet established other institutions that the public might accept.

The struggle between reformers and conservatives, moreover, was by no means resolved; what Iakovlev called "the frozen superstructure" still remained in place.[34] Gorbachev could not be sure of his position, and he hesitated to call another Central Committee plenum lest the committee not support him.[35] For the moment he put his hope for party endorsement in the Nineteenth Party Conference scheduled for the latter part of June.

Despite the uncertainty within the party apparatus, however, the Politburo's criticism of Nina Andreeva's letter and its implicit rebuke to the conservative forces in the party opened the way for greater public discussion on the processes and imperatives of reform. In Moscow the Politburo's statement evoked "an outbreak of genuine euphoria in left-liberal intellectual circles."[36] Even activists in the "provinces" now became increasingly bold in challenging established truths. Critics of the Soviet order had more safe "space" in which to voice their thoughts.

For Lithuania the Andreeva "flap" opened a new era. As recently as February 1988 the authorities were still sternly restricting public discussion in the republic, but in the aftermath of the Andreeva affair, Soviet authorities began to surrender control of public discussion across the country. The balance of power in Moscow was still crucial for developments in Lithuania, but Gorbachev's strategy and tactics in his own struggle for power gave the Lithuanians more space in which to stage their own discussions.

2

THE LITHUANIAN TANGLE

As the political struggles in Moscow reverberated through the "provinces," local party officials, although long experienced in interpreting the messages from the center, lapsed into uncertainty. The news from Moscow was confusing and unclear, the directives of yore were absent, and now glasnost had aroused public discussion. All this bewildered local officials: They did not understand what Moscow wanted, they could not even be sure whether Moscow wanted them to act. Under the old command-administrative structure, usually it was advisable to err on the side of enthusiasm in carrying out directives, but now, feeling the ground quivering underneath them, they did not know which way to turn.

As a branch of the CPSU, the Lithuanian Communist Party (LCP) was particularly vulnerable to the forces of change because its authority had depended heavily on the sheer weight of the repressive forces at its command. The CPSU had tried to sink roots in all the national regions of the Soviet state, a process called *korenizatsiia*, by recruiting locals and then advocating a "socialist consciousness," insisting that these regions had prospered under Soviet rule. Lithuanians resisted both the pressure and the thought, and in the 1980s "the percentage of party members in the population of Lithuania (5.25%) was still below the corresponding USSR average (6.75%)." Lithuanian nationalists responded by idealizing the independent state that had existed between the world wars, and in practice, a pragmatic style of thinking came to predominate in the republic, whereby Lithuanians inserted a considerable national content into their socialist style.[1]

This pragmatic behavior infiltrated the LCP through the very roots that the CPSU was trying to sink. V. Stanley Vardys wrote, "Membership [in the party] was now considered a ladder for personal career advancement which could also help to protect Lithuanian interests." Aleksandras Shtromas has characterized 90 percent of Lithuanian party members as "conservationists" and the other 10 percent as destructive to the national interests of the Lithuanians. According to Vytautas Skuodis, half of the members of the LCP had joined because it had been necessary in their occupations "where they thought they could be more useful to Lithuania and to the Lithuanian people"; another 40 percent were "materialists," seeking the benefits that membership could bestow; 5 percent had joined as "careerists," seeking power and privilege, leaving only 5 percent who had genuine "internationalist" feelings or truly believed. Although these analyses lack "objective" data, they indicate an ideological hollowness in the party organization and make clear the party's dependence on Moscow for its position.[2]

Supported by the controlled press and their repressive forces, Soviet authorities claimed to have reeducated the Lithuanians, although party officials were clearly of two minds about the stability of their system. Liberals, mostly in the lower ranks of the party, could believe the essence of the propaganda and argue that the population was trustworthy and therefore capable of using Gorbachev's initiatives to useful advantage; the conservative leadership, while asserting that the people had indeed been reeducated, stood on guard watching for dark currents in the Lithuanian character and demanded constant vigilance and control. As the tectonic political shifts in Moscow exposed the party's vulnerability, the conservatives feared for the worst.

Outside the ranks of the party, liberals and dissidents alike were unsure how to understand Gorbachev's activity. As one writer later put it, "Then, in the winter of 1987–1988, the authorities of the republic were paralyzed with fear and uncertainty, but we could not believe this and until the end of spring we fought among ourselves."[3] The dissidents, outspoken supporters of nation and church, were becoming bolder. The KGB, to be sure, probably had infiltrated their ranks, but in contrast to the past, the authorities now seemed reluctant to move against them. After the dissidents had demonstrated on August 23, 1987, the authorities had harassed them but had left them free. The dissidents then announced their intention to demonstrate on February 16, the seventieth anniversary of the Lithuanian declaration of independence of 1918. Then the regime mounted a propaganda campaign against such a demonstration, thereby raising the issue for public discussion.

Lithuanian intellectuals watched the battle between the dissidents and the authorities uncertainly; an intellectual challenged the system only at considerable personal risk. He or she could lose all the rights and perquisites that came with belonging to the intelligentsia in a Communist system. Conservatives did not want to rock the boat; liberals might sympathize in spirit with the dissidents but would fear compromising themselves; conservatives and liberals alike might even distrust the demonstrations as KGB provocations aimed at exposing "unreliable" elements. Nevertheless, in 1987 and 1988 intellectuals were beginning to push the frontiers of the permissible.

The intellectuals had first challenged the regime in 1986 with a campaign to block oil explorations on Lithuania's Baltic Sea coast. Writers such as Vytautas Petkevičius protested this threat to the fragile ecology of the Couronian Spit, and the authorities eventually agreed to atop the explorations. In 1987 Petkevičius, a member of the party, demanded that the historians of Lithuania, who "fear everything," show more initiative in teaching the youth to appreciate Lithuania's history and culture. As a collective force, however, Lithuanian intellectuals still hesitated to challenge the party leadership.

In the first weeks of 1988 LCP leaders spent an enormous amount of energy arguing publicly that February 16 was not a significant date; for the first time they were trying to impress the public with words rather than force. To emphasize the "meaninglessness" of the date, they organized petitions and mounted large demonstrations, charging that western radio "voices" were intervening in Lithuanian affairs. Moscow sent Andrei Gromyko, the president of the Soviet Union, to assure the Lithuanians that they were happy. "Soviet power was reestablished by the Lithuanian people in 1940," Gromyko lectured. "Now it is stronger than ever. Perhaps there are lunatics somewhere abroad who do not understand this. Well, life will help to cure them."[4]

When February 16 came, police patrolled the streets of Vilnius, and the city was seemingly quiet. The authorities banned meetings of groups that might raise untoward questions. Foreign correspondents, flown in for the occasion by the USSR Ministry of Foreign Affairs, confirmed that they saw nothing.[5] The authorities in both Moscow and Vilnius prided themselves on having proven that the population of Lithuania was obedient and loyal, but as one observer suggested, "Wishing to unthrone the enemy, official propaganda advertised it."[6]

The absence of clear directives from Moscow left the Lithuanian leadership uncertain as to what to do next. Ringaudas Songaila, who had become first secretary of the LCP in October 1987, seemed the very model of a modern machine politician; he had yet to give his first public speech. The party's second secretary, Nikolai Mitkin, a Russian sent by Moscow, kept an even lower profile, sending out his orders and recommendations through the party network. Representing the Soviet order in public were: Lionginas Šepetys, LCP Central Committee Secretary for ideology; Vytautas Sakalauskas, chairman of the Council of Ministers; and Vytautas Astrauskas, the chairman of the Supreme Soviet.

Šepetys had the job of publicly explaining the party's dilemma. In an interview published in *Moscow News* of April 24, 1988, he declared, "Every one of us knew there were complexities and difficulties in intra-national relations. But we believed that once the national problem had been solved in principle, it had been solved in fact." The Soviet system, he declared, had actually contributed to the emergence of "extremist" views among the nationalities: "We did this by not telling the truth and concealing facts.... We did not teach Lithuania's history properly." He called "national pride" the most important aspect of the "internationalist world view" of the day. Several months later he spoke of Lithuania's emerging from "asphyxia."[7]

The publication of Nina Andreeva's letter bolstered the confidence of the LCP leadership—Moscow seemed to be reestablishing order—but the Politburo's resolution condemning the letter brought new disorder and confusion. The Lithuanian press opened the new era modestly enough: On April 14, apparently encouraged by Andreeva's effort, a party loyalist published an essay claiming that the tens of thousands of Lithuanians deported to Siberia in the 1940s and 1950s had deserved their fate. A week later a young economist compared this essay to Andreeva's and questioned why Russians could denounce the Stalinist years but the Lithuanians could not. In response to such insolence, Juozas Jermalavičius, a party historian, took up the cudgel, arguing that the deportations had been just and proper and that the press should not be suggesting otherwise. Despite Moscow's rebuke of Nina Andreeva, Jermalavičius's essay, published in the party newspaper *Tiesa* on April 30, seemed to signal a new tough line for party policy in Lithuania.[8]

Behind Jermalavičius's essay stood Mitkin, the second secretary of the LCP since 1986. That post traditionally went to a Russian, who directed party cadres and generally oversaw the ideological orthodoxy of party and republic. Mitkin, a native of Karelia, had previously worked in Moscow as a CPSU Central Committee specialist for Estonia, and since coming to Lithuania he had pressed the LCP leadership to increase the representation of non-Lithuanians in the administration of the republic and to repress all signs of Lithuanian "nationalism" or "exclusivism." He had also directed the campaign to discount February 16.[9]

Although Mitkin had apparently commissioned Jermalavičius's essay, when protests arose the author stood alone. The director of the Institute of Party History, an agency of the LCP Central Committee, denied responsibility for the essay as did Šepetys. Jermalavičius now acquired the sobriquet of "Lithuania's Nina Andreeva": As one writer put it, "...without wanting to do so, [Jermalavičius] matured the revolutionary situation in Lithuania."[10] In 1990 and 1991, on the other hand, he would return to the Lithuanian political stage as one of Gorbachev's loyalists.

In 1988 the hostile public reaction to Jermalavičius's essay contributed heavily to the crumbling of the LCP's control of public discourse, as new forces emerged from the intelligentsia. On April 20 Arvydas Juozaitis, a philosopher, electrified an audience with a lecture entitled "Political Culture and Lithuania," denouncing the "falsified history" that the Communists had imposed on Lithuania and calling Lithuania "the last bastion of Stalinism in the Baltic." He later explained to me that he had felt the need to make some sort of protest, and since he was "not a terrorist," he "decided to deliver a public lecture, pure truth, to say everything." Juozaitis's talk constituted a breakthrough—as an American scholar put it, "This was the first time of which we were aware that the legitimacy of Soviet rule was publicly and not so subtly questioned by an intellectual who did not belong to familiar dissident circles."[11]

At the end of May the LCP lost its last semblance of control over public discussion. The issue was the naming of delegates for the Nineteenth Party Conference. Debate about who should represent Lithuania at this gathering had been intense, but on May 28 the LCP leadership announced its list—a who's who of the old guard in the party, including Mitkin and the head of the Lithuanian KGB. Intellectuals in Vilnius screamed their protests.[12]

A flurry of activity resulted on June 3 in the formation of a new association, called the Movement for Perestroika in Lithuania (*Lietuvos Persitvarkymo Sajudis*), better known thereafter simply as Sajudis. The Initiative Group of thirty-five persons that took the lead in the movement consisted of party and non-party intellectuals—artists, writers, musicians, philosophers, and economists. The artists and writers gave the group instant visibility in the society, the people who worked for the Academy of Sciences gave it political clout, and the younger members in the group gave it its energy and daring. The party members in the group helped smooth the way in the early negotiations with the authorities.

In the Byzantine convolutions of Soviet society, charges later arose that Sajudis was Moscow's tool, that Gorbachev had directed its formation, that it was an instrument of the KGB. Variations on this theme have suggested that the organizers were dupes of the authorities, that the group was simply doing Moscow's bidding, and that eventually "healthy" elements—nationalists—took the leadership of the movement away from the suspect intellectuals and made it a genuine national movement.

In the absence of any evidence to prove the more fanciful arguments, one can presume that KGB agents were present at the founding of Sajudis and that Moscow and Gorbachev welcomed the ideas that it first advanced. Sajudis leaders expressed support for Gorbachev, but there is no proof that Sajudis was Moscow's tool. The then-chief of the Lithuanian KGB, General Eduardas Eismuntas, later declared, "Although we had our agents in its structures, we, frankly, missed out on the beginning of the formation of Sajudis."[13] It appeared to be a local movement of the sort that Gorbachev claimed to be encouraging, but it quickly headed out on its own path.

The LCP looked askance at Sajudis from the moment of its founding. Mitkin personally pressured Raimundas Rajeckas, a member of the Academy of Sciences, to withdraw from the Initiative Group, threatening to void Rajeckas's appointment to the presidium of the academy; Rajeckas refused to yield. Šepetys offered the group a place as an advisory body to the party leadership, but Sajudis leaders rejected the proposal out of hand.[14]

The Sajudis Initiative Group chose to become a public organization independent of the party. This in itself was something new in the Soviet order. In the "old days," social or public organizations served essentially as auxiliaries for the state authorities. The Sajudis Initiative Group forged a new type of identity for itself, an identity unlike anything previously conceived in Lithuanian society under Soviet rule.

Without the "space" that Gorbachev's reforms had given to Soviet society, such an idea would have been unthinkable, but in the course of the next two months, the group led an explosion of Lithuanian national feeling. It brought forth the long-banned national symbols of the Lithuanians—the tricolor flag, the "pillars of Gediminas," even the simple chant "Lie-tu-va, Lie-tu-va" (Lithuania, Lithuania)—and it awakened national pride. It evoked a rising tide of emotion, a feeling of unity and pride, and ultimately a conviction that Lithuanians could handle their affairs best by themselves.

The Sajudis Initiative Group at first approved a program emphasizing ecological and cultural issues and eschewing political issues apart from denouncing the process that had chosen the delegates to the Nineteenth Party Conference. To their previous opposition to drilling for oil in the Baltic, they now added concern about the functioning of the Ignalina atomic energy plant, built on the Chernobyl model, and opposition to a newly announced expansion of the chemical industry in Lithuania. They organized a series of public meetings, each one drawing a larger crowd than the last. On June 24, when Sajudis staged a going-away party for the delegates on their departure for Moscow, a crowd of some 20,000 persons, replete with pro-Gorbachev banners and anti-Mitkin slogans, challenged the delegates to represent the interests of Lithuania. Two weeks later, on July 9, Sajudis brought 100,000 people to Vilnius's Vingis Park to meet with the delegates upon their return.

That gathering shattered the spiritual bonds imposed by almost half a century of Communist rule. People arrived in the park carrying the national tricolor flags, yellow-green-red, that had been banned in the early 1950s. Showing the flag and singing "The National Hymn" were still not legal, but the authority of the Communist regime had so deteriorated that no one seemed afraid—quite to the contrary. That day the Lithuanian people surged into a new era and experienced their "primordial" explosion, while the LCP met the future.

For the party leadership the gathering in Vingis Park posed a number of challenges, and it failed to meet them. Party leaders simply stared at the showing of the national symbols. Sajudis officials won the crowd's approval for a boycott of the party newspaper *Tiesa*, on the charge that it had been distorting the news. Although the boycott had small if any impact on subscriptions—party members were obliged to subscribe—newsstand sales dropped sharply. In the following weeks, when the other major daily newspapers disappeared from the kiosks in minutes, *Tiesa* lay on the table for hours, unsold. Party leaders looked to Moscow for advice, while Mitkin and others complained that the Lithuanians were getting out of hand.

Mitkin fully understood the danger inherent in Sajudis's embodiment of the idea of Lithuanian national sovereignty, that is, that the Lithuanian people, who constituted 80 percent of the population of the republic, should control the republic's affairs. Such a conception ran totally counter to the fundamental *raison d'etre* of the Soviet Union and to CPSU's self-image as the "vanguard" of the working class. Mitkin quickly seized on the issue of the rights of the minority 20 percent of the population—Russians made up just under 10 percent, Poles under 8 percent—as a weapon to maintain the integrity of the Soviet Union, the authority of the party, and of course his own position. He could only despair when Moscow remained silent.

Taking advantage of Sajudis's growing strength, the dissident Lithuanian Freedom League (LFL, *Lietuvos Laisves Liga*), heretofore an underground organization, began to work in public. Headed by Antanas Terleckas, a prison camp veteran, the league demanded independence for Lithuania. Sajudis leaders wanted to keep their distance from the radical dissidents, but Terleckas and his comrades made a show of their presence at Sajudis meetings. While noting "Moral courage and not erudition has been the major distinguishing feature of Lithuanian dissidents," Kestutis Girnius of Radio Free Europe's Lithuanian broadcasting praised the dissidents of the Freedom League for having "appropriated successfully and probably unintentionally the Socratic role of public gadfly."[15] Émigré news sources tended to qualify Sajudis as "government approved," while they applied the adjective "patriotic" to the Freedom League and its partisans.[16]

The disorganization and confusion of party and government, both in Moscow and in Vilnius, lay exposed to view. The party conference in Moscow duly ratified Gorbachev's calls for reform, but its promises meant little to the Lithuanians as they began their revolt against Moscow's *diktat*. Although many Lithuanians welcomed Gorbachev's acceptance of the idea of regional economic self-sufficiency, which they understood as administrative decentralization, no one could be sure where this would lead. With the erosion of Moscow's heavy hand, reformers in Lithuania paid less and less attention to the events and developments in Moscow; this bode ill for the LCP.

The Lithuanian party apparatus retreated in disarray. When Sajudis began to organize its mass meetings, a party figure had to participate, but none of the leaders wanted to. The job fell to Algirdas Brazauskas, an economic specialist in the Central Committee, who at times had been in disfavor among the leadership but who was not afraid to face a crowd. By daring to appear on a platform with Sajudis leaders, Brazauskas won considerable popular sympathy and laid the groundwork for his own installation as party chief in the fall of 1988.

Mitkin and other LCP leaders appealed to Moscow for help. "Lithuanian nationalism" was on the rise, they complained, and they spoke of threats to the other nationalities of Lithuania. Although the party still had a monopoly on armed force in Lithuania, there was no agreement on whether it should use that force. Mitkin wanted to restore law and order; many Lithuanian party leaders hesitated to resort to force. What the party leaders thought they needed most of all were clear directives from the center.

Adding urgency to the deliberations was the approach of another historic date—the forty-ninth anniversary of the Nazi-Soviet pact of August 23, 1939. The Freedom League announced that it would stage a demonstration to mark the day, and Sajudis's irregular newspaper published the text of the secret protocols to the Nazi-Soviet pacts of 1939, protocols that Moscow still insisted did not exist, whereby Hitler and Stalin divided up Eastern Europe between them. The lingering specter of Stalinism intensified Moscow's growing problem of containing the Lithuanians.

Moscow finally told the LCP it would send an investigator, but the question was who should do the job. According to Šepetys, the Lithuanians did not know until the last moment whether they would see Egor Ligachev or Aleksandr Iakovlev. They knew that the KGB was watching them suspiciously. In 1987 KGB chief Vladimir Chebrikov had considered the Lithuanians relatively peaceful and orderly, but now he was expressing concern: "I can repeat wherever necessary what is written in our information for the CC of the party. The situation is disturbing, restless, the consolidation of nationalist forces has begun." Ligachev wrote later, "Not in vain many at that time warned that the Baltic, and particularly Lithuania, would serve as a proving ground on which radical, destructive moves would be tested."[17]

The conservatives in Moscow obviously would have sent Ligachev had they been able to. Ligachev, however, was not in the picture. As he wrote in his memoirs, "...because of circumstances I was unable to watch over the Lithuanian question, I was essentially kept away from participating in its resolution." Instead, Gorbachev sent Iakovlev, and conservatives in Moscow hastened to warn their Lithuanian friends that the visitor would mean trouble.[18]

Iakovlev embodied the most sympathetic response Lithuanian reformers could have hoped for from Moscow at this time; of all the possibilities, he was the one most ready to recognize the justice of minority nationality complaints. In instructing journalists on the results of the recent party conference, Iakovlev had linked "the creation of a state based on law" with "the solution of the national problem." Union republics, such as Lithuania, should enjoy greater autonomy, but of course the center would have to guard against "a revival" of destructive nationalisms. "National relations are an extremely delicate, an acutely sensitive problem. They require tactfulness, the highest possible competence, and real intelligence," he had warned.[19]

A. Tsvetkov, deputy director of the Cultural Division of the CPSU CC, preceded Iakovlev to Vilnius and made sure that the Lithuanians knew that they could have been meeting Ligachev. He told Sajudis representatives that Moscow had been receiving "panicky characterizations of Sajudis," but he assured them that he himself had a positive opinion. At the same time he advised the Lithuanians to cooperate more closely with the party and government and to steer clear of the "extremists."

The Lithuanians delivered their own preliminary statements. Sajudis representatives complained about Mitkin, and party leaders protested Sajudis's boycott of *Tiesa*. Tsvetkov in turn advised Sajudis representatives to avoid the "moral 'totalitarianism' of the Armenians," and at the same time he agreed that Sajudis should have its own official newspaper. He suggested, however, that Sajudis not become a political organization.[20] The conservative nature of Tsvetkov's advice belied the startling impact that Iakovlev subsequently would make.

When Iakovlev arrived at Vilnius airport on August 11, the party delegation that greeted him had a conservative flavor, headed by Songaila, Mitkin, and Stasys Giedraitis, the party's specialist for agricultural affairs. During his visit, which lasted until August 14, Iakovlev met with "representatives of the Academy of Sciences" and with the "creative intelligentsia" of Vilnius—both audience identifications were code names covering the fact that he was meeting with Sajudis. He also met with party leaders, but Mitkin later complained that Iakovlev had not spoken with him privately and instead had gotten his information about the party from Šepetys.[21] From the first the visitor supported Sajudis, and at a private dinner with party leaders he even clashed with Mitkin over developments both in Lithuania and in Moscow.[22]

Publicly Iakovlev instructed the party to accept Sajudis's existence and motives. Praising the "the boldness of social thought and the unusual ideas" stimulated by perestroika, he declared that the party must "study politics" and learn to deal with the initiatives of the intelligentsia. "Perestroika," he declared, "began as an intellectual explosion," and "the intelligentsia is the expression of the self-consciousness of the people."

In speaking with Sajudis supporters, Iakovlev offered a stunning image of the future reorganization of the Soviet Union. He asserted that Lenin had identified defense and foreign policy as the only concerns that must be directed by the central government. He himself, he added, was not so sure about foreign policy. Iakovlev's statements and encouragement, carried on television and published in the press, electrified the Lithuanians. As Lionginas Šepetys later put it, "A new revolution came from above."[23]

When word of Iakovlev's activity got back to Moscow, Ligachev and the conservatives in the party hierarchy rose in anger. Iakovlev argued that "unlawful repressions" and "distortion" of "internationalist principles of socialist democracy" had fomented the unrest in the Baltic, but the conservatives took a darker view. "This is how it was in all difficult situations—whether the question was about radical mass media or about Lithuania," Ligachev complained later. "This was his position—do not be nervous!" Chebrikov declared, "I see the situation in Lithuania as critical. There is obviously an activization of nationalist forces which have penetrated the ranks of the Lithuanian Communist Party and will lead it to a split." The Soviet Right would never forgive Iakovlev for his statements during these three days in Lithuania; they seemed to believe that if he had strangled Sajudis in the cradle, the Soviet Union would have survived.[24] The Politburo, however, let the matter go, simply insisting that the party watch events closely.

Iakovlev had opened a door for the Lithuanians, and once they had passed through, Moscow could no longer restrain them. The Lithuanians gleefully accepted Iakovlev's judgments, and they loudly sang his praises. "Iakovlev is a nice fellow," exclaimed Virgilijus Čepaitis, a Sajudis organizer. "We couldn't imagine that we had such bosses!"[25] For months

Lithuanian political figures would quote Iakovlev, and indeed, in Moscow the opponents of Gorbachev and Iakovlev would be quoting his statements for years to come. Gorbachev's camp had welcomed Lithuania into the process of perestroika, but the Lithuanians were about to set off on their own course.

3

DEFINING THE PROBLEMS:
SECOND INTRODUCTION

Aleksandr Iakovlev's visit constituted a watershed in Lithuania. As Kazimiera Prunskiene later declared, "In 1988 Sajudis divided time into 'pre-Iakovlev' and 'post-Iakovlev.'"[1] In the aftermath of his visit, almost anything seemed possible, almost nothing seemed impossible. On August 20 the CPSU organ *Pravda* published an essay by Petras Braženas, secretary of the Lithuanian Writers' Union, sharply critical of the Lithuanian Communist Party leadership, and CPSU officials generally spoke of the events in the Baltic as resulting from "serious departures from internationalist principles of socialist democracy."[2]

Iakovlev's opponents would later accuse him of having stimulated the nationalists in Lithuania. This interpretation of course presumed that there were only two alternatives—servitude to Moscow or nationalist separatism. (Many western writers as well as nationalists have looked at the issues in these same terms.) What Iakovlev had in fact done was to open the way for the pragmatists, the people who had found their place as Lithuanians in the Soviet system, to act in a more open, coordinated way. As yet, the issue was still reform; the more radical nationalists would find their openings later.

The party leadership in Lithuania, who dutifully mouthed slogans of reform but attributed little meaning to them, now lacked any sense of direction; Iakovlev's directive that they find ways to work with the new forces disarmed them. Mitkin later complained, "This visit did the Lithuanian Communist Party no political good, and it gave life to Sajudis leaders—whether Aleksandr Nikolaevich [Iakovlev] wanted to or not is irrelevant."[3] By attributing such power to Iakovlev's brief visit, Mitkin, however, was in fact implicitly recognizing the fragility of the system that

he was so vehemently defending. By urging the party to hear out the intelligentsia, Iakovlev had destabilized the Soviet order in Lithuania.
Therefore, the structure that had appeared so sound and sturdy suddenly
resembled a house of cards.

Gorbachev later admitted that he had not anticipated his troubles with
Lithuania; he had presumed that political changes would help resolve troubles with the nationalities. As one Soviet writer put it in August 1988, "The
reform of the political system, in particular democratization of ethnic relations in our country, is a decisive factor for practical implementation of the
new thinking on the nationality question." In September 1989 Gorbachev
still considered national feelings a secondary factor in the problems facing
his regime, declaring "These problems have a general character, but in the
conditions of our country they have acquired a national coloring."[4]

In May 1992, when U.S. librarian of Congress James Billington asked
him what was his greatest surprise in office, Gorbachev replied, "The
national question." Blair Ruble, director of the Kennan Institute in
Washington, followed up by asking when had he recognized the intensity
of the problem. Gorbachev responded that it was in the fall of 1990, when
the republics withheld tax payments. If these answers were true, they eloquently illustrated Gorbachev's understanding of the events in Lithuania.

Gorbachev and Iakovlev had presumed that the Soviet system was
earthquake-proof. They believed the outward signs of success of the
CPSU's nationalities policies: industrialization and the economic integra-
tion of the parts of the Soviet Union, the cultural establishments that had
grown up in the republics, even the gold medals won by Olympic con-
tenders from all parts of the state. The party program of 1986, adopted
under Gorbachev's guidance presumably with Iakovlev's help, proclaimed,
"The nationalities question, inherited from the past, has been solved in the
Soviet Union." Soviet leaders had believed that "nationalism" was a phenomenon of the capitalist order that could not exist in their "socialist"
order; what problems existed were the consequence simply of faulty education. Blinded by their own propaganda, they did not recognize the fault
lines that ran through their state.[5]

Entangled in the myths and contradictions of the Soviet system,
Moscow could not find answers to questions that it could not articulate.
The Soviet constitution had guaranteed the constituent republics the right
of secession, and an authoritative commentary had called this right unrestricted. On August 30, a week after the meeting in Vingis Park, the head

of the Lithuanian KGB called thoughts of Lithuanian independence "anti-Soviet," but at the same time he had to admit that they were not "unconstitutional."[6] Once the myths of the Soviet system became subject to debate, the Soviet ideologists had no fixed *point d'appui* from which to attack.

Least of all could the authorities in Moscow understand their own contributions to compounding the national question. The administrative divisions of the Soviet Union bolstered the identification of nationality and territory, or "ethnoregional identity," but "national policy" meant the development of "internationalism" at the cost of national individuality. Soviet spokespersons had even advocated the concept of *sliianie*, or "merging," of the nationalities. The new surge of national feeling on behalf of language, culture, and environmental protection was in part a revolt against *sliianie*, and the Soviet leadership did not comprehend the integral relationship of political visions to cultural programs.

The explosion of national feeling posed unprecedented problems for Soviet specialists on the nationalities question. In the past they had responded on order to provide the rationale for what the leaders wanted. In 1989, even as nationalist sentiments grew, a Soviet specialist spoke of "the Soviet people" as "a new ethnic entity with its own parameters"[7]; as late as September 1992, a Russian political figure, Arkady Volsky, claimed that scientists had proved that there was a single genetic code for "the Soviet people." Suddenly the old verities were no longer valid: Should the specialists scrap their old theories altogether and create something new? They were not sure where such "new thinking" should start, and they were not even sure how to identify the problems they were supposed to address.

When Aleksandr Iakovlev visited Lithuania, his words went far beyond the traditional framework for the "national question," and they left the ideologues stranded outside their well-established territory. In the resulting disorder, the specialists, with the support of party conservatives, reached back for their old truths, however irrelevant they might have been. Iakovlev soon had to retreat from this new territory.

Traditionally, commentators had discussed the national question in almost mystic terms. Trying to define the nature of the Soviet state, for example, one specialist declared, "The Union of SSRs is a single union state, and at the same time a union of states (republics). For those seeking a harsh dichotomy—either this or that—such a definition is obviously a complete absurdity. But from the positions of the dialectic, as we say, everything is in order."[8] As of 1988 and 1989, however, the specialists were no longer preaching just to the faithful; they were trying to convince nonbelievers, to whom such appeals to the dialectic looked absurd. In any case, the central authorities could no longer resolve tensions with the nationalities simply by words and orders; party and governmental officials had to come up with both a new understanding of the question and a new modus operandi.

The first recourse for the specialists was to call for a return to "Leninist principles." They offered platitudes on "crude infractions of socialist legality in the 1930s to the 1950s" and spoke of the problem of "stagnation" in the '70s and '80s, but then added that the "infractions of socialist legality" and the violations of Lenin's ideals had probably begun even during Lenin's lifetime.[9] (Lenin died in 1924.) They eventually had to admit their own contributions to the problem, namely their "thesis about the unconditional resolution of the national question," the assertion that the Soviet Union had long before "resolved" the nationalities question in a unique way. The task now was "to speak not about the improvement of national relations but about their restructuring."[10]

The specialists found their vocabulary inadequate for dealing with the new situation. They of course deplored "nationalism," but they could not agree in defining the phenomenon. Some Soviet theorists saw "nationalism" as the result of an "alienated, 'inadequate' consciousness,"[11] thereby repeating the thought that Marxist education should have eradicated it. Nationalism, said another commentator, is "an expression of a nation's weakness and not of its strength."[12] Almost all, however, agreed that "opponents of perestroika" were exploiting legitimate national grievances. While reassuring believers, the specialists offered Gorbachev little help.

Gorbachev's camp began from the principle that they were regulating the relations between nationalities, a subject to which they applied the name "interethnic problems" *(mezhnatsional'nye problemy)*.[13] Françoise Thom, a French writer, has suggested, "Nationalism breeds forms of opposition which communism can handle"; therefore Soviet leaders much preferred the concept of "interethnic" conflict between nationalities rather than thoughts of "concerted political opposition" on the part of an ethnic region aimed against the center.[14] In this framework, the Soviet government could serve as the peacemaker between nationalities rather than as the target of grievances, thereby blaming locals for whatever tension existed. "We do not have political differences in republics like

Azerbaidzhan and Armenia," Iakovlev told American journalists in December 1988; "We have ethnic problems."[15] Correspondingly, Soviet leaders had trouble understanding what distinctions could be made between the political thoughts of "decentralizing" and thoughts of "secession."

When the specialists turned to problems posed by the Lithuanians, they carried strong prejudgments with them. During several extended stays in Moscow in the 1970s and 1980s, I repeatedly heard Muscovites speak of Lithuanians as a stubborn people who somehow refused to accept Soviet values, who refused to move to other parts of the Soviet Union even when offered good jobs. Many Russian tourists felt as if they were going "abroad" when they went to the Baltic. Some commentators spoke of historic Lithuanian "expansionism" that had served western interests in Eastern Europe.[16] The specialists began with negative feelings about the Lithuanians.

Beginning with the slogan "A powerful center and powerful republics," they identified undesirable forces such as the "second economy" behind the new national consciousness.[17] They recognized that the Baltic peoples had a certain right to condemn their forced incorporation into the Soviet Union in 1939 and 1940 and the subsequent deportations—so-called "Stalinist aberrations"[18]—but they concluded that the center had mistakenly encouraged irresponsible behavior by the Lithuanians: Soviet industrialization policies had created a working class of Russians in the Baltic, allowing the locals to concentrate on intellectual pursuits that failed to give them a proper "internationalist" outlook.[19] Such mechanical interpretations of national feeling, picturing it as a relic that had escaped reeducation, left Gorbachev's ideologues far "behind the curve" in understanding developments in Lithuania.[20]

Prescriptions for action likewise lagged behind developments. After discussions that emphasized the party's role as the instrument of perestroika, the specialists could agree only that the major problem with which they had to be concerned was how to keep the Communist Party in power and how to deflect the challenge of "other political organizations."[21] This interpretation left the CPSU leadership totally unprepared for the decision of the leadership of the Lithuanian Communist Party to join the movement toward strengthening local sovereignty.

When forced to take action in 1988 and 1989, Soviet authorities fell back on their established stereotypes and sought to combat "nationalism" with other "nationalisms," encouraging "interethnic conflict." In Lithuania this meant encouraging Russians and Poles to object to the behavior and demands of the Lithuanians. According to Gorbachev's last KGB chief, "The Committee of State Security [KGB] stood at the sources of founding 'international fronts' in the union republics displaying obstinacy in relations with the center."[22] Moscow wanted to fall back into its preferred role as "peacemaker," restoring order among its unruly children who were presumably incapable of striking out on their own.

As the tensions between Moscow and Vilnius grew, Lithuania became a prototype of what would be happening in Eastern Europe a year later. The party's authority was already in ruins; the political structure was beginning to crumble; and over the succeeding months the citizenry attacked the remnants of the old order with increasing vigor and force. Ever more radical images of reform and change arose. In contrast to Eastern Europe, of course, the veil of Soviet authority still hung over Lithuania, held in place by the military, but the fermenting process changed the character of the society at a pace equal to anything developing in the further western marches of the Soviet empire.

In the first days after Iakovlev's departure on August 14 and especially during the mass gathering of Lithuanians in Vingis Park to mark the anniversary of the Molotov-Ribbentrop pact on August 23, one could almost feel the earth moving in Vilnius. Although Hedrick Smith has written, "In the summer of 1988, nationalist movements in the Baltic republics of Lithuania, Estonia, and Latvia were practically born on local television-discussion shows,"[23] in Lithuania this was definitely not so. Until Iakovlev's visit Sajudis had no access to the official media, printed or electronic; it spread its word with a small irregular newsletter, *Sajudžio žinios* (Sajudis News). Only after Iakovlev's visit did the party open the airwaves and the newspapers to Sajudis spokespersons, and then in only limited fashion.

The thaw proceeded quickly. On August 17 the party finally agreed to legalize the Lithuanians' national symbols—by the weekend fans at the local major league soccer match were enthusiastically waving large tricolor flags. The party agreed to permit Sajudis to hold its observance of the Molotov-Ribbentrop pact, and party officials agreed to stand on the platform. Hunger strikers demanding the release of political prisoners set up camp in Gediminas Square alongside the wall of the historic cathedral that the Soviet authorities had converted into an art gallery. Even Mitkin directed party workers not to discriminate against party members who participated in Sajudis support groups: "Membership in Sajudis should not be a block to the selection of Communists to party posts."[24]

I arrived in Vilnius on August 16 to begin a three-month stay as a guest of the Institute of History of the Lithuanian Academy of Sciences. Compared to my previous visits, first in 1960 and most recently in 1984, I found the atmosphere astonishing. The situation most reminded me of what I had seen in Poland in the summer of 1957—after a long silence, after bitter oppression, people dared to say what they thought, to discuss their own past and experiences. They dared to look into their own souls, and they found depths of feeling that, under the self-censorship that the Soviet regime had imposed, they had concealed even from themselves.

The party still controlled the forces of repression in Lithuania, no one could be sure just what the authorities would allow or when they would choose to act, but Sajudis was capturing the hearts and minds of the people. After years of living under Moscow's heavy hand, of struggling to protect the autonomy of their private lives and their private thoughts, the Lithuanians began to express their feelings openly, to make their private thoughts public. The emergence of this emotional and intellectual sovereignty, openly challenging the weaponry of the authorities, laid the basis for political confrontation with Moscow.

When some 150,000 people gathered in Vingis Park on August 23 to mark the anniversary of the Nazi-Soviet pact, this process of emotional and national growth completed the first stage of its development. Moscow still insisted that the Nazi-Soviet agreements of 1939 had included no secret protocols, and the speakers that night in Vilnius had taken the stage nervously, unsure of what might happen. When the evening ended, the Lithuanians were ready to pursue the issue of the Nazi-Soviet protocols much more aggressively, and Sajudis had firmly established its place in Lithuanian hearts and minds.

THE MOLOTOV-RIBBENTROP PACT

Since much of the political struggle between Moscow and Vilnius in 1988–1989 revolved around the question of "the secret protocols," a brief review of the history of the Nazi-Soviet pact, its consequences, and its historiography seems in order.

The Molotov-Ribbentrop pact of 1939 took the form of a nonaggression agreement. In general, one normally might not find fault with this type of agreement. As Soviet diplomatic historians themselves made clear, however, the Germans used nonaggression pacts to disguise aggressive intentions, and in this case the Soviets conspired with them. The two parties added a secret protocol to the pact dividing up Eastern Europe between themselves "in the event that borders should change." A week later, on September 1, the Germans attacked Poland, and borders changed drastically.

According to the secret protocol of August 23, Lithuania was consigned to Germany, but in a subsequent protocol, signed on September 28, Germany traded Lithuania to the Soviet Union for another piece of Poland. The Soviets, who had occupied eastern Poland for themselves, then forced the Lithuanians, along with the Latvians and the Estonians, to sign mutual assistance agreements, whereby the three republics admitted Soviet troops into their territory. Moscow sweetened the pact with the Lithuanians by ceding to them the city of Vilnius (Wilno in Polish) and its environs, which Soviet forces had just taken from Poland.

In the summer of 1940 Moscow cashed the blank check that it had received from Berlin. The Soviet government forced the three Baltic republics to admit additional troops, and under Moscow's direction, newly elected "People's Diets" proclaimed Soviet rule and requested incorporation into the Soviet Union. In later years Soviet historiography described this as a voluntary action by the Lithuanian people, a "simultaneous revolution" in all three Baltic republics. In 1990 and 1991 the Lithuanian Right used the image of the "People's Diet" as a bugbear to forge an emotional unity among the people opposed to finding compromises with Moscow.

Since the Soviet Union and Germany were allies when the Baltic states were incorporated, and since Germany was then at war with Great Britain, the western powers, including the United States, refused to recognize the Soviet annexation of the three Baltic republics. After the German attack on the Soviet Union in June 1941, the interests of the Grand Alliance against Hitler dictated that the Baltic question had to stay on a back burner. At the end of the war, however, as the Grand Alliance disintegrated in the early stages of the Cold War, the status of the Baltic republics became a significant and sensitive question.

At the end of the war, the United States, which still did not recognize the incorporation of Lithuania and even sent clandestine aid to Lithuanian partisans resisting the reintroduction of Soviet rule after 1945, came into possession of the German foreign ministry archives. There researchers found copies of the secret protocols to the agreements of August 23 and September 28. Western prosecutors mentioned the protocols at the Nürnberg War Crimes trial, but as there were no competent international courts and international law in which the documents could be used, they became the objects of an impassioned historiographic dispute that buttressed Cold War postures.

Soviet authorities claimed that the texts published by the Americans were forgeries, "falsifications." The "nonaggression pact" had been just that, they insisted, and anyone who argued that Stalin could have agreed to divide up Eastern Europe with Hitler was in the service of the dark forces of anticommunism in the West. They insisted that Soviet troops had had to enter the Baltic in 1940 because of the perfidy of the Baltic governments, and that the people had joyfully carried out a revolution that enabled them to come under Stalin's rule.[25]

For Lithuanians the controversy caused a split in thinking that became a part of the contradictions of Soviet life. For almost fifty years they publicly had to repeat the official Soviet line about a popular revolution. Yet despite the obligatory public rituals, many of them knew that the protocols had existed and had perhaps even read them. Other Lithuanians, however, may well have dismissed the issue as not worth worrying about in the face of all the other problems they faced under Soviet rule.

Lithuanians who knew of the protocols drew a direct connection between them and the introduction of Soviet rule. Western historians had developed distinct issues: the existence and nature of the protocols, the relationship of the protocols to the movement of Soviet troops in 1940, and the nature of the decisions by the newly elected "People's Diets" in the Baltic republics to request incorporation into the Soviet Union. The Soviet system, however, had not allowed such hairsplitting in writing history— there were only broad truths. Therefore, the broad truth that many Lithuanians held quietly in their hearts was that Soviet rule in Lithuania was a direct result of the alliance between Hitler and Stalin in 1939. The essence of this belief was that a hostile, foreign army had occupied Lithuania and had forced its people to behave like trained circus animals.

Moscow could not understand the resentment about these events that persisted in Lithuania. Soviet propaganda taught the simple axiom that good Lithuanians were loyal to the Soviet Motherland, and therefore

Gorbachev was very slow to comprehend facts to the contrary, no matter how obvious. He did not feel the earth moving, and he did not see the house of cards shaking.

THE GAME OF SOVIET POLITICS

The struggle between Lithuania and Moscow proceeded according to rules and traditions peculiar to the Soviet system, and efforts to explain the issues without understanding that background can confuse more than elucidate. Both Moscow and Vilnius employed the Soviet "artistic method" called "Socialist Realism," whereby writers had to "light the road ahead," to show the way to a "brilliant future." Artists had to give an optimistic spirit to the drudgery of daily life; will and words had to mold grim reality into inspiring ideals. This belief in the primacy of words and ideals carried over into the post-Soviet era and intensified the problems of communication between contending groups that did not share the same verbal codes.[26]

A great part of Gorbachev's public struggle with the nationalities of the Soviet Union, and with the Lithuanians in particular, became a war of words, words that lacked definition and certainly did not serve to communicate. Outsiders, foreigners, attempting to participate in the struggle, tended to expect the words of one side or another to have meanings that they could understand; they tended to believe that the words used by principals with whom they otherwise sympathized had the same meaning as cognates in other languages. In fact, the combatants, trained in the principles of Socialist Realism, were employing ideals such as "democracy" or "human rights" as weapons rather than goals.

In explaining their "Lithuanian problem" to Americans, for example, Soviet spokespersons liked to draw a constitutional analogy to Abraham Lincoln's war with the secessionist-minded southern states of the United States. The Soviet constitution, however, not only represented completely different political imperatives than did the U.S. Constitution, but it also guaranteed the right of secession that the U.S. Constitution denied. In seventy years of Soviet rule, moreover, no one had ever successfully appealed to the constitution as a limitation on governmental authority. As one friend of mine heard his KGB interrogator say, "Here *I* am the constitution; *that* constitution is for the international exhibition in Paris."

Gorbachev viewed the constitution as a flexible weapon, a means of bringing obstreperous regions and groups into line. As party secretary, he was above the constitution and could choose for himself which parts to observe and which not to, and he expected others to accept his judgment. Nevertheless, many of his American sympathizers, *gorbomanes* so to speak, uncritically accepted the analogy with the U.S. Constitution.

Soviet citizens understood the political order under which they had to live, and they fitted their lives to it. Educated to think of grand visions as more real than physical deprivations, and restricted by careful censorship from identifying the contradictions of life, the citizenry fulfilled their public obligations and retreated to inner circles of family and friends for discussions. As Hedrick Smith put it, "I had come to understand that I could not judge someone by what he said in public."[27] Few, however, could comprehend just where their own public posture ended and where their personal beliefs began. "We believe nothing we are told," cynics frequently declared, but in fact in their thought and behavior patterns they had accepted much from the society in which they had been raised.

The Soviet order, for example, was the model of government that its own critics knew the best. In the furor and confusion of the late 1980s and early 1990s, new forces, eager to move from "opposition" to "position," conceived of the "position" in terms of what they had grown up with. Once they entered into public affairs, while embracing the vocabulary of "democracy," they worked in ways inherited from the old "command-administrative system." Moscow's challengers in Lithuania and in other republics were almost all products of the Soviet order, its educational system, and its culture; when they rose against Moscow, they used the weaponry they had been trained with. The result was a war of words, posturing, and shadows that only partially reflected the deeper struggle.

One other factor in the struggle must still be mentioned here, namely the role of the KGB. As a network of informants and agents that enforced the will of the Soviet leadership over the years, the KGB had penetrated and permeated the society in ways that will take years to uncover and to neutralize. The organization was still functioning in 1991; after that it lived on in spirit if not in flesh and blood.

The Lithuanians obtained KGB files after the collapse of the "August Putsch" in 1991, and information from the files—some authentic, some not—entered Lithuanian political life. Charges and countercharges filled the air—this organization, that person, those institutions, "as everybody knows," were all under the influence, if not the direction of the KGB—and historians may never be able to prove or disprove the various allegations. Nevertheless, the historian has to say something, and he or she must therefore remember to tread carefully through this minefield laid by the Soviet system.[28]

4

THE BATTLE IS JOINED

In just three hours on August 23, 1988, Sajudis changed Lithuania. Some 150,000 persons gathered in Vilnius's Vingis Park to commemorate the Molotov-Ribbentrop pact of 1939 and its consequences for Lithuania. One after another, speakers condemned the pact, and by the end of the evening only dedicated party faithful still could insist that the secret protocols of 1939 were a myth, a fabrication by western intelligence services. The meeting amounted to a mass demand that Lithuania's relationship to the Soviet Union be examined and redefined. Lithuanians identified themselves as a distinctive community, and they demanded greater control of the space in which they lived. A duel was taking shape—the collapsing culture of the Moscow-based Soviet structure against the rising culture of Vilnius.

In contrast to the days when the Communist Party set the tone for public life in Vilnius, the Lithuanians' political life now admitted new forces and new groups. Some looked to their history for models, others wanted to create new models, and still others forged forward without any plans, driven by nationalist emotions. The result was a new political culture—not necessarily what Arvydas Juozaitis or others had had in mind in April 1988, but a distinctively Lithuanian process.

CPSU leaders in Moscow, still claiming to be the all-knowing arbiter of what was right, watched this process uneasily, while at the same time they floundered in the restructuring of their own system. Glasnost was creating such turmoil that the possibilities of enacting a coherent plan were rapidly evaporating. The escalation of reformist hopes and the development of embittered opposition polarized the Soviet leadership, and Gorbachev resorted increasingly to tactical measures aimed at short-term survival while he exalted the evanescent image of "perestroika" as some sort of Holy Grail that only he could find.

The questions of the future relations between Gorbachev and the Lithuanians were multifold. Could Gorbachev integrate the emerging Lithuanian culture into his Moscow universe? Would he even want to? Could he expand Moscow's political culture so as to incorporate such regional cultures as the Lithuanians'? Was he willing to try? What place would the Lithuanians leave Moscow in their own cultural renaissance? Was Gorbachev willing to give up Moscow's practice of controlling Lithuanian political culture and to accept simply a place in it? And to what degree would the interaction between Moscow and Vilnius affect decision making in both capitals, or for that matter in other capitals around the Soviet Union?

The first news from Vilnius at the end of August passed through the filter of the Soviet information services in incomprehensible form. TASS, the Telegraph Agency of the Soviet Union, asserted that the meeting in Vingis Park had "noted that Hitlerite Germany, by violating the nonaggression treaty, unleashed World War II...The USSR was then the only real force on whose help Lithuania could count."[1] The Soviet propaganda machine was not yet ready to deal with the news from Lithuania.

Conservatives in the Politburo could endorse the TASS dispatch as a representation of what *should* have happened in Lithuania, but they knew that that meeting had said something quite different, and they viewed the events with grave concern. They questioned Iakovlev's sanguine image of the forces in action in Lithuania, but they did not pursue the subject. Subsequently they enshrined his visit as a turning point in perestroika's road to disaster. As Ligachev put it, "A social and class-based analysis of the processes in Lithuania was replaced by maneuvering, warping the truth, and a policy of appeasement." Nevertheless, in September 1988, they only grumbled as Gorbachev went ahead, for the moment, on the path forged by Iakovlev.[2]

At the same time, Gorbachev carried his own power struggle one step deeper into the party hierarchy. In the words of an American observer, the Soviet leader had created "two opposition elites, one official, the other unofficial, who were to play a crucial role in the formation and consolidation of the popular movements."[3] At the end of September, on very short notice, Gorbachev summoned a plenum of the Central Committee and supervised a series of startling changes in the leadership that still confuse analysts.

To many observers, the changes represented a triumph for Gorbachev, who now took the presidency for himself: "Then, in October [sic] 1988," wrote Hedrick Smith,

> he really cut into their power, with a swift surgical behind-the-scenes coup at a Party Central Committee meeting. Vladimir Kriuchkov replaced Chebrikov as head of the KGB. Gorbachev forced President Andrei Gromyko and three other senior Brezhnev holdovers into retirement; he stripped Ligachev of the ideology portfolio—responsibility over the press and media; he disbanded the Party Secretariat; and he began to lop off Central Committee staff departments that dealt with economic management.[4]

Lost in that glowing account of what seems complete triumph was the fact that Iakovlev surrendered his role in the nationalities question to Vadim Medvedev and turned to concentrate of Soviet foreign relations. The historian Roy Medvedev (no relation to Vadim) said of these changes: "Not everything that happened in September is clear to me.... Aleksandr Yakovlev [Iakovlev] was shifted from ideology to international problems 'in exchange' for the simultaneous removal of Ligachev from ideology. Medvedev was temporarily assigned to ideological issues to prevent Ligachev's defeat from becoming visible."[5]

For the Lithuanians and the other nationalities of the Soviet Union, Iakovlev's transfer was the first item of note in these changes. Medvedev was an unknown quantity. Roy Medvedev considered him a "centrist," while Ligachev saw him as Iakovlev's man.[6] Some foreign observers accepted the image of Medvedev's being close to Iakovlev,[7] but Dmitry Mikheyev, an émigré, called Medvedev "much more ideologically conservative" than Iakovlev. Pointing to the fact that Gorbachev also brought Kriuchkov and Boriss Pugo into his inner circle at this time, Mikheyev argued that the September CC plenum represented "the onset of a more conservative policy."[8] The Lithuanians understood that, with Iakovlev's reassignment, they had lost a major source of support in Moscow.

Iakovlev himself now publicly denied everything that he had said in Lithuania. When Philip Taubmann of *The New York Times* asked him about the situation in the Baltic, Iakovlev accused the Balts of advocating "many ideas that are out of touch with reality." In August he had said that "pere-stroika began as an intellectual explosion" and would have been impossible without the support of "the forceful activity of the civic-minded intelligentsia.... It is commonly known that the intelligentsia is the expression of the self-consciousness of the people" and also "the architect of this self-consciousness." Now he dismissed Sajudis leaders as simply "performers and musicians and people of this sort."[9] Close associates of Iakovlev's later insisted to me that "he *had* to speak this way" at this time.

Out of the glare of the American press, Iakovlev struck more of a balance in amplifying his views. He told a German journalist a short time later: "I was in the Baltic states once. Many of the questions that are being raised there are very sensible. Of course there is a borderline—it runs between national and nationalistic." He insisted that Moscow was concerned with protecting the rights of Russians in the Baltic, but he admitted that the national question had emerged "a bit suddenly." Indicating sensitivity toward attacks from the Right, he argued that perestroika had not caused the problems between the nationalities of the Soviet Union; it had simply brought them into the open.[10] Whatever the evolution of his views, Iakovlev obviously felt the need to cover his tracks.

In all, the shakeup at the end of September and the beginning of October represented a personal victory for Gorbachev but also a compromise for various of his policies. A few weeks later, when the authorities published Gorbachev's proposals for constitutional changes, it became clear that he had pulled back from many of the decentralizing ideas advanced by the Nineteenth Party Conference and was instead trying to reconstruct centralizing institutions. One might view this either as a surrender to the Right or as a tactical measure aimed at installing his own people in power before launching a new campaign, but in fact Gorbachev's own time horizons seemed to be contracting as he spent more and more effort on simply maintaining his own position of power from day to day.

In Lithuania the party leadership seemed more disorganized than ever. At a meeting of the party Bureau (the LCP's equivalent of the CPSU Politburo) on September 5, Mitkin argued for forceful action: "We are disgracefully wasting time, we have already lost a great deal, we must more self-critically evaluate our work, analyze the political situation in the republic more deeply." The party must retake the offensive; it must regain momentum in this rapidly changing situation. Sajudis, he warned, was aiming at taking power, and the party must act before it was too late.[11]

The party leadership's efforts to assert itself, however, only escalated its problems. After intense negotiations with Sajudis leaders over plans for a popular protest at the Ignalina power plant on September 17 and 18, party authorities suddenly banned the holding of a meeting. In a momentous challenge, Sajudis leaders immediately decided to go ahead with their demonstration, simply eschewing the formal trappings of a rally such as speeches and resolutions.[12]

Perhaps encouraged by reports of the September CC plenum in Moscow, on September 28 party conservatives tried again to assert their authority. They called in troops from Minsk to suppress an unauthorized Freedom League rally marking the anniversary of the supplementary Nazi-Soviet agreement of September 28, 1939. The troops forcefully broke up the meeting, and Lithuanians protested en masse. At noon on September 29, Sajudis leaders, including Vytautas Landsbergis, stood together in public with Antanas Terleckas of the Freedom League to denounce the actions of government and party; the party's recourse to violence only brought Sajudis and the LFL closer together.

Sajudis's strength was growing apace. On September 23, the group published the first issue of its newspaper, *Atgimimas* (Rebirth), edited by Romualdas Ozolas: "...the samizdat, rotoprint stage of Lithuanian journalism ended, and a legal one began."[13] The first issue appeared, after several reprintings, in a total edition of 100,000 copies, and a Russian edition, *Vozrozhdenie*, with a circulation of 30,000, followed. Sajudis would soon have the weaponry and public support necessary to challenge the party dictatorship and even to publicize its cause in other parts of the Soviet Union.

In the face of mass protest, reform elements in the party demanded change in the leadership, and Ringaudas Songaila faced a call for his resignation. Although he survived the first challenge, the Lithuanian CC, on October 4, took two momentous steps: It relieved Nikolai Mitkin of the job of overseeing party organization, giving it instead to a Russian-Lithuanian, Vladimir Beriozovas, and it held its discussions in Lithuanian rather than Russian. On October 7 party officials watched as Sajudis raised the Lithuanian tricolor over the Gediminas tower in Vilnius—another sign of a new era.[14]

As Sajudis prepared to hold its formal founding congress in Vilnius on October 22 and 23, public attacks on Songaila and Mitkin increased. Sajudis leaders announced that the congress would consider resolutions declaring no confidence in both the LCP and the Lithuanian government: "Sajudis supports M. Gorbachev's radical reform policy and appeals to the Central Committee of the Lithuanian Communist Party to take resolute steps to reconstruct the national economy and culture of the Republic."[15]

Political infighting among the party leadership intensified. A faction within the Bureau, led by Lionginas Šepetys and Algirdas Brazauskas, pressed for a change in the secretaryship. Mitkin criticized the move as "an adventure" and complained to Moscow.[16] CPSU leaders in Moscow wanted no splits or divisions in the Lithuanian party. On Sunday, October 16, Songaila visited Gorbachev, who told him that the party leaders should attend the Sajudis convention, but with "a clear, thought-out program" in their hands. In the company of several representatives of the CPSU, Songaila returned to Vilnius and on Monday, October 17, told the Bureau that he would not resign.

Songaila's opponents refused to back down. Communist Party members in the Writers' Union and unions of other "creative workers" sent a telegram to Gorbachev demanding Songaila's ouster. Moscow finally withdrew its support: Songaila had to resign. On October 18, the head of the Lithuanian section in the organizational division of the CPSU CC, E. N. Trofimov, flew to Vilnius to confer with Mitkin and other party leaders about a possible successor: the major candidates were apparently Stasys Giedraitis, a conservative, and Brazauskas. With great misgivings, Mitkin endorsed Brazauskas.[17] The Bureau chose Brazauskas, and after the CPSU representatives had agreed to the Lithuanians' decision, Brazauskas flew to Moscow to meet with Gorbachev.[18]

Brazauskas's trip to Moscow aroused debate about his relationship to Gorbachev. Hedrick Smith declared that the Lithuanian "had been installed by Gorbachev," but Brazauskas himself has insisted that his trip was just a "get-acquainted" visit: "There was no decision; he did not know me." This was, he declared, "an ordinary conversation," but he went on to meet other Politburo officials with whom he would have to deal, including Georgy Razumovsky, the CC secretary in charge of the party's organizational division.[19] Upon his return to Vilnius on October 20, the LCP Central Committee elected him first secretary.

Brazauskas still had to pay his dues to Moscow: He informed the LCP that it had no power to remove Mitkin because Moscow had appointed him; he conveyed Gorbachev's "best wishes to the Lithuanian people"; he continued to deal with the CPSU's envoys investigating the situation in

Lithuania. On the other hand, Mitkin soon resigned, and Beriozovas replaced him as second secretary.[20] As Saulius Girnius of Radio Free Europe (RFE) summarized the situation, "The election of Brazauskas suggests that the central authorities in Moscow realized that the current leadership had lost the respect of the Lithuanian populace and that the Lithuanian Restructuring Movement was replacing the party as the most important social force in the republic."[21]

At the Sajudis Constituent Congress on October 22-24, Brazauskas received a warm welcome from the delegates, telling them that Gorbachev "asked me to pass on his most sincere greetings and wishes to all the creative and industrious Lithuanian people, whom he very much values and respects. Comrade Gorbachev said that he sees Sajudis as a positive force that can work to benefit perestroika and raise the prestige of Soviet Lithuania still higher."[22] Brazauskas then won great popular support by announcing his decision to return the Vilnius cathedral to the Catholic Church. On Sunday October 23, however, he took the podium to caution the gathering about untoward nationalistic enthusiasm.

Sajudis itself underwent a profound change in the course of its congress. Although during the summer the Sajudis Initiative Group had kept its distance from the Freedom League, Antanas Terleckas and other radicals spoke at the congress to tumultuous applause. When the congress accepted the principle that Sajudis was not a membership organization, the way was open for more active participation by the radicals; the Freedom League became Sajudis's left wing. The very experience of holding the congress, moreover, sharpened the feelings of Sajudis leaders; they became ever more demanding and aggressive in their attitudes toward the LCP and Moscow.[23]

For Brazauskas the next month was a honeymoon marred by a dark cloud on the horizon. He enjoyed his popularity, and he even manipulated and played with it. He ordered the release of political prisoners; he appeared at meetings and ceremonies in the company of Sajudis leaders. He knew, however, that a crisis was coming in Lithuania's relations with Moscow.

The immediate issue in the crisis was a clash of constitutions. The Lithuanians had been discussing changes to their own constitution since early in the summer, and Gorbachev's proposals for constitutional reform, published in the same weekend as the Sajudis congress, raised the stakes in the debates. The Sajudis Seimas, a body established to coordinate the organization's positions, demanded that Soviet laws not be effective in Lithuania unless approved by local authorities, something akin to the idea of "nullification" in the antebellum American South, and it condemned Gorbachev's package of constitutional amendments. Sajudis was now unreservedly entering the political arena.

Concerned about attitudes in the Baltic, Moscow sent emissaries to all three Baltic capitals over the weekend of November 11-14, 1988. When Nikolai Sliunkov arrived at the Central Committee building in Vilnius at about noon on November 11, a crowd of demonstrators protesting the constitutional revisions was waiting for him. He waved and tried to smile at the crowd, but the demonstrators just looked on silently—the tension with Moscow was almost palpable. That evening Moscow television reported, "The conversations between Nikolai Nikitovich Sliunkov and the residents of Vilnius in the streets and squares of the town were full of profound interest and political activeness." As a witness to his arrival, I disagree with this effort to indicate that Sliunkov evoked anything but a negative reaction from the Lithuanians.

Sliunkov's mission could not have been more different from Iakovlev's visit in August. Sliunkov demonstrated little understanding either of the debate about constitutions or about local thoughts of economic self-sufficiency. Although Moscow quoted him as asserting "that the new provisions of the constitution not only do not lessen, but considerably expand the rights of the Union Republics,"[24] the Lithuanians heard him insist that he was not prepared to discuss constitutional changes. He also angered the locals by calling Lithuania a "territory" rather than a "republic." In all, he embodied Moscow's desire to pull the strings tighter again, and Lithuanians wanted no part of it. Brazauskas even had to extricate Sliunkov from an unfriendly crowd in Kaunas.[25]

A few days later, on November 18, Brazauskas confronted his dilemma at a meeting of the Lithuanian Supreme Council. Tension was high: a western analyst argued, "No Lithuanian First Secretary has ever moved so decisively to satisfy the public.... Nonetheless, a confrontation seems inevitable with either the Kremlin or the Lithuanian Restructuring Movement."[26] Associates later disclosed that Brazauskas was at this point taking medication for tension.

Brazauskas tried to pacify the nationalists by making Lithuanian the official language of the republic and by adopting the Lithuanian national symbols, but he resisted the demand for a constitutional change asserting the primacy of Lithuanian laws—Estonia had just two days earlier adopted similar legislation. While not rejecting it outright, through parliamentary maneuverings directed by Šepetys, the council's speaker, the party succeeded in tabling the proposed constitutional reform. Observers concluded that Brazauskas had surrendered to pressure from Moscow.[27]

The official Lithuanian media celebrated the Supreme Council's meeting as a triumph for government policy,[28] but for this effort to find a middle road between Moscow and Vilnius, Brazauskas paid heavily. Demonstrators outside the parliament building spit on the deputies as they left the meeting. Sajudis leaders stopped traffic in Vilnius as a protest, and on November 27 the party Bureau criticized the leaders of Sajudis who wanted to "restore the bourgeois order in Lithuania."

Brazauskas's program at this point seemed to fall into three basic spheres. Culturally he supported all the basic demands of the Lithuanians, and he endorsed the use of the Lithuanian language and the national symbols. His economic program called for strengthening the republic's "self-sufficiency," and as an economic specialist in the party, he could provide forceful leadership in this direction. His political program was considerably less forceful; he advocated Lithuanian "sovereignty" within the Soviet federation. It was on this last point that he clashed with Sajudis.

Although Gorbachev proved to be completely unsympathetic to his dilemma, Brazauskas subsequently denied that Gorbachev was putting any pressure on him at this time, explaining that he was acting on his own responsibility. Moscow had made no explicit threats, he insisted, but he feared that Gorbachev might establish presidential rule in Lithuania and place a governor in charge. He claimed simply to have understood Moscow better than those around him did.[29]

When Lithuanian deputies went to Moscow for the Supreme Soviet session at the end of November, Gorbachev berated them for the disorder in their land. They did not take this lesson kindly. "What kind of dialogue was that?" Vytautas Astrauskas, Lithuania's chief of state, later complained. "We sat there for an hour like a schoolchild at a tribunal.... I then understood that M. Gorbachev was totally uninformed, that no one here even wanted to understand us."[30] In his speech to the Supreme Soviet, however, Astrauskas praised Gorbachev's program, saying that the gensek's report and recommendations "inspire confidence that the reform of the political system will guarantee conditions for the further free development of each nation and ethnic group."[31] Gorbachev pushed his constitutional changes through the Supreme Soviet over the protests of deputies from the Baltic republics.[32]

One constitutional change that was to have great significance for Gorbachev's dealings with the Lithuanians provided for the establishment of a new legislative body for the USSR, to be called the Congress of People's Deputies. Gorbachev was obviously not yet ready to move his center of power from the party to the government, but he hoped to recruit a new set of local representatives from across the county who would help him to establish stronger control of the political order.

At this same time, however, he banished the Lithuanians and the Estonians from the ranks of his perestroika, telling the presidium of the USSR Supreme Soviet, "No matter what attire such elements might don, no matter with what pledges and assurances they might try to cover up their real attitude, they are parasites of perestroika, and it is necessary to see through their actions."[33] The Balts might protest that they were in fact realizing perestroika's highest ideals, but the Soviet leader rejected the thought that others had any right to their own interpretations of his perestroika.

As was to be expected, the Moscow press turned on the Lithuanians. Moscow correspondents had already targeted Terleckas and the Freedom League for criticism, but they had expressed sympathy for the main lines of Sajudis activity. Now the press spent far more energy in criticizing Sajudis than in praising Brazauskas. Less than two weeks earlier, Leonid Kapelushny, *Izvestiia*'s correspondent in Lithuania, had won praise from the Lithuanians for his reporting of the Sajudis congress. Now he suggested that Sajudis's day had passed, and he singled out Vytautas Landsbergis as the symbol of the new extremism that seemed to have taken over the Lithuanian reform movement.[34] In response, the Sajudis Seimas broke with the organization's tradition of not designating a single leader, and it named Landsbergis the chairman of its council.

Brazauskas tried to act the peacemaker. On December 15, over Moscow radio, he insisted that although relations between Sajudis and the party were strained, Sajudis did not constitute "opposition to the party." The next day on Lithuanian radio he expressed sympathy for Gorbachev's understanding of problem of Lithuanian sovereignty. Neither Gorbachev nor the leaders of Sajudis were paying him much heed.

By the end of the year Gorbachev probably regretted what Iakovlev had done in Vilnius. Decentralization could mean surrendering power to political opponents; it was better to stress the need for centralized leadership. On December 19, Vadim Medvedev, the party's ideological supervisor, declared that at this "extremely crucial stage" in the development of Soviet society, the party's attention had to focus first of all on economic development. He took pains to insist that perestroika was not the cause of the upsurge in national consciousness—he spoke of "the exacerbation of interethnic relations"—and he urged party ideological workers "to embark on a profound analysis of pressing problems." He offered no substance other than to reassert that the party, and obviously Moscow, must take control.[35]

Seeking ways to undermine Sajudis's democratic image, the CPSU and the central government now came to the defense of minority rights, arguing that the presence of other nationalities in the three Baltic national fronts was "purely symbolic."[36] The Muscovites, to be sure, could find no *point d'appui* among Lithuania's small Jewish population, who were supporting Sajudis; instead the Soviet authorities concentrated on rousing and defending the interests of Russians and Poles. The Russian-language party newspaper *Sovetskaia Litva* had warned of interethnic clashes for some time: "I must admit," declared its reporter after the demonstration of September 29, "that I, as a non-Lithuanian, felt uneasy in the middle of this crowd and was afraid to utter a word of Russian." The Lithuanians, readers were to conclude, were becoming threatening.[37]

At the beginning of November, the "Socialist Movement for Perestroika in Lithuania—*Edinstvo*" announced its existence as an "informal group." Its platform criticized the "indecisiveness" of the Lithuanian Communist Party, called for continued ties with the "union of sovereign republics of the USSR," and reaffirmed its faith in "Marxist-Leninist ideology." The Soviet military, expressing itself through its newspaper *Krasnaia zvezda* (Red Star), enthusiastically supported Edinstvo, trumpeting reports of discrimination against Russians in this republic.[38]

Moscow loyalists paid special attention to advancing the interests of the Poles in Lithuania, although the Poles previously had enjoyed few favors from the rulers of the Soviet Union.[39] Poles were particularly numerous in the two southeastern Lithuanian districts of Šalčininkai and Vilnija and were a significant minority in the districts of Trakai and Švenčioniai, in addition to making up about 18 percent of the population of the city of Vilnius. (In the post-Soviet period Belarusian nationalists have laid claim to this same territory.) Although in the past local Poles had shown a strong inclination to choose Russian schools for their children, a number of Poles had moved to Lithuania to take advantage of the Polish-language schools there. Now CPSU and KGB representatives encouraged people in these regions to register complaints and make demands of the authorities in Vilnius.[40]

Ironically, Polish leaders in Warsaw looked askance at this activity in Lithuania. Adam Michnik, editor of *Gazeta wyborcza*, called upon all Poles to reject thoughts of servility to Moscow and to support the Lithuanians; Lech Walesa clearly stated his support for the Lithuanians; and a Club of Friends of Lithuania sprang up in Warsaw.[41] The pro-Moscow Poles in Lithuania rejected such advice, saying that their compatriots across the border did not understand the situation.

As the year 1988 waned, Moscow and Vilnius were entering new dimensions of conflict. Sajudis, feeling ever more confident, was radicalizing its program and its demands. Moscow, seeking to undermine the Lithuanians, searched for new allies within the republic, mobilizing the Polish and Russian minorities. In addition, the Baltic military district was voicing its concerns about security in the region. Caught in the middle were Brazauskas and his supporters, who were trying to bridge the growing gap between the two camps but who soon would have to choose on which side to stand.

5

SOVEREIGNTY OR INDEPENDENCE?

In preparation for the elections to the USSR Congress of People's Deputies (CPD), which Gorbachev scheduled for the end of March 1989, Vilnius surged ahead of Moscow in putting some of Gorbachev's own ideas into practice. While Moscow was musing the possibilities of a "multiparty" system, the Lithuanians were proceeding with genuinely contested elections. Sajudis won four seats in by-elections to the Lithuanian Supreme Council, and although Sajudis leaders denied any intention of making their organization "a political party," their actions spoke far more eloquently. Swept up in what Kestutis Girnius of Radio Free Europe called "the revolution of rising expectations," the Lithuanians could be expected to aim higher.[1]

The developing struggle between Gorbachev and the Lithuanians made Brazauskas's work difficult but also constituted his political bread and butter. He wanted to bridge the differences between the two sides, but he had troubles with both. On the one hand he feared the possibility of Moscow's forceful intervention, and on the other he deplored the Sajudis's aggressiveness. And he had to work under Moscow's suspicious eye: "Those who then accused the LCP CC of cowardice, should remember how we were constantly being watched," he later complained. "The CPSU CC brigades, especially from the organization section, would not leave Lithuania. The leadership of the Baltic military district also paid a great deal of attention to us.... The security was also active."[2] The question of the day was whether Brazauskas was Moscow's man in Lithuania or Lithuania's man in Moscow.

Brazauskas chose to take his case "to the people," and he startled Moscow by deciding to run in a competitive election for a seat in the CPD rather than take a guaranteed place as a representative of the party. (Gorbachev himself took one of the reserved party places rather than face open election.) The Lithuanian leader later explained the situation as one in which he had a more radical constituency than Gorbachev did, and his efforts to build support within his own community complicated his efforts to find common ground with the Soviet leader.[3]

Brazauskas's freedom of movement was hampered by the fact that he himself could not change the makeup of his Central Committee, and he rejected demands that he convene an extraordinary party congress to deal with this problem. As Bronius Genzelis later put it, "the leadership of the LCP CC changed, but not the apparatus, which tried to take its revenge."[4] In December 1988, to be sure, Brazauskas had formalized some changes that had already taken place: The CC accepted Mitkin's resignation and approved the naming of Mindaugas Barysas as editor of *Tiesa*. (Barysas's appointment resulted in the unprecedented situation that the editor of the party newspaper, a veteran journalist, was not a member of the Central Committee.) The party apparatus nevertheless was still in place.

In order to bolster the party's popular support, the LCP took several new, unprecedented initiatives. Brazauskas supervised the preparation of two major documents, one the LCP program for the upcoming elections and the other the LCP's recommendations to the proposed CPSU CC Plenum on the nationalities question. The party also advanced a new slogan, "A Lithuania without Sovereignty is a Lithuania without a Future." The word "sovereignty" was, of course, an indefinite term in the Soviet political lexicon, but since the word was already in the Soviet constitution, Moscow could not object to it.[5] The party went on to endorse the principle of republican economic self-sufficiency, including economic relations with foreign countries and even the possibility of a separate currency, and to call for a full scale review of the Nazi-Soviet agreements of 1939 to 1941.[6]

On January 26 Brazauskas met with Sajudis leaders for the first time since the crisis in November; the talks were lively. The Sajudis representatives complained that the party's fear of Moscow's intervention was hindering the resolution of crucial issues; the party agreed to celebrate February 16, permitting all political groups including the Freedom League to participate. The Sajudis representatives came away from the meeting with a feeling of victory, but Brazauskas believed that he had made his point about dangers: "We also spoke very concretely about tanks and about the possible reaction of the Soviet Union."[7]

Moscow did not look kindly on Brazauskas's initiatives. The LCP's electoral program and its position paper on the national question represented the first such documents to be adopted in Vilnius without having first been cleared in Moscow. "The material has already been sent off," Brazauskas publicly told the Lithuanians, "Some there may not like it, but truth is truth." Vytautas Astrauskas later said with a laugh, "We were pulling the threads with the Kremlin; there was a peaceful parliamentary liberation.... We began to send not projects of laws, as before, but already passed laws!"[8]

In Moscow, both the party and the military disliked what they saw happening. Radicals in all three Baltic republics were already demanding the withdrawal of Soviet "occupation forces" from their territories. On January 6 Gorbachev boldly told a meeting of intellectuals in Moscow, "It is not in vain that we say that there is currently a revival of faith in socialism in the Baltic region,"[9] but the authorities in Moscow were uneasy. In mid-January the Lithuanians helped Belarusian reformers, who had not received permission to gather in Minsk, to meet in Vilnius, and at the end of the month Lithuanian radicals sponsored a meeting of "representatives of national-democratic movements of the nationalities of the USSR."

The plans to celebrate Lithuania's Independence Day caused particular concern in Moscow. On January 25 the Politburo accepted a report indicating that foreign "centers of ideological diversion" and "anti-Soviet organizations" were urging the Baltic peoples toward "confrontation with the organs of power."[10] The CC dispatched an ideological commission "to acquaint itself with the situation in the republic."[11] Authorities in Moscow blocked visas for eight prominent Lithuanian-Americans who wanted to attend the festivities. On February 16 the army's newspaper, *Krasnaia zvezda*, used adjectives such as "alarming," "irresponsible," and "extremist" in describing preparations for the holiday.

In early February, amid rumors that the CPSU leadership was dissatisfied with his "flirting" with the "nationalists" and that it was perhaps planning to remove Brazauskas from office, the Lithuanian leader visited Moscow. (A YAK-40 airplane stood always ready at Vilnius airport for special flights to Moscow.) The Politburo now formed a special commission to study the Baltic question and Lithuania in particular. Vadim Medvedev, as ideological secretary, chaired the group, which included Georgy Razumovsky (the organizational secretary), Vladimir Chebrikov, Iu. D. Masliukov (Gosplan), Dmitry Iazov (Defense), Vladimir Kriuchkov, and Nikolai Sliunkov.

Brazauskas had to explain to the Muscovites what he meant by "sovereignty," what was involved in drafting a new Lithuanian constitution, and why the party had agreed to celebrate February 16 as a national holiday. The Soviet leaders also challenged the behavior of LCP members who were active in Sajudis and complained about Sajudis's agitation among other nationalities; Kriuchkov shouted, "What, you want to destroy the Soviet Union?" Brazauskas later said of his interrogators, "Their understanding was very primitive."[12]

Upon his return home, Brazauskas publicly dismissed the reports of Moscow's displeasure, joking "I think there are no grounds to spread such rumors in Lithuania. I am alive and well and, as you can see, am in my office." He nevertheless added that the radical thoughts emanating from some corners of Lithuania "are disturbing not only us, not only me as First Secretary. They are also disturbing other people." His reference was obvious as he went on to urge restraint.[13]

On February 15 Brazauskas was again in Moscow, this time giving Gorbachev an account of his stewardship of the LCP and demanding a freer hand from interference by Moscow bureaucrats. Gorbachev rejected out of hand Brazauskas's request to postpone the elections that were scheduled for Easter Sunday. The Soviet leader went on to complain that the words to the Lithuanian National Hymn did not mention socialism, and he suggested that the LCP postpone its planned publication of a draft constitution for the republic. When Brazauskas urged that Moscow publish the secret protocols to the Nazi-Soviet agreements, Gorbachev insisted that they were not to be found in Soviet archives. The meeting seemed to end in a stalemate, but Brazauskas left Moscow feeling reassured that he could negotiate with the center.[14]

Moscow waged a vigorous campaign against the Lithuanians' February 16 celebration. Edinstvo organizers denounced LCP leaders for having agreed to the celebration, staged their own demonstration on February 12, and organized work stoppages on February 15. (Soviet authorities seemed to approve of such "strikes.") Chebrikov denounced popular movements like Sajudis as having caused "great harm to our mighty, positive social movement." On February 14 Gorbachev declared "Those who demand Lithuania's secession from the USSR are people who are guided by personal ambitions, career considerations, or are simply extremists.... We must give them a determined rebuke." He offered instead the slogan, "Strong center, strong republics."[15]

Sajudis leaders, however, wanted to challenge Moscow still more aggressively. Kaunas members of the Sajudis Seimas had persuaded the group to meet in the republic's "second city" for the occasion. This would separate Sajudis's celebration from whatever Brazauskas and the Communist authorities in Vilnius might do, and Kaunas would provide the setting for a more radical statement. The move also symbolized the passing of Sajudis from the control of the Vilnius intelligentsia to a broader coalition of nonintellectual, even antiintellectual, forces that were driven by deep antipathy and resentment toward a half-century of Soviet rule and were therefore that much less interested in reforming the existing structure.

The celebration, which took the form of a special meeting of the Sajudis Seimas, began in the state theater at 6:45 P.M. on February 15, and in testimony to the power of the Kaunas group, it first paid tribute to the memory of Romas Kalanta, a young man who in May 1972 had immolated himself in protest against Soviet rule. Organizers planned to make a climactic declaration at midnight, but through the evening they were still arguing about what they should say. As Audrius Butkevičius, a member of the Kaunas radical faction, later recalled, "It was already time to go and we were still discussing the text.... We surrounded [Romualdas] Ozolas [a prominent figure in Sajudis]. He must decide, this is why the Seimas was invited to Kaunas, so that its declaration would clearly speak of the drive for restoring independence." The Kaunasites asserted that they would not sign any declaration that did not mention independence, and when they won the support of representatives of other cities, in Butkevičius's words, "We felt that we had the power to squeeze those Vilnius professors. And we squeezed."[16]

At the meeting some speakers urged moderation. Algis Klimaitis, an émigré living in West Germany and an active participant in the work of the European parliament, warned that the western powers above all wanted stability in the Soviet Union and therefore favored Gorbachev. When Brazauskas showed up unexpectedly, organizers allowed him to address the gathering, and the party secretary repeated his slogan: "A Lithuania without sovereignty is a Lithuania without a future." Most Seimas members nevertheless wanted to make a forceful statement.[17]

As a result, the Sajudis Seimas adopted a declaration denouncing the Molotov-Ribbentrop pact and reiterating "the Lithuanian nation's aspiration to create a democratic state": "The Lithuanian nation never reconciled itself to the loss of its state sovereignty." The declaration stopped short of calling for independence but made clear that that was Sajudis's long term program. At a public rally on February 16, Sajudis leaders added: "Our goal: a free Lithuania!"[18]

Bobbing between Sajudis and Moscow, Brazauskas attempted to quiet the storm by claiming to have won Gorbachev's agreement to Lithuania's "economic self-sufficiency," and he criticized some of the thoughts expressed on February 16 as "unacceptable." He tried in turn to dismiss his problems with Moscow as being natural: "Everything is ahead, and we have to work hard because we are first. It is hard for the ones in the lead to break the ice."[19]

Moscow's pressure on Brazauskas intensified. At a plenum of the LCP Central Committee on February 21, speakers denounced Sajudis, and even Brazauskas accused it of leading Lithuania to ruin, warning that unless Sajudis eschewed thoughts of independence, the LCP would cease to work with it. Pointing to what appeared to be the lame-duck status of the Central Committee members, Lithuanians characterized the gathering as "the plenum of the victims of perestroika"; Brazauskas later called it "one of the most oppressive events in party life in 1989."[20] In any case, Moscow seemed to be regaining influence in the LCP.

The clearest sign of Moscow's pressure came in the restructuring of the ideological work of the LCP. Having lost its traditional foothold in the LCP with Mitkin's departure, the CPSU created a new one: It directed the Lithuanians to form an Ideological Commission, similar to the Moscow reforms of September 1988, and to accept Valerionas Baltrunas as the CC secretary for ideology and chairman of the Ideological Commission. (Baltrunas had previously worked the Central Committee in Moscow.) This meant Šepetys's retirement as party ideological chief, and it gave Moscow entry into the inner workings of the LCP. The plenum went on to call for greater control of party members taking part in Sajudis.[21]

In explaining the plenum to the Lithuanian public, Brazauskas insisted that on the one hand, the LCP had made significant progress in asserting the principles of political sovereignty and economic self-sufficiency, and that on the other, radicals in Lithuania were creating tension by raising irrational demands. "Therefore our basic goal," he asserted, "is to establish goals toward which we can go together.... But if there are no common goals, if they diverge, cooperation becomes difficult, even inconceivable." Whatever the current tactics of the party, he further emphasized, the party had not changed its goal of genuine reform.[22]

Although angered by Brazauskas's position, Sajudis leaders feared the consequences if Moscow should remove him, and therefore they chose, in the words of Bill Keller of *The New York Times*, "to avert an open confrontation with the Communist Party." Brazauskas had chosen to run in the difficult district of Antakalnis in the city of Vilnius, where the university's influence was strong. Opposing him was the popular Sajudis leader Arvydas Juozaitis. If Brazauskas lost, he would have no credibility in Moscow.

Sajudis observers believed that despite their current leanings, Brazauskas and Beriozovas were closer to their views than any other leaders of the LCP, and therefore, as they explained to Michael Dobbs of *The Washington Post*, "It was unwise to risk the public humiliation" of the LCP leaders. The Sajudis council therefore directed Juozaitis to withdraw from the electoral campaign, and it also withdrew its candidate against Beriozovas. As Landsbergis put it, "We wanted to show our conditional support for the progressive forces in the party." Juozaitis seemed to agree: He had earlier told the London *Independent*, "I am a radical, and fear is a bad counsellor in politics—but I am afraid. If Brazauskas loses, it could mean a political crisis."[23]

For his part, Brazauskas tried to show both his constituencies that he was indispensable. In Moscow he continued to press for a discussion of the Molotov-Ribbentrop Pact, and he insisted that the western powers' continued refusal to recognize the incorporation of the Baltic states put Lithuania in a qualitatively different position from republics in the Caucausus or other regions of the Soviet Union. Speaking to a Lithuanian audience, on the other hand, he reported Gorbachev's goodwill toward them and announced that the Soviet leader had in principle accepted an invitation to visit the republic "when he is more free."[24]

For the moment, it seemed as if Gorbachev had no choice in Lithuania but to work with Brazauskas. In the words of a British journalist:

Mr. Brazauskas talks only of economic sovereignty, while Sajudis wants political rights too. Semantic nuances—sovereignty versus independence, group versus party, and phrases like 'for the time being'—are used to fox friend and foe alike. Mikhail Gorbachev is weighed down with problems of his own and shows no appetite for attempting to kick Mr. Brazauskas into line.[25]

Another western analyst suggested, "Gorbachev has a hefty political stake in helping [Brazauskas] navigate the narrow straits between nationalist extremists and conservatives within his party apparatus."[26]

The elections on March 25 threw all these calculations into confusion. In the first round of voting, Sajudis won thirty-one of the forty-two seats at stake, and in the second round it added five more. Brazauskas and Beriozovas swept to victory, thereby demonstrating their personal popularity; the only LCP leader to win a seat without Sajudis's endorsement was Kestutis Zaleckas, the head of the Vilnius city party organization. Vytautas Sakalauskas and Vytautas Astrauskas both lost their bids for seats. Sajudis had an organizational victory; Brazauskas had a personal victory; and the Communist Party stood rejected.[27]

Brazauskas concluded that he had to move closer to his Lithuanian constituents, even though this would risk antagonizing both Moscow and also conservatives in his own organization, perhaps even splitting the party. As he told an audience in Klaipeda, "the party must rethink its tactics and strategy in order to regain people's trust." Beriozovas called the results not "altogether unexpected, although obviously they were unsatisfactory for most party members." He admitted that the tone of the recent party plenum may have alienated voters, but he insisted that the February CC plenum had not signified "a return to old times." From Brazauskas's point of view, all this dictated the need to cooperate with Sajudis, and he called on the newly elected CPD deputies to work out a common program in order to have a strong impact in Moscow.[28]

For Sajudis the election results constituted a great step forward. Meeting on April 1, the Sajudis Seimas declared that the voting had shown the people's lack of trust in the LCP, and it resolved to press yet more forcefully for Lithuania's economic self-sufficiency and for the republic's "sovereignty." Although one still could argue that "a major part of the Sajudis candidates are members of the Lithuanian Communist Party who are active champions of the current reform policy in the Soviet Union,"[29] it was clear that new forces were emerging onto the political stage. As Mečys Laurinkus, a Sajudis victor, told his electors in Taurage, "I think that the people gave us an 'advance.' Most of those elected have no political experience.... I consider what happened as the people's thanks for our 'movement.' This is a great responsibility."[30]

Sajudis's victory brought the Lithuanian question home to Moscow; a delegation of Lithuanians, dominated by separatist if not secessionist thought, would now have official status in the Soviet capital and would have access to both national and international media. Commentators in Moscow reacted uncertainly. Linking Sajudis's victory with his own election as a deputy, Boris Yeltsin declared, "It is interesting to note that those of us who promoted the process of change had the most resounding victories in the elections."[31] Writing in *Sotsialisticheskaia industriia* on April 4, Iury Kurbatov welcomed Brazauskas's election and credited the LCP as having been "the cementing cause that brought all reasonable forces together." Others in Moscow were not so sanguine in their evaluations.

In preparation for their new activity in Moscow, the Lithuanians first met privately with Soviet leaders. On April 1 a group of Lithuanian deputies urged Iakovlev to make public the work of a commission that under his direction was considering the publication of Soviet foreign policy documents from 1939 and 1940.[32] On April 6 Sajudis representatives— Landsbergis, Ozolas, Kazimiera Prunskiene, Genzelis, accompanied by Baltrunas as a representative of the LCP—met with Anatoly Lukianov, deputy chairman of the USSR Supreme Soviet.

Lukianov was not ready to promise the Lithuanians anything. Landsbergis opened the meeting by complaining about the information on which Moscow seemed to be relying, and he insisted that Sajudis's goal was "the sovereignty of Lithuania." Genzelis declared that the LCP, and especially its Central Committee, was out of touch with the Lithuanian people. Ozolas urged the formation of independent Communist parties in all the republics of the Union, and Prunskiene argued in favor of the principle of economic self-sufficiency.

Lukianov questioned the group closely. Landsbergis assured him that the Lithuanians still accepted "the principles of socialism," but he complained that perestroika was moving too slowly. The Sajudis representatives urged the reorganization of the Soviet Union, arguing that the Soviet state must establish a new basis for "mutual trust" between the nationalities, and they repeatedly emphasized their demands for greater economic autonomy, insisting that their republic's economy was more mature than other republics' and that therefore the Soviet government should permit it greater independence. Lukianov concluded with the thought that "he knows the Lithuanian character and therefore is very attentive to what is being said there; decisions, however, will be adopted by all the republics."[33]

Lukianov's cautious response epitomized the way in which the Soviet leadership manipulated the constitution. When desirable, the authorities in Moscow could assert the unrestricted power of the center or else insist they could do nothing without the agreement of "all the republics." On the other hand, they would not allow the republics to block Moscow's will or, even worse, to band together to impose a decision on Moscow. The Lithuanians, in turn, put little faith in the wording of the constitution or in the legal system.

In Vilnius, Brazauskas, amid rumors that he would be summoned to work in Moscow, struggled to keep his place in the middle. In dealing with Moscow he emphasized four points: economic self-sufficiency, condemnation of the Molotov-Ribbentrop pact, the necessity of a new treaty of union between the constituent republics of the USSR, and the status of the LCP within the CPSU structure. He shocked CPSU officials by suggesting that Gorbachev reverse the order of his titles, putting his role as USSR president ahead of his position as CPSU general secretary. He visited USSR defense minister Dmitry Iazov to discuss problems of Lithuanians in the Soviet armed forces. On May 18 the Lithuanian Supreme Council asserted the republic's "sovereignty," proclaiming that "only the laws adopted or approved" by the Supreme Council "will be valid on the territory of Lithuania."[34] Carefully publicizing his efforts by means of regular Friday interviews, he projected the image of a man determined to stand up to Moscow.[35] As a result of the publicity that he received, he became a role model for moderates throughout the Soviet Union.

At the same time, he conferred with Sajudis leaders. According to his memoirs, he met frequently with Landsbergis: "He would visit me in my office, and we would drink coffee." Convinced that they were under KGB surveillance, they would take walks together in Vingis Park: "We would discuss the most sensitive questions of Lithuanian statehood, economic self-sufficiency, our deputies' work in Union matters, and generally relations with the Soviet Union."[36] Out of such meetings came a plan of action for the Lithuanians who would take seats in the USSR CPD.

For Gorbachev the convening of the Congress of People's Deputies would open a new era in his efforts to reform the Soviet Union. He had hoped that this would constitute a victory for "his people" and provide support for his program, whatever it might be. To the contrary, however, centrifugal forces were continuing to grow, and not just in Lithuania. On April 9, just a few days after Sajudis's meeting in the Kremlin, Soviet troops killed demonstrators in the Georgian capital of Tbilisi. In Lithuania the news evoked demonstrations of support for the Georgians, and it also aroused new concerns. The Sajudis Seimas called for clearer definition of the "legal and political aspects of the stationing and use of the Interior Ministry troops and other special military units in Lithuania."[37]

At the same time Gorbachev faced growing pressure to act more forcefully in the Baltic. In May the Politburo's special commission on the Baltic presented him with a statement that one of his advisors called "thunderous, panicky," and it summoned the three Baltic party secretaries to answer their charges. Gorbachev tried to calm his comrades, declaring "We have to trust all three, it cannot be otherwise," and insisting that none of the three Baltic republics, "not even Lithuania," wanted to secede." One must think rationally and not fear experimentation, he cautioned, and he ruled out the use of force.[38] The meeting of the Congress of People's Deputies promised to be exciting.

6

THE BALTIC WAY

During the summer and fall of 1989, as Lithuania and Moscow continued to diverge, Gorbachev tried to appease the Lithuanians while controlling them. In government he made cautious concessions, allowing an investigation of the Molotov-Ribbentrop pact and eventually accepting the principle of economic self-sufficiency; the system, however, moved glacially in the direction of making these concessions reality. In party affairs, which still constituted the more important political arena in the Soviet system, Gorbachev and other CPSU leaders strongly disapproved of Brazauskas's efforts to build a popular following. Brazauskas nevertheless persisted, and by the end of the year, the gap between Moscow and Vilnius was too great to be bridged by words and promises.

The formal opening of the Congress of People's Deputies in May portended an effort by Gorbachev to move the base of his power and authority from the party to the government. The congress, however, proved to be a disappointment for him. The deputies he could rely on to accept his parliamentary moves were averse to extensive changes in society; the deputies representing the new forces that he wanted to recruit tended to be more independent. He had to face questions about Afghanistan and the killings in Tbilisi, and he displayed considerable pique when 87 deputies (out of 2,210) voted against his candidacy for the chairmanship of the congress. A deputy even dared to question whether the same person should serve both as chairman of the CPD and as gensek of the party, saying "When a man is torn between two stools, you know that nothing sensible has ever come out of it."

The congress sessions also had the effect of stripping the party of the last vestiges of its previously mystical powers. Party leaders came to the sessions as ordinary human beings and had to defend their views. Nevertheless, Gorbachev made clear that he would continue to rely on the party as the foundation of his power; as he explained early on in the congress's debates, "Without the position of the party, without being able to lean on the party, so to speak, this process will go badly."[1]

Gorbachev demanded followers rather than colleagues. Speaking on behalf of his own candidacy for the chairmanship of the CPD, he affirmed his devotion to "democracy" and his readiness for "dialogue," but he insisted that he knew best what the country needed: "I know everything. I maybe even know more than you." In particular he called for orderliness—and obedience: "We are taking [the situation] in hand, but it is still escaping our grasp. Reform is breaking loose, the political process is breaking loose.... The realization has now appeared after such head-on skirmishes that it is time for consolidation for the sake of our supreme interest." As for the "interethnic question," he warned that "If we start separating our peoples and ethnic groups now.... if we start recarving our country, it will be the road to disaster, I assure you."

At this point, Gorbachev still seemed to have little comprehension of the problem that was developing with the Lithuanians. His references to "interethnic conflict" seemed aimed at the Azeri-Armenian clash over Nagorno-Karabakh rather than at the quieter Lithuanian situation. He seemed to be assigning the latter a low priority among his problems and thought he could still handle it with words.

The Lithuanians, however, had come to Moscow not just to talk but also to win attention. Before leaving Vilnius, the Lithuanian deputies had decided as a group to press their demands for political sovereignty, for economic self-sufficiency, and for an examination of the Molotov-Ribbentrop pact. Brazauskas later asserted, "Of course our delegation traveled to the Congress rather aggressively inclined against Moscow and even M. Gorbachev personally."[2] The Lithuanians voted for Gorbachev as chairman of the CPD, and in interviews they seemed to be wishing him well. Romualdas Ozolas spoke of working toward "a common goal—the building of a just law-governed state" and of supporting "Mikhail Gorbachev so that the transformations that he is initiating are not artificially slowed down," but only Brazauskas would seem to have argued that Gorbachev understood the Lithuanians' concerns, calling his position on the study of the Molotov-Ribbentrop pact "positive, as we understand that."[3]

On the first day of work in the CPD the Lithuanians demanded that the government suspend its ban on demonstrations in Moscow, and they objected to the assembly's voting procedures. Then, calling the constitution "bad," Landsbergis on May 26 objected to the system of voting proposed for elections to the new Supreme Soviet, and he warned that the assembly should "not be surprised that we will be unable to take part in the voting." Gorbachev responded, "We respect the Lithuanian comrades' stand," but he rejected their "ultimatum." The assembly supported Gorbachev.[4]

Parliamentary rules permitted the Lithuanians to present three speakers in the general discussion of Soviet affairs. Brazauskas spoke of the necessity of decentralizing the Soviet system, of the desirability of "economic self-sufficiency" for the republics, and of the urgency to reexamine the Molotov-Ribbentrop pact. Landsbergis suggested that "new thinking" was primarily a product for export, and he argued that perestroika must provide a new base for union between the republics. Kazimiera Prunskiene spoke to questions of economic self-sufficiency.[5]

On June 8 the Lithuanians threw congress deputies into a furor when fifty members of their delegation walked out of a discussion on the formation of a Committee for Constitutional Compliance, insisting that their participation in such a vote would compromise the principle of Lithuania's sovereignty. The "aggressive majority" (Iury Afanasiev's words) shouted insults at them, but Gorbachev persuaded the deputies to suspend their deliberations while he consulted with the Lithuanians.[6]

Gorbachev met with the Lithuanians for a half hour on the morning of June 9, and for many this constituted their first opportunity to meet the Soviet leader in person. He sat down beside Prunskiene and declared his readiness to defend the rights of the republics. The Lithuanians raised other issues concerning the republics' rights, but Gorbachev insisted that the state had to be centralized—all confederations were unstable and doomed. Gorbachev then agreed to postpone the formation of the constitutional commission. Brazauskas, who as a member of the congress presidium had not participated in the walkout, called the meeting "a friendly conversation."[7]

All in all, the Lithuanians felt that they had accomplished much in this CPD session. Gorbachev had backed off on the establishment of a constitutional commission, and he had agreed to consider economic self-sufficiency for the Baltic and to investigate the ramifications of the Molotov-Ribbentrop pact. The deputies also claimed to have won the respect of the congress: Vitas Tomkus declared that the Lithuanians had "found themselves in the center of attention." Landsbergis called the congress a great "political forum" and asserted that the Lithuanians had "earned a certain respect, even among the country's leadership"; on June 11 he told a crowd in Vingis Park, "We have progressed from relations between a great all powerful center and poor subjects into a new, honorable relationship of partners."[8]

Winning agreement to a commission to study the political and legal significance of the Molotov-Ribbentrop pact was an especially significant accomplishment. The congress approved the action on June 2, and Aleksandr Iakovlev became the commission's chairman. As late as April 1989 former foreign minister Andrei Gromyko still called the protocols "forgeries"; and even in September *Pravda* denied their authenticity.[9] Gorbachev had approved a giant step toward recognizing their existence.

Sajudis members in the Lithuanian delegation nevertheless continued to express considerable reserve about Gorbachev's intentions. Prunskiene called the Soviet leader a "situation manager" and suggested that he was better at controlling an unruly gathering such as the CPD than he was in developing a program. Like other Lithuanians, she recognized his seeming readiness to talk about almost anything, but at the same time she noted "the wall" that arose when the discussions became substantive. The Lithuanians also understood that Gorbachev intended to leave the Communist Party in charge of the country and to keep it under his control.[10]

By way of contrast, the Lithuanians expressed growing sympathy for Boris Yeltsin. Prunskiene wrote that she first met Yeltsin when the deputies "goosestepped" to vote for Gorbachev as congress chairman; he assured her that he supported the Baltic republic's claim to sovereignty. In a newspaper interview, Landsbergis spoke approvingly of Yeltsin's endorsement of "decentralization" and his concern about "concentrating power in one pair of hands." Mečys Laurinkus, however, argued that Yeltsin had not voted properly on the formation of the constitutional control committee and had taken an ambiguous stance on the issue of power to the people.[11]

After the CPD session, Gorbachev was very slow to carry his concessions to the Lithuanians through to completion. On July 19 members of the commission studying the Molotov-Ribbentrop pact completed a draft resolution specifying that the alliance with Germany had led to Soviet incorporation of the Baltic states. On July 20 a new draft, while condemning the pact and the protocol, did not draw any direct link between the secret protocols and the incorporation of the Baltic states. Even as altered, the document remained in a drawer; Iakovlev insisted that nothing would be official until approved by Gorbachev and by the CPSU Central Committee.[12] Within a few days, the Sajudis Information Agency was informing the world of the drafts.[13] In a similar vein, the Supreme Soviet, a smaller parliament elected by the CPD, now approved the principle of "economic self-sufficiency" for the Baltic republics, but in the absence of enabling legislation, this remained an empty promise.

While Gorbachev maneuvered, the central media in Moscow denounced developments in Lithuania. Although the Lithuanians liked to speak of the sympathy that they were winning,[14] Soviet spokespersons talked about the Lithuanians' "isolating" themselves—this, of course, in contrast to the complaints that the Lithuanians were trying to "revolutionize" the Soviet Union. The CPSU organ *Pravda* objected to the thought "of dividing people living in a region into the indigenous people and inhabitants belonging to other nationalities" and called for a new union treaty that would make clear that "only the USSR has complete, unlimited sovereignty."[15] The Soviet military chimed in with complaints about the behavior of the Lithuanians toward its forces in the Baltic.[16]

Behind the scenes, the Lithuanian Communist Party and the CPSU were coming into even sharper conflict. In June 1989 the CPSU Control Commission demanded that the LCP dismiss Romualdas Ozolas, Justas Paleckis, and Bronius Genzelis on the charge of "splitting and antiparty activity." Brazauskas refused and urged the LCP CC to assert its own freedom of action—he variously used the words "self-sufficiency" and "autonomy."[17]

On June 24 the LCP CC called for a special party congress to consider separation from the CPSU. As Brazauskas put it, the party had to "renew itself" and "dissociate itself from its past."[18] (This was, to be sure, the same Lithuanian CC that had indulged in the revenge of "the victims of perestroika" in February, but as Paleckis later explained, this time there were "invited guests who created a different atmosphere.")[19] According to Brazauskas, the CPSU central organs now dropped the Lithuanians from their circulation list for important documents such as summaries of Politburo meetings. The CPSU again sent special representatives to

Lithuania to investigate the situation, but the Lithuanian leader publicly continued to assure his people that Gorbachev "understands us."[20]

Much to Moscow's chagrin, the LCP continued to cooperate with Sajudis. At the beginning of July Kazimiera Prunskiene took Sajudis's first step into government by accepting the post of deputy prime minister. When she consulted Sajudis leaders, they told her to do as she wanted and that the experience would be good for her and for Sajudis.[21] At the beginning of August, Paleckis, the head of the LKP CC ideological division, joined with Landsbergis, Antanas Terleckas, and Kazys Bobelis, an émigré leader, in a declaration affirming their common goal to be the independence of Lithuania.[22] On August 4 Brazauskas had to appear before the Politburo's Baltic Commission to respond to denunciations of his work as well as of the activity of Paleckis and Beriozovas.23 On August 15, with another commission from the CPSU CC in Lithuania, *Pravda* again denounced "nationalists" who seemed to be taking over Popular Fronts in the Baltic.

Activists in the Baltic only put forth still greater challenges. As the fiftieth anniversary of the Molotov-Ribbentrop pact approached, they called for a human chain to extend from Gediminas hill in Vilnius to the Tompea tower in Tallinn, to be called "the Baltic Way," demonstrating the solidarity of the Baltic peoples. In mid-August Sajudis leaders announced that they would demand a change in Article 6 of the Lithuanian constitution eliminating the special power and privileges of the Communist Party.

Lithuanian party and governmental institutions kept pace with the surge of national sentiment. On July 17 the Lithuanian Communist Youth League, the *Komsomol*, declared its independence from the parent organization in Moscow. On the eve of the anniversary of the Nazi-Soviet pact, a commission of the Lithuanian Supreme Council declared that the process of Lithuania's incorporation into the Soviet Union in 1940, resulting from the Molotov-Ribbentrop pact, had been illegal: "The People's Diet's Declaration on the Entry of Lithuania into the Union of Soviet Socialist Republics of July 21, 1940, and the USSR Supreme Soviet's Law on the Acceptance of the Lithuanian Soviet Socialist Republic into the Union of Soviet Socialist Republics of August 3, 1940, are unlawful."[24]

In addition to the demonstration on August 23, which won them wide publicity, the Baltic Popular Fronts issued a joint statement to the world, warning "Many have let their conscience be lulled" and scornfully speaking of "apologists of imperialism and red fascists." Although much of the world had hidden behind "double standards and security," the Balts "have remained faithful to democracy and human rights." The appeal concluded, "Brothers and sisters in East and West, we are prepared to forget about your double standards, if you will find in yourselves courage to demand the application of the principles of international law not only in Africa and Asia but also in Europe." The leaders of the Popular Fronts of the three Baltic nations also appealed to the United Nations to denounce the Molotov-Ribbentrop pact.[25]

Moscow waxed apoplectic. On August 23 *Pravda* published a list of grievances against the Lithuanians, entitled "Only the Facts" and compiled by the "Ideological Section of *Pravda*." In *Izvestiia* of August 24, Leonid Kapelushny reported that the Lithuanian Supreme Soviet's latest declaration constituted nothing less than an effort to upset the Helsinki agreement, and the next day the newspaper called "the Baltic Way" a dangerous action: "Whether the Lithuanians who joined the human chain like it or not, the shadow of anti-Soviet and anti-Russian appeals lies over the entire event." Turning on the Communist Party, *Pravda* of August 25 declared that the LCP "has in the last 18 months or so basically been avoiding the political struggle and showing signs of confusion and appeasement." Lithuania, the newspaper added on August 26, was headed for confrontation with the entire Soviet Union.

On the evening of August 26 Moscow television news read a declaration in the name of the CPSU Central Committee condemning "the growing persistence and aggressiveness by certain forces in Lithuania, Latvia and Estonia." Charging that "nationalist, extremist groups" had "misappropriated the role of true proponents of national affairs," the declaration noted that "some of the mass information media" had joined in this "unhealthy" development. "The existence of the Baltic peoples is in serious danger," the document warned. Despite "the deep understanding" shown by the CPSU, "leaders of these republics," including "party committees and functionaries," had failed "to convince the people of the harmfulness of the plans and practices of opposition forces." Calling on the working class and the peasants to defend "the new revolution and perestroika" and on party members to set a good example, the document concluded, "Let's preserve the single family of Soviet peoples and the unity of the Communist Party of the Soviet Union."[26]

Moscow believed that it had a significant audience in the Baltic to which it could appeal. *Pravda* of August 25 quoted Baltrunas as demanding that the Center provide leadership. Gorbachev was on vacation, and his role in the declaration remains unclear. According to Ligachev, the Central Committee's declaration arose in reaction to news from the Baltic "of discrimination against nonnative populations and of the sharp growth of interethnic tension." Healthy forces in the Baltic, he asserted, received the declaration "approvingly, with hope." The declaration sought to "guarantee full freedom for national traditions" while at the same time pointing out "the dangers of nationalism." Had the mass media carried through the spirit of the declaration, he argued, "further events would have developed completely differently and would not have led to political crisis in the Baltic."[27]

The world, however, had changed. As the Lithuanian journalist Algimantas Žukas declared, "The days have passed when reprimands could turn the course of developments in one direction or another."[28] A plenum of the LCP CC adopted a counterdeclaration, trying to sound moderate but nevertheless rejecting the complaints. It trumpeted its slogan "A Lithuania without sovereignty is a Lithuania without a future," it called the Soviet actions of 1939–1940 "political violence," and at the same time it recognized that history could not be erased: "The Lithuanian Soviet Socialist Republic is politically and economically integrated into the USSR." The Lithuanian Supreme Council resolved that it did "not approve of the categorical tone" of the CPSU's "statement and unsubstantiated assessments.[29] The major Lithuanian media supported the LCP's stand.[30]

While Gorbachev himself remained silent, the major Moscow news media took up the cudgel on behalf of the CPSU's declaration.[31] *Krasnaia zvezda* of August 27 complained of mistreatment of soldiers in the Baltic, and *Sovetskaia Rossiia* of August 30 told of Russians there who were frightened and wanted to leave the region. On August 30 Baltrunas told Moscow television viewers that the LCP CC plenum had "expressed its understanding of the concern and anxiety of the CPSU Central Committee." In a speech marking the opening of the Soviet school year, Chebrikov called the CPSU declaration "a precise and clear position" that should help "all honest people to avert disaster in our multinational home." Party members, he urged, must regain their posts of leadership and "adhere to clear philosophical and class positions." *Pravda* of September 2 suggested that western information agencies had a strong interest in fostering trouble in the Baltic. In Vilnius pro-Moscow forces organized as the Committee for the Defense of Soviet Power in Lithuania.[32]

Among themselves, however, Politburo members could only gnash their teeth. In a resolution on August 30 it declared, "LCP CC First Secretary A. Brazauskas, having a certain authority in the republic, could more actively influence the course of events in a positive direction. But he is not demonstrating firmness, he is drawing no conclusions from CPSU CC decisions and from conversations in the Politburo commission." Brazauskas, the Politburo resolved, was too soft on "separatist strata," and he was not "mobilizing the healthy forces in the party and in the society."[33] Although the Politburo could lecture Brazauskas and denounce him all it wanted, it nevertheless could not remove him; instead it lapsed into what Ligachev disgustedly called "impermissible passivity."[34]

Gorbachev himself continued to try to restrain the Lithuanian Communists. On September 4 Brazauskas told a press conference in Vilnius that in a recent telephone conversation, Gorbachev had emphasized the seriousness of the situation and had complained that "certain people lack a sense of proportion and forget in what time, in what epoch, and in which state we live." Gorbachev had then requested him to inform the leaders of Sajudis of his displeasure: "If processes continue developing like this in Lithuania, in such an extreme direction, I will not be your friend."[35] The Lithuanians nevertheless continued on their own path.

Over the succeeding months, the CPSU declaration became a source of embarrassment for the authorities in Moscow. When it appeared, there was some question as to whether Gorbachev had participated in its writing, since he was at the time not in Moscow; but according to Georgy Arbatov, a CC member, the gensek had personally approved the document. One of Gorbachev's advisors later commented that "he succumbed to emotions (also his own term)." Brazauskas considered it the work of the Politburo's Baltic Commission.[36] When the CPSU failed to follow up on its threat, the Lithuanians began demanding to know exactly who had written the document. CPSU leaders sullenly offered only vague responses or refused to answer altogether; Vadim Medvedev privately told the Lithuanians that he had signed it without reading it.

In January 1990, when Medvedev held a press conference in Vilnius marking the end of Gorbachev's visit to the Lithuanian capital, I asked him, "Who wrote the declaration?" Medvedev angrily lectured me on how various agencies of the Central Committee could issue statements in the committee's name, scolded me for being interested in such an old document, and urged me to seek happier thoughts and to study the Central Committee's resolution on the nationalities question in September 1989. The CPSU leadership obviously wanted to forget the August declaration.

The Central Committee's resolution on the nationalities question to which Medvedev referred was the product of the CPSU CC plenum on the national question, convened in Moscow, September 19–20. Although Gorbachev had issued the call for this meeting early in 1988, the party leaders had kept putting it off as they struggled to understand the problem. On the eve of the session Gorbachev told Brazauskas that he would support "sensible steps to consolidate all the forces" in Lithuania but added "harsh words" concerning the Lithuanians' "very bold steps and decisions."[37] The plenum then recognized that in the past "deformations" had entered the system and had lingered on to the present day, hurting not just smaller nationalities but also the Russians themselves. Now a strengthened "Soviet federation" must establish institutions respecting "national and international values and interests" while respecting their "sovereignty."[38]

In addressing the plenum, Brazauskas insisted on the necessity of a "real union of equal sovereign states," as promised in the constitution, and he insisted that republican "sovereignty" would open the way to greater economic and cultural achievements. The developments in Lithuania, he argued, had relevance for the entire country. but observers must distinguish between more significant and less significant events and statements. The CPSU, he insisted, must properly understand what the LCP had to do in order to gain the trust of the people, and he criticized the CC's resolution for not speaking out strongly enough about Stalinist crimes against specific nationalities. Changes in the party, he concluded, must move faster than changes in the society.[39]

The plenum, which also called for a CPSU congress in 1990, did not slow the sharpening confrontation. At home Brazauskas reported simply "The plenum was difficult" and admitted that Lithuania had "very few sympathizers" there.[40] In October a plenum of the LCP CC decided to schedule the decisive extraordinary LCP congress for December. Gorbachev warned Brazauskas to move more slowly, telephoning him before every major meeting in Lithuania and urging him accept the decisions of the CC plenum; in Lithuania, Sajudis leaders demanded that the government publish the Iakovlev's commission report on the Molotov-

Ribbentrop pact. Together, the leadership of the LCP and the leadership of Sajudis prepared a constitutional amendment to change Article 6 and to remove the Communist Party's special status in the government and society.

By now—the fall of 1989—it can be argued that the question of Lithuania's political future had been essentially resolved; as a result of the cooperation of Sajudis and the party, Lithuania was moving rapidly in the direction of independence (or "sovereignty"). In December the Lithuanian Supreme Council established a commission to prepare a plan for achieving Lithuania's independence; its membership included Ozolas, Brazauskas, and the poet Justinas Marcinkevičius. The question of the day in internal politics was now one of political power: Would the party or Sajudis be the driving force in determining the details of that future? In effect, the next election campaign had now begun.

A preliminary skirmish arose over the issue whether Lithuania should have a president. Although Brazauskas was a popular figure in Lithuania, his position as party secretary would have no political significance when the Lithuanians altered Article 6 of the constitution and if the basic threads holding Lithuania to Moscow were broken; therefore his supporters began to toss about the idea of establishing a formal presidency, which he would presumably occupy. Sajudis leaders, on the other hand, welcomed the shifting of power from party to government, but they did not want to see Brazauskas in charge of a strong executive branch. Therefore they opposed the establishment of a presidency in the republic.

For the moment, however, the LCP was still the moving force in Lithuania, and in response to his perception of his constituency—Sajudis leaders were now calling the LCP an agent of the authorities in Moscow—Brazauskas was loosening all ties with Moscow. In turn, he could count on the support of Sajudis only in his confrontation with Moscow, and even there many criticized him as being too soft because he worried too much about Moscow's responses. In Ozolas's judgment, Brazauskas "reflects Moscow's viewpoint, is always having dealings with those people, and bears in mind the danger which they represent, but if we are to act while always thinking about what other people will say, it is better not to begin."[41] Win or lose in his dealings with Moscow, Brazauskas would yet face political opposition at home.

Sajudis leaders were preparing to challenge the party's role in the government, and in this they had the support of leaders of the Lithuanian emigration. Émigrés provided Sajudis with microcassettes, dictaphones, typewriters, paper, ink, and computers; they also financed travel abroad for Sajudis leaders, on occasion complaining that Sajudis was simply issuing orders. On the other hand, the émigrés backed away from Brazauskas: In November the doyen of the émigré Lithuanian diplomatic service, Stasys Lozoraitis, informed Brazauskas that his presence would at the Lithuanians' Vasario 16 (February 16) gymnasium in Germany be unwelcome.[42]

Moscow demonstrated little understanding of Brazauskas's problems. At an eight-hour meeting of the Politburo on November 16, which Brazauskas and others attended, Kriuchkov, Iazov, Pugo, and Nikolai Ryzhkov angrily criticized the Lithuanians. Ligachev declared, "What is there to discuss with them, with Brazauskas? They have already accepted their Supreme Council's resolution on the superiority of Lithuania's laws to the laws of the Soviet Union. Juridically they have already separated from us." After denouncing thoughts of economic self-sufficiency, he continued, "And now they are preparing to take the final step, that is, the political separation from the CPSU. Let us look squarely at these events and evaluate them for what they are."[43] When the meeting broke up, Beriozovas, the second secretary of the LCP, refused an invitation to stay for a "private conversation" with members of the Politburo.

A few days later the Politburo denounced the Lithuanians as the worst offenders "in trampling on the freedoms" of the republic's citizenry. In particular the bureau on this occasion objected to the progress the Lithuanians were making in developing a multiparty system and in their characterization of the Lithuanian Communist Party as an "agent of a foreign power."[44]

Rather than remove Brazauskas as it would have of old, the Politburo now sent Vadim Medvedev to Vilnius to teach the LCP about orthodoxy and party discipline. Meeting with the Lithuanians on December 1, Medvedev delivered a message from Gorbachev and lectured the Lithuanians on the dangers of their chosen path, warning that they were endangering the very success of perestroika. Moscow, he warned, was reaching the end of its patience in the face of the talk of independence. "We favor broad independence for the Lithuanian Communist Party," he declared, but "we cannot fail to express our negative attitude toward the desire to separate from the CPSU."

Gorbachev's message spoke warmly about the support of his program shown by the Lithuanian people and admitted that progress was coming only painfully. The CPSU, he insisted, was fighting resolutely against all the negative phenomena of the Soviet past, but the LCP was succumbing to "the alarming elements that are accompanying the processes of renewal." Therefore the Politburo believed that Lithuanian independence "and the formation of a republican Communist Party independent of the CPSU would nullify the results of Lithuania's development."

In response Brazauskas argued that the Lithuanian CP could "play an important political role in the life of Lithuania today" only by cutting the strings of Moscow's control. He rejected Moscow's quotations of Lenin's opposition to "party federalism," arguing that the Bolshevik leader had been reacting to qualitatively different situations, and he insisted that the LCP would be a party representing all the people of Lithuania, not just the ethnic Lithuanians. "Our goal at this stage" was the restructuring of "a new union of free republics."

When members of the LCP Central Committee had the opportunity to speak, individuals came out both for and against separation from the CPSU. "The Communists of the Šalčininkai District [Poles constituted a majority in this district] are categorically against leaving the CPSU," said one speaker, but Šepetys argued in favor of separation, saying "If we are seriously concerned about building a common European home, it would be a crime not to be concerned about our own home." Sigizmundas Šimkus, rector of the Vilnius Higher Party School, declared, "Conscience commands us to renounce Article 6 of the constitution.... It is annoying that Moscow is spreading disinformation, making groundless accusations."[45] In the end, the Medvedev mission accomplished little. "V. Medvedev did not understand the Lithuanian situation at all," Brazauskas wrote. "He tried to educate us, that was the most important purpose of his trip."[46]

As the confrontation intensified, Moscow threatened the Lithuanians with a variety of measures. Soviet spokespersons expressed concern for the future of the minority nationalities in Lithuania: Medvedev criticized Brazauskas as a nationalist and urged Poles and Russians in Lithuania to oppose the establishment of an independent LCP. At the same time, Moscow threatened the territorial integrity of Lithuania: It encouraged Belarusian specialists to lay claim to the Vilnius region (which Moscow otherwise seemed to consider inhabited by Poles) and declared that it had the right simply to take Klaipeda away from Lithuanian control. Gorbachev also began to speak of the millions and even billions of rubles that the Soviet government had invested in Lithuania, warning that in the event of secession, the Lithuanians would have to pay compensation. (He made clear that the payment would have to be in dollars, not rubles.) Gorbachev's ultimate option, of course, was the use of force, but for the moment that did not enter into consideration.

Brazauskas nevertheless still hoped to cooperate with Gorbachev. At the end of November, after long delays and considerable opposition, the USSR Supreme Soviet approved legislation enabling the Baltic republics to embark on their policies of economic self-sufficiency as of January 1, 1990. Ryzhkov, Masliukov, and others had opposed the plan to the end; Lukianov had declared that a separate Baltic economic autonomy law was not necessary and that all problems would be solved in the context of all-union economic reform; but at Brazauskas's urging Gorbachev accepted the idea. As events developed, the idea was stillborn, killed by Moscow's resistance to the thought and of course by Gorbachev's blockade of Lithuania in the spring of 1990. Moscow had failed to offer a viable answer to the question "sovereignty or independence?"

7

AT THE CROSSROADS

The end of 1989 and the beginning of 1990 constituted perhaps the most crucial period for Gorbachev's Lithuanian policy; this would be his last chance to find a means of controlling the course of events in the republic. He objected to the initiatives the Lithuanians were showing in forming a separate Communist Party and building a multiparty political system. Some observers expected him to use force to bring the Lithuanians back into line, but instead he plodded forward, complaining but not offering any significant new initiatives, never able to catch up with the flow of events.

If anything, he reluctantly, resentfully, followed the lead of the Lithuanians; perhaps he recognized a logic in their arguments. In February 1990 he persuaded the CPSU CC to approve at least the thought of developing a multiparty system, and in April the CPD approved a law on secession. Like his belated enthusiasm for rewriting the treaty of union between the republics—another idea that originated with the Lithuanians—his actions were too little and too late. Gorbachev's fundamental concern, it would seem, became the question of maintaining his own position, while Lithuania, originally a testing ground of his proposals for decentralizing the command-administrative system, was spinning out of his control.

Besides the problem of taming Vilnius, Gorbachev had to recognize that his troubles with Lithuania were attracting international attention. When he met U.S. president George Bush in the stormy waters off the coast of Malta in early December 1989, the situation in the Baltic constituted "the most sensitive and potentially the most explosive matter on their agenda." The Bush administration, having come into office in January, had at first taken a cautious line toward Gorbachev, but when it concluded that it could work with Gorbachev, it feared that national dissent, as seen in

Lithuania, could undermine his position in Moscow. "It is not necessarily in the interest of the United States to encourage the breakup of the Soviet Union," declared presidential advisor Brent Scowcroft. On the other hand, the White House feared that if Gorbachev resorted to force, "his image as a peacemaker in the West would vanish," and that too was an undesirable prospect.[1]

Bush and Gorbachev reached an understanding, but in the words of Jack Matlock, the U.S. ambassador to the Soviet Union, there was no "explicit or implicit deal" giving Gorbachev a free hand in the Baltic. Bush welcomed Gorbachev's assurance that the Soviet government was "determined" to avoid the use of force, and he told the Russian that "we don't want to create big problems for you." As Matlock has put it, the Americans assured Gorbachev that "we will not go out of our way to embarrass him."[2]

The understanding left considerable latitude for Gorbachev's policy in the Baltic. The Soviet side already had occasion to appreciate the American president's caution; in April 1989, when Soviet troops killed demonstrators in Tbilisi, Georgia, the Bush administration had issued only muted sounds of concern. Bush seemingly accepted the Soviet code word "ethnic conflict," with all its connotations justifying Moscow's intervention, but "violence" against the Baltic republics would bring the U.S. government to act more forcefully. Therefore, Gorbachev at least had to avoid use of the word.

Lithuania nevertheless remained a severe test. Despite Gorbachev's objections, the LCP approved the abolition of the party's special position, and on December 7 the Lithuanian Supreme Soviet amended Article 6 of the constitution of the Lithuanian SSR, thereby eliminating the formal basis for the one-party system.[3] Speaking to a plenum of the CPSU CC on December 9, Gorbachev made clear that he opposed any such action in Moscow: "The Central Committee will wage a resolute struggle against attempts to minimize the Party's importance and undermine its authority among the working people."

The question of an independent Communist Party was even more delicate than the constitutional question; for Gorbachev this promised repercussions within his own camp in Moscow. When the LCP's Twentieth Congress assembled in the Opera and Ballet Theater in Vilnius on December 20, the atmosphere was both expectant and tense. Brazauskas's nationalist critics thought that he was holding back, that he was unsure whether he should really split with Moscow. Brazauskas himself felt that he had the support of the people, but he feared the consequences if the conservatives in the party should break away in protest against the party's independence from Moscow. At noon of the first day Gorbachev telephoned him; "in a particularly angry voice," the Soviet leader asked, "Have you passed that resolution about the separation of the party?" Brazauskas replied, "No, we have not accepted such a resolution, but we will," to which Gorbachev exclaimed, "Do you know where this all can lead?"

Brazauskas, fearing that Soviet troops might disperse the congress, hurried back to the hall and urged immediate action on his colleagues. "One could feel that threat in Gorbachev's voice," he later recalled. Soviet leaders had often promised him "help" in reestablishing "order" in Lithuania, but Brazauskas had always rejected Moscow's prodding, insisting that "neither I nor my colleagues nor our party leadership could resort to force. The democratic processes had to proceed naturally." The LCP now declared itself an independent organization.[4]

The pro-Moscow camp in the LCP immediately rebelled. A rump group of the congress broke away and declared that it did not recognize the decisions of the congress. Instead, the dissidents spent the night—hence their nickname "the nighttimers"—organizing themselves as the Sixth Conference of the LCP (the fifth had met in 1933) and proclaiming their loyalty to the "Moscow program"—hence another of their nicknames, *programininkai*. They organized a provisional Central Committee and appealed to Moscow for help.[5]

Elected secretary of the provisional LCP/CPSU CC was Mykolas Burokevičius, a professor of Marxism-Leninism, who had distinguished himself by his opposition to the winds of reform in 1988 and by his avowed sympathy for Edinstvo. As late as 1972 Burokevičius had praised Stalin's infamous "Short Course" history of the CPSU for its role in reeducating the Lithuanian intelligentsia.[6] Also prominent in the new group were Juozas Jermalavičius, "Lithuania's Nina Andreeva" of the spring of 1988, and Vladislav Shved, party secretary for the October District in the city of Vilnius.[7]

Brazauskas's LCP, now called the "independent" LCP, won an unprecedented show of popular support in Lithuania, but at the same time it had a full plate of problems. Although some prominent figures from Sajudis entered the LCP Central Committee and even the Bureau, the LCP's conversion to the cause of independence aroused suspicions and concern among more radical Lithuanians as well as among pro-Moscow forces. Was

Sajudis taking over the party or was the party co-opting Sajudis? Nonparty Sajudis leaders declared that they would support the party insofar as it opposed Moscow, but otherwise Sajudis must remain in the opposition to the party. Brazauskas, however, had little time now for the power struggle; once the LCP's congress had ended, he hurried to face a special plenum of the CPSU Central Committee in Moscow.

Gorbachev was openly angry. On December 21 he had sarcastically addressed Lithuanian delegates in the USSR Congress of People's Deputies as "comrades, communists, nonparty Bolsheviks." When Landsbergis began to speak, Gorbachev inquired, "Nonparty Bolshevik?" "Yes," answered Landsbergis, who apparently had not heard the "Bolshevik" reference, and an exchange of barbs ensued. In a private meeting with Brazauskas, the Soviet leader showed a sadder face, sighing "Ach, Algirdas, what did you do with the Communist Party, what did you do, who will be responsible for that!"[8] Brazauskas understood that the CC plenum would be difficult.

Moscow nevertheless made one more concession to the Lithuanians in the political arena: The USSR CPD finally accepted the Iakovlev commission's denunciation of the Molotov-Ribbentrop Pact. To be sure, it first rejected the report when Iakovlev presented it on December 23. After some confusion, Lukianov won agreement to give the commission time to reconsider its motion. "For the delegates from the Baltic this was vitally important," said one of Iakovlev's aides, "but the outcome of the voting was no less important for the democratic part of the congress." The next day, December 24, Iakovlev persuaded the congress to accept the report. Gorbachev gained nothing with the action: The Lithuanians gave him little credit, and the conservatives in Moscow registered this in their dossier cursing Iakovlev for the troubles in Lithuania.[9]

In the CC plenum Brazauskas found little understanding. After Gorbachev had opened the meeting by recalling Moscow's warnings to the Lithuanians, Brazauskas responded that the formation of an independent Communist Party had been essential. He argued that the Lithuanian Communist Party had led the drive "to strengthen the sovereignty of the republic." If the LCP had not acted, the reformers would themselves have split from the party: "Parallel party structures had been created and were beginning to operate," he declared; "an alternative congress could take place with hard to predict consequences." The independence of the LCP, he insisted, "does not mean cutting off ties or a split" with Moscow, and certainly not cutting economic ties.[10]

The overwhelming majority of the members of the Central Committee rejected Brazauskas's arguments. They muttered and scolded when he or his colleagues spoke, and they cheered the "nighttime" leaders Burokevičius and Shved. Some committee members challenged Brazauskas's naïveté, others his integrity. Questioned as to whether he had met with the American ambassador, Jack Matlock, Brazauskas, with a touch of relief, responded, "The easiest question, because I once again assert that I never visited nor met with Mr. Matlock nor with other ambassadors of other governments." Nevertheless speakers kept returning to the thought that foreign intrigue lay behind the Lithuanians' actions.

Central Committee members seemed convinced that Sajudis had captured the Lithuanian Communist Party and that Sajudis posed a threat to the country as a whole. Vadim Medvedev pictured the Lithuanian party congress as the merging of the LCP with Sajudis. Egor Ligachev called the LCP "in fact a tool of the nationalist goals of Sajudis." Juozas Kuolelis, of the LCP/CPSU, called the new LCP Bureau "the flower of Sajudis." Sajudis representatives had reportedly captured the media in Lithuania and were flooding the public with their propaganda. Sajudis representatives were moreover traveling throughout the Soviet Union and mobilizing dissident forces. Several speakers called for a ban on extremist, nationalist organizations; there was no serious consideration of finding a compromise.

The party leaders were also concerned about the challenge that the Lithuanians were posing to the party's position. Kriuchkov called the LCP's action in amending the constitution "a detonator for events of the same sort in other republics." N. A. Nazarbaev, the first party secretary in Kazakhstan, accused the Lithuanians of wanting "to deprive the CPSU of its role as the political avant garde of Soviet society, to emasculate the basic political essence of party activity, without which the party, as such, would cease to exist," but he went on to urge the restructuring of the CPSU Politburo to represent the nationalities of the Soviet Union. The Ukrainian Vladimir Ivashko denounced the Lithuanians' actions as a blow against "our entire party, the sole integrating force of Soviet society."

The CC members seemed particularly responsive to two anti-Brazauskas speakers from Lithuania. On the first day Valerionas Baltrunas denounced the "psychological terror" that the Lithuanians had exerted against Moscow loyalists in the party, and on the second day Vladyslav

Shved emotionally argued that Moscow had to intervene if it wanted to maintain a loyal party organization in Lithuania. Shved's speech lost a bit of its impact when Gorbachev had to correct his arithmetic, but the Central Committee members welcomed his passion.

Amid the soaring rhetoric two speakers stood out because they focused their attention on concrete questions. Iu. D. Masliukov, the chairman of Gosplan, the state economic planning agency, spoke in detail of Lithuania's economic development, how it was tied to the Soviet economy, and how the Lithuanians would suffer if they chose to cut ties with Moscow. On the second day, Boriss Pugo, a former chief of the Latvian KGB and former Latvian party boss, who was then head of the Party Control Commission, recounted his agency's vain efforts to get the Lithuanian party leadership to root out the dissident elements within its ranks. The party leadership, Pugo argued, should move more aggressively against its foes.

Brazauskas and his allies had little opportunity to defend themselves. Beriozovas appealed to logic by pointing to the upcoming elections to the Supreme Soviet in Lithuania: If the LCP wanted to do better than it had in 1989, it had to appeal to the population. If Sajudis won a strong majority of seats in the new Lithuanian parliament, Beriozovas warned, it would soon thereafter declare the independence of the republic. His argument fell on deaf ears: The Central Committee wanted to know nothing of election campaigns; it was concerned with the status of the CPSU.

Gorbachev called the Lithuanians' action "a blow to the CPSU" and "a blow to perestroika," and he repeatedly joined in the attacks on Brazauskas and the LCP. When Vadim Medvedev pictured the LCP as a tool of Sajudis, Gorbachev interjected, "A Trojan horse!" When Masliukov spoke emotionally of the streams of Russians who would soon be fleeing Lithuania, the general secretary exclaimed, "Comrades, we cannot allow this to happen!" and he offered his own idea of a renewed federation. Masliukov thanked him for providing an end to his talk, and Gorbachev commented, "Good conclusion."

On the second day CC members attacked Brazauskas personally. Shved argued that Brazauskas was incorrigible, and speakers demanded that Moscow intervene. V. M. Nikiforov, USSR Deputy Minister of Foreign Affairs, called for the expulsion of Brazauskas, Beriozovas, and Paleckis from the CPSU; Brazauskas, he insisted, was "all the more dangerous" because he was "a man of sense, an authoritative man." A. A. Dzharimov, from Krasnodar, suggested that the Central Committee revoke its decision of October 1988 approving Brazauskas's appointment as first secretary of the LCP.

A semblance of calm returned only when Vytautas Astrauskas warned that if the Lithuanians returned home with the news that Brazauskas, Beriozovas, and Paleckis had simply been expelled, "this will not help us." Subsequent speakers, including Boris Yeltsin, urged restraint. (Brazauskas claimed also to find some sympathy from Eduard Shevardnadze.) To punish Brazauskas now "could arouse unpredictable things in the republic.... Why, in a struggle over the party line is it immediately necessary to call the KGB?" asked M. A. Ulianov, but Burokevičius returned to the rostrum to plead for action: "Please consider the situation in our republic!"

Gradually the group came around to a temporizing response, agreeing that the two factions in Lithuania could not reach agreement among themselves and therefore Moscow should send a delegation to teach them. The Kirgiz A. M. Masaliev was the first to suggest that Gorbachev himself should go; Yeltsin agreed; and finally Burokevičius argued that Gorbachev's presence would mobilize the "many and many" who supported the program of the CPSU. In conclusion, the Central Committee officially recessed until Gorbachev and other party representatives had had a chance to visit Lithuania to make their own observations.

The gathering had embodied all the contradictions of Gorbachev's policies, and its work made clear that those contradictions would continue. At a time when most persons admitted the necessity of change, Gorbachev called on the CC, which he called "the brain of the party," to maintain its "principles," and, as he himself recognized, those principles were in fact very conservative. "We all now have to read Lenin very carefully," declared T. G. Ivanova, deputy chairman of the Presidium of the RSFSR Supreme Soviet. Although in just six weeks Gorbachev would reverse himself and persuade the CC to end the party's special status, many speakers had insisted that protecting the party's status was the key issue in their view of the events in Lithuania.

Closely tied to the status and power of the party was the control of public opinion and discussion. Most of the speakers at the plenum seemed convinced that loosening the party's reins on the press and media in the Soviet Union had delivered these institutions into the hands of their enemies. Ultimately, the fear that any further loosening of the reins of power would stimulate and release the dark forces in the society testified to the distrust with which the party leaders viewed the masses.

After the plenum, Gorbachev scolded some of his advisors for having remained silent during the discussion, and one responded that since the gensek had not made his own position clear, his allies "did not know how to support you." His advisors despaired of his tactics in the CC, saying "You have to be done with such a CC if you want to save the party for perestroika." Iakovlev reportedly told Gorbachev that he should have walked out of the meeting and that Medvedev, Kriuchkov, Shevardnadze, and Sliunkov would have walked out with him. Gorbachev's supporters argued that their chief was still making too many concessions to Ligachev and the conservatives.[11]

In preparing for his trip to Lithuania, which the Politburo duly approved on January 2, Gorbachev summoned the Bureau of the independent Lithuanian Communist Party to Moscow on January 4. Flanked by Iakovlev and Medvedev, he told them that he was having trouble educating his colleagues. Although the Lithuanians considered Iakovlev more sympathetic than Medvedev, in public statements there was little to choose from. Speaking over Soviet television, Iakovlev warned that Lithuania could start a "domino" effect that threatened the very structure of the Soviet Union; Medvedev told the Lithuanians that their actions constituted "an expression of no-confidence in the party." Standing in the center as was his wont, Gorbachev tried to impress the Lithuanians with both his power and his problems.[12]

In this turmoil, Moscow welcomed all the support it could find in the West. After *The New York Times* of January 3 had carried an op-ed essay that strongly warned the Lithuanians against thoughts of secession, Moscow loyalists in Vilnius enthusiastically recommended it to the foreign journalists who had flocked to follow Gorbachev in Lithuania, and Soviet Foreign Ministry spokesperson Gennady Gerasimov, who had little good to say about foreign journalists, subsequently singled the essay out for special praise.[13] On February 5 *The New York Times* called on the peoples of the Soviet Union to remain true to Gorbachev's ideals. Moscow could only wish that the western press had the impact on the Lithuanians that Soviet conservatives frequently attributed to it when they blamed it for their problems.

Officially Gorbachev's visit to Lithuania, which extended from January 11 to January 14, 1990, was party business (to confer with Lithuanian party officials), but he obviously planned to appeal to the Lithuanian people over the heads of the Lithuanian Communist Party. "I do not think," he told

Brazauskas in December, "that you have adequately expressed the will of the people." Upon arriving in Vilnius, he declared, "We are here to find a way out, to block the way for the development of dangerous centrifugal forces in the USSR. We cannot hurry the process of history." He still believed in his own power to rally mass support; the Lithuanians, he discovered, talked back.

The leaders of Sajudis seized the opportunity of being at the center of the world's attention to talk of independence, welcoming Gorbachev as the president of the Soviet Union and not recognizing any special role for him in Lithuania as general secretary of the CPSU. They called on the people to show him respect as the "leader of a neighboring country," "a friendly neighbor," and, mindful of the flood of reporters that would come with him, they urged the people to come out carrying banners, especially in foreign languages, for the benefit of television cameras.

Sajudis's elaborate welcome intensified the Soviet leader's dissatisfaction. A month later, in front of the CPSU CC, he scolded Brazauskas: "...you prepared to receive me as the president of a neighboring country." Brazauskas responded, "Mikhail Sergeevich, I never prepared to receive you as president. You know this very well. These were others who wished to do this, and it is very difficult for me to answer for them."[14] Brazauskas insisted that even the independence of the LCP should not be interpreted as breaking off communications with Moscow. Gorbachev, however, could not accept this new concept of political life and statehood that the Lithuanians were advocating.

The key slogan of Gorbachev's delegation in Vilnius was that "the national question was not the main question in life," meaning that the Lithuanians should direct their efforts at economic revival and moderate political reform. (Gorbachev, it should be noted, had brought Vadim Medvedev but not Aleksandr Iakovlev to Vilnius with him.) The Muscovites, down to the journalists accompanying them, kept repeating this message, and they could not understand the Lithuanians' response that national feeling is deeper than any other emotion. The Moscow journalists themselves, however, seemed to have more elemental feelings that they refused to admit: After lecturing me on this theme, the Muscovite sitting next to me at a press conference loudly and angrily objected when a Lithuanian journalist used her own language to pose a question.[15] Once again, in this struggle between Vilnius and Moscow, the words being used did not represent the essence of the conflict.

In the standard style of such visitations, Gorbachev went to factories, traveled out of town to Šiauliai, and held public meetings first with the intellectuals of Vilnius and then with the party *aktiv*. In his own fashion, Gorbachev played the crowd, staging intense conversations with individuals standing near him. When he laid a wreath at Lenin's statue, for example, he spoke at length with people by his car. Where I was, on the fringe of the crowd, people were complaining that he should use a microphone so that everyone could hear him, but I believe that he was using this as a photo and television opportunity to show a much larger audience how well he communicated with the people on the street.

The Moscow press corps duly reported that bystanders, the Lithuanians on the street, were declaring their support of Gorbachev's program. On January 13 Moscow radio declared that "the absolute majority" of Lithuanians supported Gorbachev's efforts, but television broadcasts told another story. Obviously surprised by the vigor with which individual Lithuanians argued with him, the Soviet leader berated the Lithuanians for their "narrowmindedness," urging them to realize that the Soviet Union promised them the best future and then bluntly warning that Moscow was not about to abandon its military and industrial investments in the Baltic.

Gorbachev nevertheless made several major public concessions during the visit, indicating that his government was preparing a law establishing procedures for secession and also accepting the idea of a multiparty state. While both statements represented startling changes in his program, these announcements had a stronger impact on the foreign journalists than on the Lithuanians. The Lithuanian government had already declared that Soviet law was not necessarily Lithuanian law, and in any case, it remained to be seen what Gorbachev's ideas would look like in practice.

Gorbachev did what he could to give the "nighttime party" equal status to the independent LCP. Everywhere he went he traveled in the company of both Brazauskas and Burokevičius, and on January 12 he held a special, unannounced meeting with the provisional Central Committee of the *programininkai*. According to Moscow TASS, the group put special emphasis on "the role of the CPSU as a guarantor of the irreversibility of perestroika." While paying lip service to "perestroika," the theme underlined the conservative conception of the party as the source of order in the society, something of a contradiction to Gorbachev's newly discovered sympathy for a multiparty system.

Taking advantage of the presence of world media, Sajudis leaders held daily press conferences and also sponsored two major demonstrations in Cathedral Square, one in anticipation of Gorbachev's coming and the second shortly after his arrival. (The gatherings also manifested considerable support for the LCP; as Justas Paleckis and Vladimir Beriozovas walked together down the center of Gediminas Prospect to the square, shouts of *Valio*, "Hurrah," greeted them.) The demonstrators demanded that the Soviet government denounce the movement of its troops into Lithuania on June 15, 1940, and that it remove its army from Lithuania. They also demanded that Moscow compensate Lithuanians for the human and physical costs of Soviet rule, and that the USSR Supreme Soviet approve opening negotiations with Lithuania on the question of independence.

After Gorbachev had left for Moscow on Sunday, January 14, Justas Paleckis commented that the most positive conclusion to be drawn was that nothing had happened—no one had become angry, no bad scenes had taken place.[16] Direct conflict had been averted, but then nothing had been resolved. Each side continued on its own path, and as the Lithuanians forged on, this meant a defeat for Gorbachev. It was only a matter of time until Moscow would issue another challenge, this time stronger because the sides were moving even farther apart.

Two days after Gorbachev's departure, Brazauskas took the post of chairman of the Presidium of the Lithuanian Supreme Soviet, in essence Lithuania's president, although the post did not come with strong executive powers. By this act, he was of course preparing to deal with Gorbachev as president to president, rather than as party secretary to party secretary, but he was also moving the font of power in the society out of the party into the Supreme Soviet. When he became first secretary in October 1988, no governmental appointment was necessary to confirm his power; now he had subordinated the party to the government; and when he was ousted as "president" in March 1990, he remained party secretary but he no longer controlled Lithuania's destiny. In the tumultuous fifteen months since the fall of 1988, the political structure of Lithuania had changed drastically. Brazauskas had accomplished what Gorbachev had apparently dreamed about, and as his reward the authorities in Moscow were about to drum him out of the official ranks of the perestroika faithful.

Once back in Moscow, Gorbachev declared that the trip had not changed his mind, but as he prepared for the resumption of the Central

Committee's deliberations on the crisis, his position seemed a bit softer: He spoke of passing laws to define the procedure for secession; he spoke of possibly defining a new relationship between republican parties and the CPSU; and he called for consideration of a multiparty system in the Soviet Union. On the other hand, when he sent Soviet troops into Baku on January 20 to quell "ethnic conflict," Washington remained silent, and he could therefore assume that U.S. president Bush now accepted the principle of using force to put down "ethnic conflict."[17]

On February 7 the CPSU CC reassembled to hear Gorbachev's account of his visit to Lithuania, and the gensek reported that the "majority of people" in Lithuania "support perestroika" but that "at present separatist attitudes dominate in the republic." The Lithuanians, in their passion, had not considered all the consequences of secession from the Soviet Union. Arguing that the LCP had had no right to declare its independence from the CPSU, he proposed that "the two wings" of the LCP both send delegates to the upcoming Twenty-eighth Congress of the CPSU: "We are leaving the doors open in the hope that Lithuanian comrades will use this possibility for a common search for a way out of this situation."[18]

In the ensuing discussion the vast majority of speakers took a much harder position, calling for measures to put the Lithuanians in their place. Driving the speeches of many was the fear they might fall victim to an upheaval like the Romanian revolution of December 1989 that had summarily executed the Communist dictator, Nicolae Ceausescu. At the December CC plenum, only one speaker, Vladimir V. Karpov, secretary of the USSR Union of Writers, had expressed concern for his own safety, and another, M. A. Ulianov, the director of the Vakhtangov theater in Moscow, had pointed to Ceausescu's fall as a warning that an uncompromising stance did not ensure survival in these troubled times. In February, however, the pro-Moscow Lithuanian Communists exploited the "Ceausescu syndrome" and pictured Sajudis leaders as bloodthirsty nationalists. The conservatives in the Central Committee resolved to protect their cohorts in Lithuania and thereby of course to prevent such thoughts from spreading elsewhere in the Soviet Union.

The conservatives also reacted negatively to the LCP's newfound popularity in Lithuania. The reformers in the LCP had themselves found it difficult to become "politicians" in order to win popular support. "A year ago I was not a politician," Brazauskas had told party workers, "but now we all must be politicians." Such ideas, however, ran counter to tradition in the CPSU, and Central Committee members one after another told Gorbachev that the CPSU should not seek the kind of popularity that the LCP claimed to enjoy.

LCP/CPSU members focused considerable hostility on Iakovlev and thereby, however indirectly, on Gorbachev. At the December plenum Stasys Giedraitis had complained that in 1988 Iakovlev had misrepresented events in Lithuania. At this February plenum, although Burokevičius dated the development of Lithuanian separatism from the second half of November 1988, Shved insisted that many Lithuanian Communists dated their problems from Iakovlev's visit. In his own defense, Iakovlev called the split in the ranks of the Lithuanians "a blow to perestroika in a most difficult moment," and he complained about "political infantilism" in the Lithuanian party. Another Lithuanian, V. J. Kardamavičius, nevertheless indicated that the pro-Moscow camp was unforgiving: "We once again want to inform the comrades that the visit of comrade Iakovlev in Lithuania truly began the series of bad things in our republic."

In the end, Gorbachev yielded to the conservatives, and he formulated the plenum's resolution as (1) a denunciation of the leadership of Brazauskas and Beriozovas for having contributed to weakening "the unity of the CPSU," (2) a declaration of "all possible support" for the Burokevičius group, and (3) a call for Lithuanian communists to participate, through the Burokevičius group, in the preparations for the Twenty-eighth Congress of the CPSU. Burokevičius accepted the resolution, but when Brazauskas stated, "I do not know what to say," Gorbachev angrily scolded him:

Everything is objectively stated. You took a decision, this was a split. The first point establishes this. The second establishes the formation of a parallel organization with a provisional Central Committee, that we must deal with it. This is also a confirmation of reality. And the third point—we once again turn to you: reconsider everything and work together with the CPSU. Is there anything to be added?

Brazauskas nodded, saying "We understood everything," and when Gorbachev put the resolution to a vote, the plenum accepted it unanimously.[19]

Although Gorbachev subsequently declared, "The doors are open, party comradeship has been shown, and a hand extended," the doors were in fact closed. The plenum's action marked a turning point in Moscow's policy toward Lithuania. Gorbachev's supporters might argue that the Soviet leader had made only a tactical retreat, but in fact he had moved out of positions that he was never to retake. He apparently thought that Burokevičius & Co. represented a force in Lithuania akin to what the conservatives in Russia seemed to wield, but he was wrong—Burokevičius had no political following in Lithuania other than what Moscow could deliver to him.

The reforms that Gorbachev had proposed in the course of January proved to be ephemeral and in any case irrelevant to the Lithuanian situation. The laws on secession came in April and modified the constitution, thereby making clear once again that the constitution was not the "fundamental law" of the Soviet Union, but in any case the Lithuanians had already chosen to ignore this line of action. The Central Committee, to be sure, approved the revision of Article 6 of the constitution, but its debate on the Lithuanian question and Soviet practice of 1990 and 1991 in general made eminently clear that this action changed nothing as far as the party's actual position was concerned. Gorbachev continued to rely on the party apparatus as his basic political and social organizational support, even as he pushed forward plans to expand the powers of the Soviet presidency.

Gorbachev had now essentially lost Lithuania. He had placed his wager there on forces that in the past had resisted his programs; he cut himself off from the reform elements in Lithuania that had supported perestroika. By cutting off institutional contacts with Brazauskas, he had weakened the elements in the Lithuanian body politic that were more ready to cooperate with what he had left of a reform program. The leaders of the Lithuanian CP had thought that they could work toward independence with Gorbachev's help[21]; now they could no longer work with him—although some still tried.

Without a dynamic tension with Moscow, the independent Lithuanian Communist Party lost its vital role in Lithuanian society and even much of its reason for existence. Gorbachev had thereby committed himself, his party, and his government to a policy of force and intimidation in Lithuania, with all the ensuing complications that such a policy would create for him elsewhere. This guaranteed his failure both in Lithuania and on the larger Soviet stage.

8

RECONSTITUTING THE
LITHUANIAN STATE

During Gorbachev's visit to Lithuania in January 1990, visitors and natives alike openly discussed when—not whether—the Lithuanians would decide to declare their independence. Many suggested July 12, which would be the seventieth anniversary of the Soviets' recognition of Lithuanian independence in 1920, but the discussions generally missed the essence of the issue as it developed: Specifically who would issue the declaration, and what form would it take? Then: What would be Gorbachev's reaction?

Although Lithuanians were agreed on the idea of independence, there were two major lines of thought on how to translate words into action. On the one hand, LCP leaders favored going slowly and evoking a minimum of conflict with Moscow; on the other, the radical wing of Sajudis anticipated that conflict with Moscow was inevitable and therefore believed the Lithuanians should act quickly without fearing Moscow's reaction. In between these two extremes, perhaps leaning this way, perhaps that, stood probably most of the Lithuanian public.

Brazauskas of course advocated a slow approach—"step by step," he called it. On February 7, the day on which the CC plenum in Moscow ended, the Lithuanian Supreme Soviet annulled the decision of the People's Seimas of July 21, 1940, requesting Lithuania's entry into the Soviet Union, and the parliament invited Moscow to begin talks concerning "restoring the independence of the Lithuanian state." The LCP called for the "restoration of an independent Lithuanian state" by "parliamentary constitutional means," and Brazauskas later described this as "a revolutionary step" that cleared the way for the declaration of March 11. Sajudis leaders, however, dismissed the LCP's initiatives as election maneuvers.[1]

On February 9 Moscow TASS declared that the Supreme Soviet's action "cannot be regarded otherwise than a step towards this Baltic Republic's secession from the Soviet Union." Brazauskas later tried to discount the protests: "Of course Gorbachev made some noise and let loose a tirade of accusations against us,"[2] but after Gorbachev's visit to Lithuania, Soviet commentators followed two lines of thought on Lithuania: (1) The Lithuanians should not separate from the Soviet Union, and (2) they had the right to separate, but they had to consider the costs and their obligations to the other republics. The Lithuanians tended to seize on examples of the second approach as signs that independence could be negotiated.[3] The battle of words, however, merely provided a facade for Gorbachev's basic policy, which was to restrain and control the Lithuanians.

The Lithuanians nevertheless pushed ahead, and Gorbachev's camp suffered a humiliating defeat in the Lithuanian elections of February 24, which saw 472 candidates—401 Lithuanians, 30 Russians, 30 Poles, and 6 Belarusians—campaigning for 141 seats in the Lithuanian Supreme Soviet. The independent LCP fielded the most candidates, 210, while the LCP/CPSU put up 78, and 139 were listed as nonparty. Since Sajudis was not formally a party, official statistics made no mention of it, but a number of the LCP candidates also had Sajudis's endorsement. The first round of voting resulted in the election of 90 deputies, 72 of whom (80 percent) had Sajudis support. The LCP claimed 22 seats, the LCP-CPSU only 7, most of whom were Poles. In the additional rounds of voting in early March, Sajudis-backed candidates won enough seats to guarantee absolute control in the new parliament.

Gorbachev now openly threatened the Lithuanians. He sent a delegation headed by Burokevičius to Vilnius to help the LCP/CPSU gain control of party property, and on March 5 he warned Brazauskas that secession would cost Lithuania some 21 billion rubles—that is, $33 billion in hard currency since the Soviet state would not accept payment in rubles. (Gorbachev apparently had calculated this by figuring the Soviet national debt against Lithuania's trade balance with the other union republics and then freely translating all this into "world prices.") He also threatened to take away the cities of Vilnius and Klaipeda, reducing Lithuania to its "borders of 1939."[4]

Lithuanians flatly rejected Gorbachev's financial and territorial threats. Landsbergis declared that "if they were to present bills to each other, Lithuania's would be dozens of times greater." A Lithuanian journalist ironically noted that Gorbachev based his claim to Vilnius on the terms of the Molotov-Ribbentrop pact, which his parliament had denounced. Almost lost in the tumult was Brazauskas's warning that times ahead would be difficult: "It would be nice if we ourselves could avoid creating reasons for life to become even harder. But that could happen."[5]

When the new Supreme Soviet deputies began to gather in the early days of March, the drive to declare Lithuania's independence mounted quickly. In the words of Kazimiera Prunskiene, who became prime minister of Lithuania on March 17, "It was the unmistakable will of the people to be able to find themselves as free citizens in a free land. In this way the nation gave its future deputies very clear tasks."[6] The fact that foreign journalists were inquiring about their intentions drove Sajudis leaders to be more forceful, and they decided to convene the Supreme Soviet as soon as possible, especially in view of the expectation that the USSR CPD would give Gorbachev greater powers as president when it met on March 12. Therefore, when the supplementary elections guaranteed Sajudis at least ninety-four seats, two-thirds of the total number of deputies, Sajudis leaders called the parliament into session. The Sajudis Deputies' Club, organized by Virgilijus Čepaitis, prepared the way.[7]

As a first step, the new parliamentary majority had to decide how to divide up political offices, and after some debate Vytautas Landsbergis became the deputies' club's candidate for the post of chairman of the Presidium of the Supreme Soviet. Although Brazauskas, the current incumbent of this post, was probably the most popular figure in Lithuania, the Sajudis majority in the legislature guaranteed Landsbergis's election. Once installed in office, Landsbergis, with the support of the deputies' club, could restructure the government apparatus and control appointments to other offices—he eventually designated Prunskiene prime minister, and Brazauskas became her deputy for economic affairs.

Turning to the question of declaring independence, Sajudis leaders had to decide whether to appeal to the constitutional right of secession or to declare the entire period of Soviet rule null and void. Until Gorbachev began interpreting the constitution in his own way, the right of secession had appeared to be complete and unconditional. The document did not stipulate procedures, but the republics seemingly had the right to follow their own paths. Once the Lithuanians had begun speaking of independence, however, Gorbachev declared that he would establish a procedure for secession. The constitutional road to secession was therefore cloudy and dangerous, if one could believe in the provisions of the Soviet constitution.

A counterargument called for the Supreme Soviet to declare the restoration of the independent Lithuanian state that had existed before World War II. This argument denounced the Soviet years as an occupation of the land by a foreign power and declared the Soviet constitution inoperative in Lithuania. The Sajudis Deputies' Club adopted this line, affirming the continuity of Lithuanian statehood and eschewing any appeal to the Soviet constitution.

Holding some deputies back was the question of what aid they could expect from elsewhere—what would be the response of western governments and especially the United States? In light of Washington's cold response to their declaration of independence after the fact, Lithuanians later frequently asked how Sajudis leaders could have presumed that they would receive American backing. An American-Lithuanian professor, V. Stanley Vardys, suggested that the US State Department had been supportive but that the administration had overruled its recommendation: "...most of the State Department's recommendations (especially in important matters) 'pass' through the White House. There they soften everything, and we see the result."[8] A recently published American account of the Bush-Gorbachev relationship offers a quite different view: "[Bush] asked his aides and the State Department to devise language that would allow him to walk the delicate line between Washington's old refusal to concede Lithuania's annexation and his own desire not to create trouble for Gorbachev."[9] In fact, the situation involved misconceptions in both cities, Washington and Vilnius, compounded by confusion in Moscow.

The U.S. government was closely monitoring events both in Moscow and in Lithuania. Shevardnadze told the Americans that the Lithuanians risked military intervention if they declared their independence before the CPD had acted on Gorbachev's presidential powers. When the Lithuanians began to inquire about the possibilities of recognition, the Americans advised caution and care, refusing to promise anything and even indicating that they would do nothing without Gorbachev's consent. There were, they argued, objective standards for recognition of a government, including the question of whether the government had the support of the population and whether it controlled its own frontiers. Presumably the Americans expected these lectures to impress the Lithuanians with the complicated nature of the problem.

Lithuanians, moreover, could at times draw completely opposite conclusions from one and the same meeting with American officials. Even the
lecture on the "objective" conditions for recognition left some Lithuanians
calculating how to meet these "objective" standards. On March 8 a group
of Sajudis leaders—including Landsbergis and Ozolas—met with the US
ambassador in Moscow, Jack Matlock, who tried to discourage them.
Ozolas came away from this meeting pessimistic, saying "The conversation
was obscure," and then adding "We parted, one might say, at a dead end."
Landsbergis, on the other hand, emphasized the interest that the
Americans were showing: "The American embassy very much wants to
have information about our very latest views."[10]

Arguments over what should have been expected from the United
States eventually focused on the relationship between Landsbergis and
Stasys Lozoraitis, who represented the émigré Lithuanian diplomatic corps
as chargé d'affaires in Washington. "In the spring of 1990 some Sajudis
deputies noted that V. Landsbergis preferred to confer not with them but
with [Lozoraitis]," wrote the Lithuanian journalist Ruta Grinevičiute. As
Landsbergis himself explained, it was necessary to find just the right formula; therefore he had to seek advice from specialists.

Lozoraitis later recalled of this period, "The situation was very difficult.
The USA was most concerned with Gorbachev's fate, and our quick movement to independence was unacceptable. In Lithuania there were also
political forces who spoke about autonomy, who used the very unclear
word 'sovereignty' and avoided saying 'independence.'" This, he argued,
played into the hands of those in the West who wanted to ignore the entire
issue. Gorbachev was unlikely to agree to any gradual program of independence, Lozoraitis argued, and therefore the Lithuanians should seize
the moment and act. They must show the world their determination to be
independent.[11]

The key conversation came in the night of March 10, 1990.
Landsbergis called Lozoraitis to find out how the U.S. government stood
on the question of independence. This, according to Lozoraitis, was the
only conversation during the week specifically on the question of American
support of independence, and the diplomat urged that the Supreme Soviet
act immediately. He read to Landsbergis the position papers that the Baltic
desk of the State Department had drawn up for the White House and that
Brent Scowcroft, President Bush's National Security Adviser, had apparently approved.

The two statements, one read by the White House on March 11 and the other used by White House press spokesperson Margaret Tutweiler to explain the American government's position, reaffirmed "the Baltic peoples' inalienable right to peaceful self-determination," took note of the parliament's "intention to restore Lithuanian independence," and urged the Soviet government to enter into "immediate constructive negotiations with the government of Lithuania." Tutweiler explained that "United States practice has been to establish formal relations with the lawful government of any state—once that government is in effective control of its territory and capable of entering into, and fulfilling, international obligations."[12]

Rather than say directly that recognition was a political question, the Bush administration had chosen to put the question in "legal" terms. President Bush himself declared on March 15, "I think there are standards of control over one's country or control over one's, in this instance, territory, that guide recognition."[13] On March 19 White House spokesperson Marlin Fitzwater added, "We have a standard of control of one's territory which guides us in this matter."[14] Officials at the American embassy in Moscow had also stressed the problem of a government's "control of its territory." This legalistic argument may well have misled the Lithuanians, who considered the justice of their cause beyond doubt and therefore believed that the governments of the world should only welcome the opportunity to recognize their independence.

Lozoraitis interpreted the US State Department's papers in the most favorable way possible, and his conversation with Landsbergis finally cleared the way for action. According to a witness, after Landsbergis had finished talking with Lozoraitis, he breathed a sigh of relief and declared the matter settled; he seemed convinced that Lithuania would get American help. Speaking to the Supreme Soviet on March 11, he declared, "According to our information, specific drafts and variants have been prepared in the most important western state, how it should react to our future political actions in the Supreme Soviet." He also reported that Lithuanian émigrés in southern California had persuaded former U.S. president Ronald Reagan to intervene with George Bush on behalf of the Lithuanians.[15] The Lithuanian leadership had no contingency plan for the possibility of a sharp reaction from Gorbachev and no support from the United States.[16]

On March 11, a Sunday, the parliament worked according to a pre-arranged plan. The group elected Landsbergis as its chairman; then it decreed that "the residents of Lithuania voluntarily gave the mandate of representatives of the people to the elected deputies of the Supreme Soviet of the Lithuanian SSR and the obligation to reestablish the Lithuanian state and the sovereign power of the people." After changing the name of the state to "Republic of Lithuania," the deputies proclaimed "the reestablishment of the independent Lithuanian state."[17]

The reconstitution of the state, which had been "abolished by foreign power," took the form of abolishing the constitution of the Lithuanian SSR, recognizing the former Lithuanian constitution of 1938, and then suspending that constitution, replacing it with a "Provisional Fundamental Law" based on the constitution of the Lithuanian SSR. The institutions of government remained as they existed on March 10, although Lithuanian spokespersons henceforth insisted that the English name for the parliament should be "Supreme Council." In a message dated March 12 Landsbergis asked the Soviet leader to recognize Lithuanian independence and "begin negotiation for solving all questions related to the reestablishment of the independent State of Lithuania."[18]

The entire process took some time, and it was late evening before the deputies made their formal declaration and stood to sing the National Hymn. Although foreign journalists, including CNN television cameras, broadcast the proceedings to the world, critics subsequently spoke of this being a furtive, even unexpected, action.[19] As Hedrick Smith, a witness, recounted, "Weeks later, Gorbachev insinuated that the Lithuanian declaration of independence was done in the dark of night, as if it were an act of stealth. That was not the case. The whole procedure was wide open, to the Soviet press as well as to Lithuanian and foreign journalists." Writing in *Izvestiia* of March 7, Leonid Kapelushny had declared that Lithuanian leaders were preparing their people to "pull out" and that they shed "sober assessments" like "water off a duck's back." On the same day, Moscow Interfax reported that Sajudis leaders wanted the parliament to establish Lithuania's independence on March 11. An English journalist, Anatol Lieven, nevertheless called the entire process "a surprize."[20]

The Lithuanians apparently did not expect a strong response from Gorbachev.[21] In the deliberations of the Sajudis Deputies' Club, Čepaitis had argued that Gorbachev would just throw up his hands and accept "the will of the Lithuanian people." Several months earlier Landsbergis had predicted that Moscow would employ only "a partial" blockade, perhaps not even using the word,[22] and on Friday, March 9, he declared, "People are intimidated...by a possible blockade.... It is inconceivable that the Soviet Union through its present leadership would start smothering Lithuania in this way." Even Prunskiene had argued that action would facilitate negotiations: "We have to go to Moscow and clearly say that here, we are already a state, demanding talks between states and we are facilitating them."[23]

Publicly Gorbachev and other Soviet leaders responded only with words. Ligachev told foreign correspondents, "We must resolve this by political means. Tanks will not help in this matter." Gennady Gerasimov of the Soviet Foreign Ministry added the thought that this was an internal Soviet matter and therefore foreign powers should stay out. On March 12 Gorbachev called the Lithuanians' declaration "alarming," and on the thirteenth he called it "illegitimate" and "invalid." He declared that he would not negotiate with the Lithuanians—"negotiations," he argued, meant talks between governments—and a few days later he told Estonian representatives that the Lithuanians had turned into "a dead end." Nevertheless there was at first no sign of action, even though members of Gorbachev's administration were demanding a forceful response.[24]

On March 15, under Gorbachev's direction, the Soviet Congress of People's Deputies denounced the Lithuanians' action, declaring it null and void and "commissioning" Gorbachev to protect the rights of the USSR and its citizens in the "Lithuanian Soviet Socialist Republic." Lithuania, it was understood, continued to be a part of the Soviet Union, and the Soviet government should yet determine the conditions and procedures for secession should a republic insist on trying to do so.[25]

The Lithuanians had entertained some hopes that deputies from other republics would disrupt the work of the Congress of People's Deputies in their support, but only a few, such as Galina Starovoitova from Erevan, E. E. Inkens of Latvian television, and N. K. Kozyrev of Voroshilovgrad, spoke out on their behalf. Most criticized the Lithuanians: Roy Medvedev, the historian, declared that there should have been a referendum; a Belarusian deputy, V. M. Semenov, protested his love for Lithuania and noted that Belarus had territorial claims against the Lithuanians. The lone spokesman for the Lithuanians in the congress, Nikolai Medvedev, argued that negotiations should be the first order of business.[26] The CPD as a whole showed no sympathy for the Lithuanians.

Whatever the issues in other areas of Soviet life, the CPD gave Gorbachev the weapons he wanted for dealing with the Lithuanians, creating a new, stronger presidency that they of course entrusted to him. In strengthening his powers, the congress gave him the authority to establish "presidential rule"—martial law—in a republic without the consent of the local authorities. It eventually passed the law on secession that he wanted, thereby allowing the central authorities to intervene at will and to delay any steps taken by a republic toward leaving the Soviet Union. Nikolai Medvedev called it "not a law about leaving but a law about not leaving."[27] The Lithuanians nevertheless insisted that the decisions of the CPD had no significance for them.

After notifying the Lithuanians of the congress's resolution, Gorbachev lapsed into silence while the Soviet military called for action. At times the Soviet leader let foreign visitors speak for him; U.S. senator Edward Kennedy, for example, reported that Gorbachev had no intention "to use force unless lives were at stake." USSR defense minister Dmitry Iazov, on the other hand, told an American visitor that the army stood ready to "crush" Lithuania.

The military made its case to the Politburo on March 22 when General Valentin Varennikov, head of the Soviet land forces, presented a scenario that included presidential rule, the introduction of three regiments into Lithuania, and the formation of a pro-Moscow administration that would welcome the troops. (Although the enhancement of Gorbachev's presidential powers had appeared to mark a shift of power from party to government, crucial matters such as the invasion of Lithuania were still a Politburo matter.) Iakovlev and Vadim Medvedev reportedly remained silent during the presentation, which some later compared to Hungary in 1956 and others to Prague in 1968. After the meeting advisors went to Gorbachev to protest Varennikov's plans, but Gorbachev reportedly waved them off as so many worrywarts.[28]

The Soviet military presence in Lithuania intensified, and claiming to be acting on behalf of the LCP/CPSU and therefore the USSR CPSU, the army began seizing buildings, including the Institute of Party History and the Press House, where most of Lithuania's newspapers were printed. During the night of March 23-24, while parliament was in session, a giant convoy of tanks and trucks rumbled around the building. "We were moving them at night so that they would not disturb anyone," a Soviet officer said disingenuously. At the end of March, the Soviet authorities ordered foreign journalists out of Lithuania.[29]

The Soviets also encouraged antigovernment demonstrations in Vilnius. Military helicopters dropped leaflets encouraging Russian and Polish workers to demonstrate and strike against the Lithuanian government. The Committee of USSR Citizens in Lithuania, calling for a rally on April 4, charged, "Political adventurers are creating a society of social inequality, they are destroying the economic, political and social ties between the peoples of the USSR." When Lithuanians held a rally in Vingis Park on April 7, a Soviet helicopter buzzed the crowd and dropped broadsheets; Landsbergis told the gathering, "Those who litter will end up on the rubbish heap."

Possibly leery of American reactions, Moscow determinedly insisted that it was not using force. A Soviet journalist, Igor Sedykh, noted, "To be sure, not a day passes in Lithuania without a demonstration of Soviet military might in one form or another, but does this give cause to dramatize the situation?"[30] On the other hand, a broadside calling a protest meeting for May 18 in front of the Parliament Building, issued by the Committee of USSR Citizens, proclaimed, "Down with the government of separatists! Long live Soviet Lithuania!"[31] The potential for violence was high, but only on the part of Moscow's supporters.

Although some observers have argued that the U.S. government now became the "mediator" between Vilnius and Moscow, Washington in fact held back and limited its role to calls for "dialogue" in a situation where there seemed little room for compromise. (Since Gorbachev had ruled out "negotiations," any talks between Vilnius and Moscow would have to be subsumed under another label: hence the term "dialogue.") At the beginning of April Ozolas spoke with Iakovlev in Moscow and upon returning called the trip "truly beneficial for us," describing his meeting with Iakovlev as "a very normal talk if we keep in mind our situation as seen by Moscow, and the situation we have put them in." Gorbachev, however, demanded surrender in the form of a repudiation of the declaration of March 11, and Landsbergis would not give him that.

The crisis made Landsbergis the worldwide symbol of Lithuania's non-violent resistance to Moscow's threats and posturing. In his hands, the post of chairman of the Presidium of the Supreme Council became a powerful office, first of all directing Lithuania's "foreign relations." Algirdas Saudargas became Lithuania's new foreign minister, but in the Lithuanians' official publication, *The Road to Negotiations with the USSR*, his name does not appear as a signatory to any document sent to Moscow in 1990–1991.

Landsbergis took Lithuania's infant foreign policy out of the hands of the cabinet of ministers and brought it, through the Supreme Council, under his own purview as the chief executive officer of the parliament. When the U.S. government refused to come to his aid, Landsbergis appealed directly to western public opinion; in the absence of military might, he presented the issue as one of morality. He himself spent considerable time entertaining western visitors, and they in turn gave him publicity, referring to him as the "clever fox" and repeating his sayings, such as his quotation of Dr. Stockmann in Henrik Ibsen's *An Enemy of the People*, "The strongest man in the world is the man who stands alone." An American visitor called him "a romantic, but realistic nevertheless...a modest man, who does not seek responsibility, but who will accept it." For admiring foreign observers he seemed to embody the ideal of the intellectual come to power to bring morality into the politics of the world.[32]

In evaluating the Lithuanians, Gorbachev made a number of miscalculations. Based on the conviction that national consciousness was a false idea and therefore not the real issue in Lithuania, he apparently thought that military and economic pressure could force the Lithuanians to surrender. (Circulating among the Soviet delegation in Vilnius in January 1990, I overheard a high-ranking Soviet official saying with a laugh to his colleague, "Poland could not last three days in the face of a gasoline blockade; how long do you think the Lithuanians would last?") Gorbachev severely underestimated the Lithuanians' bad memories of Soviet rule and their passion for independence.[33] He was certainly not prepared to deal with their determined resistance.

Gorbachev's sources of information on Lithuania were at best unreliable in that they would not present information contrary to their own interests: The KGB was confused and at this point even unsure of the loyalty of its own staff; military intelligence had its own cake to bake; and the Burokevičius group insisted it represented the true will of the Lithuanian workers and peasants. Burokevičius's LCP/CPSU, moreover, criticized Moscow as being soft on the Lithuanians. In the words of Vadim Bakatin, "the president received a false impression of a lack of mass support for the governments of Latvia, Lithuania and Estonia. This although one had to be a very naive person to believe it."[34] Given, however, Gorbachev's decision to support Burokevičius, he would seem to have no alternative but to resort to force in the mistaken expectation that the Lithuanians would welcome him.

On March 31 Gorbachev addressed appeals to both the Lithuanian Supreme Council and to the "citizens of the Lithuanian SSR," urging compliance with the CPD's denunciation of the act of March 11. He warned the parliament that its "illegal decrees" had directed Lithuania into "a dead end," and he called on the people to reject "the political insanity" of the Lithuanian government. Citing popular demand "that the Constitution of the USSR be defended," he indicated that "economic, political, and administrative" measures might follow as well as a division of Lithuanian territory among its neighbors.[35]

The Soviet leadership was first of all concerned about the impact of the Lithuanian example on the other republics of the Soviet Union: "In connection with the decision of the Supreme Soviet of Lithuania on secession from the USSR the situation in the Soviet federation has acutely sharpened, and separatist tendencies in other union republics have become stronger."[36] (Although I have elsewhere translated *Aukščiausioji Taryba* as "Supreme Council," in quoting Soviet sources I have used "Supreme Soviet" in order to capture the flavor of the statement.) Government propaganda, therefore, aimed at picturing the Lithuanians as isolated, without support from either other nationalities or the reformers in Russia. The Soviet press sometimes argued, as did *Pravda* of April 10, that western agents were behind the Lithuanians, and at other times warned the Lithuanians that they could expect no aid from the West.

Lithuania received both good and bad press in Moscow. Vilnius's decision to withdraw its deputies from the CPD drew criticism from Russian reformers, who sympathized but despaired of what they considered headstrong and rash actions.[37] In a meeting on April 12, a group of liberal CPD deputies, which included Boris Yeltsin, called on the Lithuanians to suspend all their acts since March 10. At the same time, the Lithuanians received encouragement from popular front groups in Ukraine, Latvia, Belarus, Georgia, and even Leningrad. The Lithuanian mission in Moscow had an unprecedented number of visitors from other republics inquiring about citizenship.[38] Since western reporters were prohibited from visiting Vilnius, however, they had to rely on sources in Moscow for their reports home, and some accepted the picture of the Lithuanians as "isolated."[39]

Although much of the western press lionized Landsbergis, western governments demonstrated strong sympathy for Gorbachev. They came to understand that Gorbachev nurtured "deep animosity" toward Landsbergis, and they were themselves dismayed and angered by

Landsbergis's moralizing and his suggestions that the West had "sold" Lithuania or that it was engaged in appeasement on the scale of a Munich. U.S. government officials "were chary of talking directly with Landsbergis and other top Lithuanian leaders, feeling that they were dealing with amateurs who might publicly describe any United States private suggestion of flexibility as a suggestion that they give up."[40] As the Soviets tightened the noose, President Bush mixed effusive praise of Gorbachev personally with vague warnings that strangling Lithuania could have a negative effect on Soviet-American relations.

Gorbachev apparently decided on his next step in a meeting with his presidential council on April 9. Out of that meeting came indications that "economic and political measures" would ensue. His press secretary declared that the Soviet leader was ready to defend the Soviet constitution and the rights and interests of Soviet citizens. The Soviet government, he asserted, had shown its "goodwill," and it was now up to the Lithuanians to respond. Gorbachev, he added, viewed the restraint of the West positively since the Soviet Union would not tolerate foreign "intervention" in this domestic "constitutional" struggle.[41]

On April 13, Good Friday in Catholic Lithuania, the beginning of a weekend when public life would normally come to a standstill, Gorbachev delivered his final ultimatum: "If within two days, the Supreme Soviet and the Council of Ministers of the Lithuanian SSR do not revoke their aforementioned decisions, orders will be given to suspend delivery to the Lithuanian SSR from other Union republics of the type of production that is sold on the foreign market for hard currency."[42] The Lithuanians refused to give in, but by this point, Gorbachev probably did not expect them to.

Gorbachev called his dispute with Lithuania "a constitutional conflict," but insofar as he proclaimed himself the sole authoritative commentator and interpreter of the Soviet constitution, it is futile to argue the constitutionality of any action by the Soviet leadership. He played mirror games with the constitution, declaring that this clause was valid, that one invalid, and he made clear that the constitution was not the ultimate law of the land. Despite the CPSU CC's decision of February to amend the notorious Article 6, the Communist Party of the Soviet Union, as directed by its general secretary and the party Politburo, still represented the real political power in the Soviet system.

In responding to Gorbachev's actions and statements, Landsbergis found the gap between the posturing and the reality in the policies of both

Washington and Moscow easy targets for sarcasm and irony, two strong weapons in his rhetorical arsenal. Clumsy Soviet moves, such as cutting off the U.S. television line with Lithuania in the middle of David Brinkley's Sunday morning talk show, only gave the Lithuanians more favorable publicity—Sam Donaldson insisted that the show give Americans another chance to hear these people out—and embarrassed Gorbachev's American supporters. Landsbergis in turn spoke darkly of Soviet pressure on the western powers, blocking the recognition of the legitimate claims of the Lithuanians.[43] In the end, both Washington and Moscow wanted to find the quickest way out of the impasse.

Almost lost in the confrontation that followed the Lithuanians' declaration of March 11 was the action of Brazauskas and the independent LCP after they had lost the February/March elections. When the new Supreme Council met, the LCP peacefully surrendered its control of government, and Brazauskas became a member of Prunskiene's cabinet. The Lithuanians had far outstripped Moscow in moving political power from party headquarters into government offices, but Gorbachev did not approve of their example.

9

THE BLOCKADE:
LESSONS AND COSTS

Gorbachev's blockade of Lithuania began on April 18, 1990. The last drops of oil flowed into the refinery in Mažeikiai in northern Lithuania at about 10:30 in the evening. The next day Soviet officials held up the flow of natural gas from Belorussia and Latvia; Gorbachev eventually allowed Lithuania 3.5 million cubic meters of gas per day, less than one-fifth of its average consumption of 18 million cubic meters. He also blockaded a long list of items for which he said the Lithuanians should be paying hard currency, including coffee and sugar, but he rejected any suggestion of accepting hard currency from the Lithuanians for these goods, including gasoline.

Once the first shock had passed, Gorbachev was embarrassed by the action because the Lithuanians refused to surrender. Brazauskas later explained to me that Gorbachev's purpose "was to show how much Lithuania's economy depended on the Soviet Union," but others thought that the issue was the preservation of empire, pure and simple. The Second Congress of Sajudis, meeting on April 21, called on the people to stand firm and on the government to reorganize the economy to overcome shortages and to avoid unemployment. Gorbachev faced unexpected resistance.

The Soviet leader found himself in a peculiar predicament, blockading part of the country he supposedly governed but also not using the overwhelming military advantage that he had at his command in just that territory. He had promised Washington that he would not use force, and he resisted calls to overthrow Landsbergis, who everyone agreed was the legally installed leader of the Lithuanian government. (He thereby of course rejected Varennikov's scenario.) The blockade was a limited one, and some of his officials even objected to calling it a "blockade." Gorbachev seemed to fear allowing the Soviet military a free hand, but he certainly misjudged the Lithuanians' motivation.

Other than damaging the Lithuanian economy, the blockade failed in its purpose, and Gorbachev even had to cope with protest demonstrations in Moscow. During the traditional festivities on May 1, he left the viewing stand in Moscow's Red Square to escape the indignity of watching demonstrators who, among other banners, waved Lithuanian flags. The blockade of Lithuania contributed nothing to the prestige of his office.

The Lithuanians resisted in both word and deed. The restructuring of the Lithuanian economy to meet the blockade fell to Brazauskas, the deputy prime minister,[1] who undertook the redistribution of resources, setting the goal of giving agriculture 60 to 70 percent of its usual supply, public transportation 70 percent, food transport 90 percent, and rubbish removal 80 percent. He expected that fuel supplies would last for one month.[2] "Every day we adjusted the use of gas," Brazauskas later reminisced.[3] As of May 17, Lithuania reportedly had enough gasoline to last only until the beginning of June.

The problem of dealing with fuel shortages was complex. Lithuanian officials considered exporting products ranging from television sets to "Xerox paper" in exchange for gasoline. The official supply of raw materials from the Soviet Union was estimated at 15 to 20 percent of normal, and therefore the Lithuanians had to investigate means of getting materials through other channels. Brazauskas sought help from friends in Moscow and Leningrad, used false addresses in Belorussia, and sent trucks into the Soviet Union to look for goods. Food products, apart from sugar, coffee, and other "forbidden goods," were arriving in adequate supply from the Soviet Union.

The blockade lasted seventy-five days. Many Lithuanians liked to say that it failed because of traditional Russian inefficiency, but the basic hole in the system that allowed Lithuania to hold out was in electrical energy. Because of the Ignalina atomic station, Lithuania was a net exporter of electricity, and Gorbachev did not shut it down. If he had, Lithuania would have, in Brazauskas's words, faced a "catastrophe." When Moscow at one point closed down the station "for repair," Brazauskas threatened to cut off electricity for the Kaliningrad region, which received 60 percent of its electrical power from Lithuania; Ignalina soon returned to service.

Since Lithuania normally had produced agricultural goods for export, the blockade made more such goods available for the domestic market. This undermined a good part of the image that Gorbachev tried to create; visitors from the Soviet Union, only too aware of the shortages they faced at home, were shocked to see how much food the Lithuanians had in the market. "We should experience such a blockade!" seemed to be a common reaction.

The blockade quickly became a major international problem, and Landsbergis seized the role of conscience for the Great Powers. He challenged Washington, asking the Voice of America, "Will America sell us a second time or not?" When told that that statement had offended people in Washington, he opined that such controversy "will perhaps help our efforts." On another occasion in discussing American policy, he exclaimed, "Of what value then is the idea of freedom itself?"[4] In the competition for the attention of the world press, Landsbergis emphasized a "just cause," while Gorbachev's defenders spoke of necessities of state and Bush's supporters expressed regret about the tortured path that American policy had to follow.[5] Landsbergis won more sympathy than either of his competitors, but that of course did not mean practical aid.

Once entered, Gorbachev's predicament in Lithuania had no easy exit. As one Soviet commentator noted, Lithuania now had two names (Republic of Lithuania and Lithuanian SSR); there were two Communist parties, three "procurators" (attorneys-general), two ministers of defense, and a Lithuanian militia coexisting with Soviet paratroopers in militia uniforms; Soviet forces had occupied a print shop where the workers refused to obey; and both Moscow and Lithuania were putting forth laws and decrees that the other ignored. "It is difficult to predict the future of the present situation," the commentator said with a sigh.[6]

Gorbachev's action threw the Americans into confusion. George Bush thought he had a special personal relationship with Gorbachev. American officials had expected that Gorbachev would practice "Baltic exceptionalism" and give up the Baltic republics; they had done almost no "contingency planning" for a crisis in the Baltic. A Bush administration official exclaimed that this was "the first time we've seen Gorbachev draw a bottom line and remove options that would give him flexibility."[7] The Americans had not expected Gorbachev to act so forcefully.

Bush still wanted to give Gorbachev the benefit of any doubt. He repeatedly expressed sympathy for the Soviet leader's "very difficult internal problems." On March 23, to be sure, he warned that Soviet actions in

Lithuania were "bound to backfire," while administration officials privately admitted that they did not understand Gorbachev's motives. Bush continually insisted that "we are not backing away from our concept of self-determination," but he added, "Let somebody else sort all that out." He spoke of Gorbachev's good intentions and repeatedly called for "dialogue." On March 29 the American leader admitted to lawmakers "that keeping the Soviet leader in power was a higher priority than the Lithuanian independence drive."[8]

Both Gorbachev and Soviet foreign minister Eduard Shevardnadze assured the Americans that Moscow would not use "force" against the Baltic republics,[9] and US policy consisted of warnings about possibly stern American reactions and of fumbling efforts to minimize the impact of news coming from Lithuania. When reports came of the seizure of young men avoiding military service, together with television pictures of the blood spilled in the operation, White House spokesperson Marlin Fitzwater refused to define this as a "use of force," explaining "We do not want to inflame the situation." When Gorbachev expelled U.S. diplomats from Lithuania, Washington simply declared that it was displeased. By the beginning of April, Washington pundits were suggesting that the military was pressuring Gorbachev, although some officials believed that Gorbachev was manipulating the military's image so as to win more understanding for whatever he chose to do.[10]

In the end Bush refused to oppose Gorbachev. After Gorbachev had delivered his ultimatum of April 13, U.S. foreign policymakers drew up a list of alternative economic sanctions to indicate Washington's disapproval. Finally, on Monday, April 23, Bush told his staff that the United States would do nothing. He had given an indication of this position a few days earlier when he and French president François Mitterand called Gorbachev's survival a higher priority than resolving the Lithuanian imbroglio, but some people present at the meeting on April 23 thought that even National Security Adviser Brent Scowcroft and Secretary of State James Baker were surprised by the president's announcement. "The real reason the President didn't act, I was told by some of those around him, was that he didn't want to—and had never wanted to," wrote a journalist.[11]

The president insisted that he was acting in the best interests of "freedom," explaining "I'm concerned that we not inadvertently do something that compels the Soviet Union to take action that would set back the whole cause of freedom around the world."[12] Behind the smokescreen of legal and moral phraseology, however, lay summit power politics: Bush believed that the leaders of the Great Powers had the task of preserving world peace and that the Lithuanians should not have acted so rashly. He justified his position by citing public opinion polls indicating that Americans considered it more important to support Gorbachev than to back Lithuania.[13]

By the end of April the blockade was embarrassing both Moscow and Washington: Journalists around the world were fascinated with the daring of the Lithuanians, and many were accepting Landsbergis's argument that Lithuania's freedom was a moral issue. The policy options for the Great Powers were limited: Insisting that Lithuania was an internal problem of the USSR, the Soviet government opposed foreign intervention on behalf of the Lithuanians—Soviet commentators liked to note that it was then twenty-five years since U.S. marines had landed in Santo Domingo—but it in fact welcomed intervention aimed at convincing the Lithuanians to change their ways. The western governments accordingly urged the Lithuanians to be flexible.[14]

On April 26 German chancellor Helmut Kohl and French president Mitterand addressed a letter to Landsbergis urging talks, suggesting that the Lithuanians "temporarily" delay "the results of your parliament's decisions," but not mentioning the blockade. In an interview with Voice of America on April 27, Landsbergis called the letter "important and positive" for Lithuania but declared that "we will have to consider very carefully" what the "Lithuanian Parliament should do to ease the political situation of the Soviet government into which it has put itself." He understood the note to be "much more flexible" than Moscow's demands that Lithuania annul its declaration of independence, and he welcomed this European initiative as a positive new step in the confrontation, especially in view of the United States' having "washed its hands" of the matter. Either Landsbergis did not know or he did not care that Bush had encouraged his European colleagues to act.[15]

Landsbergis's response won him no new friends in Washington, and the Bush administration looked for other Lithuanians with whom it might work. To this end, it reversed a previous decision and agreed to receive Kazimiera Prunskiene, the Lithuanian prime minister who had been traveling in western Europe and Canada and who requested a meeting in Washington. Even though the American authorities insulted her by blocking the front gate of the White House, thereby forcing her to walk through security, the prime minister displayed great poise in handling the situation, and when she indicated her willingness to consider a "moratorium" on Lithuania's independence, the president "praised her patience and foresight." With Bush's endorsement, Prunskiene went on to meet with government leaders in France, England, and Germany.[16] Her trip, however, brought Lithuania no closer to recognition by the Great Powers.

Gorbachev's camp did what it could to depict the Lithuanians as inflexible. Gorbachev's first position, of course, had been to demand a repeal of the declaration of March 11, but by the end of April he was willing to consider "suspension." Iakovlev called the Lithuanian problem one of "dialogue and respect for law," he complained that the Lithuanians "had sold him out," and he challenged the Lithuanians to hold a referendum on the question of secession. Gorbachev indicated that Lithuania could be independent in two years if it suspended its declaration of independence.[17] The stalemate dragged on as the sides maneuvered for position.

On May 16 the Lithuanian Supreme Council and the cabinet issued a joint declaration that Lithuania stood ready "temporarily" to suspend the "realization of those decisions" arising "from the acts on the reestablishment of the independent Lithuanian state." As Landsbergis explained, the Lithuanian government could observe a "transitional period" in its drive toward independence.[18] In approving the declaration, the council directed both Prunskiene and Landsbergis to sign it, and Prunskiene, riding the wave of her successful trip through the West, carried the text to Moscow.

When she first requested a meeting on May 17, Gorbachev, angered by Landsbergis's barrage of public statements, responded, "If you have an unpublished letter to deliver, then come, and we can talk." The conversation, Prunskiene later recalled, "was very difficult." Soviet prime minister Nikolai Ryzhkov opened the session by warning her not to try to divide the Soviet side. Gorbachev seemed much sterner and more somber than she had seen him before, but he indicated that he might accept a compromise. Although Prunskiene was still unsure of Gorbachev's real intentions, she nevertheless thought that there was room for negotiation, and she was critical of Landsbergis's "uncompromising" stance.[19]

Time was working against Gorbachev; there were rumblings in other parts of the Soviet state. The Lithuanians in particular welcomed the emergence of a separate Russian consciousness within the Soviet system. Although many westerners had long identified the Communist system with Russian nationalism, activities in the name of "Russia" now evoked tremors in the heart of the system. A Russian Communist Party came into being, and on May 29, as Gorbachev flew to North America for summit meetings in Canada and in the United States, the Supreme Soviet of the Russian republic (RSFSR) elected Boris Yeltsin as its chairman and thereby the "president" of the republic. A confrontation was developing, and the Lithuanians watched for ways in which they might profit by it.

Gorbachev's visit to the United States in June 1990 produced mixed results. Many observers agreed that he enjoyed greater popularity in the West than at home. He basked in the adulation of the American public, while also encountering demonstrators protesting his policies in Lithuania and elsewhere. He was able to persuade Bush to sign a trade treaty without publicly mentioning the Lithuanian situation as a problem that could hamper ratification of the agreement by the U.S. Senate. Although he could claim to have accomplished much in enhancing his American image, he still had to find a way out of the quicksand he had stumbled into with his blockade of Lithuania.[20]

The Soviet leader returned home to find that Yeltsin was not only changing both Russia and the Soviet Union but was even intruding into the Lithuanian question. In Moscow on June 1, in a spectacular display of solidarity between rebellious republics, Yeltsin had talked with Landsbergis for an hour, agreeing in principle on cooperation between their governments.[21] (In April Yeltsin had criticized the blockade of Lithuania.) As if his Lithuanian problems were not enough, Gorbachev also faced new ethnic conflicts in Central Asia and a declaration by the Russian parliament to the effect that Russian laws took precedence over Soviet laws, an echo of the nullification conflict with Estonia in 1988 and Lithuania in 1989.

Yeltsin's initiatives were changing the Soviet Union in ways only a few western observers could as yet comprehend. While Gorbachev was still in the United States, Anthony Lewis, writing in *The New York Times* of June 1, called Yeltsin's activity in Moscow more significant for the future of Russia than Gorbachev's in Washington; writing from prison in 1992, ex-KGB chief Kriuchkov complained, "The decisive phase in the destruction of the union began in the summer of 1990 after the congress of RSFSR People's Deputies adopted the Russian declaration of sovereignty and the primacy of Russian over union laws."[22] The Soviet empire was crumbling at its very center.

In addition, Gorbachev could expect the Lithuanian question to come up for debate in the Twenty-eighth Congress of the CPSU, scheduled for the first days of July. Some party leaders called his Lithuanian policy the "great failure" of perestroika. In a memorandum dated May 28, Ligachev charged that anti-socialist forces with "foreign connections" were arising and that "bourgeois nationalists have seized power in Lithuania, the republic is drifting to the West." When Gorbachev ignored his complaint, Ligachev tried to work his theme of "the dangers of nationalism and separatism" into the Politburo's report to the congress; the report, however, spoke only of "serious complications" presented by the rise of national feeling.[23]

In these circumstances, Gorbachev recognized only too well the challenge that Yeltsin, who was probably the most popular political figure in the Soviet Union, posed for him. He had already accused Yeltsin of calling "for the breakup of the Soviet Union," and he told Bush that Yeltsin had "become a destroyer."[24] Nevertheless, upon his return from abroad, he declared his readiness to work with Yeltsin in a businesslike manner. He also considered it necessary to take a more moderate line toward Lithuania; it was now in his interest to end the blockade as quickly as possible.

The Lithuanians, however, were divided among themselves as to how to deal with Moscow. At a time when the democratic Left in Moscow was criticizing them for breaking away from a common reform front, Lithuanian nationalists seized on Yeltsin and the emerging Russian national consciousness as an alternative to Gorbachev's centralism. As new forces in Moscow held the prospect of a collapse of the Soviet state, the nationalists in Lithuania, including Landsbergis, displayed a growing disinclination to deal with Gorbachev. Instead they were looking at Russia's emergence as a growing, destabilizing force in the Soviet future.

Prunskiene, to the contrary, advocated more flexibility in dealing with Moscow. There would be serious costs, she warned, associated with precipitate independence; these costs would involve the loss of the Soviet market and even perhaps territorial concessions. Lithuania, she argued, should be ready to make "certain concessions, a certain retreat" so that negotiations could begin. "I am convinced," she wrote a year later, "that the period between the end of May or the beginning of June until the end of August was a historical opening with the possibility of getting the most that we could have gotten."[25] She did not consider Gorbachev and Yeltsin to be alternatives. In fact, she predicted that they would yet find common ground, and she favored negotiating with Gorbachev rather than gambling on Yeltsin.

The Lithuanians' problems of negotiating with Moscow, moreover, did not involve just the selection of policy options; there were also antagonisms and rivalries between institutions and personalities in Vilnius itself. The nationalist majority in the Supreme Council openly distrusted the cabinet, especially Prunskiene and Brazauskas, and did everything it could to limit their freedom of action. A personal rivalry between Landsbergis and Prunskiene, intensified by the international éclat bestowed on the latter in her travels through western capitals. further complicated the picture. In all, the political rivalries in Lithuania dictated that an agreement to end the blockade would be more controversial in Vilnius than in Moscow.[26]

The final steps to agreement came only with difficulty. By the beginning of June, the word "moratorium" offered the key for freeing both Moscow and Vilnius from the impasse. As a foreign import, it had no negative connotations in Lithuanian, and Gorbachev let Landsbergis know that the Soviet government would welcome any formula that the Lithuanians might choose to make just so long as that magic word appeared in it. Trying to make sure of the definition, however, was a major problem: Landsbergis and Prunskiene differed sharply in how they interpreted the word and in how each thought that Gorbachev interpreted it.

On June 16 Prunskiene's government proposed that parliament "discuss the possibility of declaring a temporary moratorium" of the act of March 11. Prunskiene argued that the Lithuanians should immediately announce the moratorium, meaning that they suspend—not abrogate—the declaration of independence, but that they do this only after Gorbachev lifted his blockade. She called this a temporary action "while negotiations with Moscow are under way." If the negotiations were broken off, the moratorium would end.

Sajudis leaders objected to the very idea of a moratorium under any conditions and organized a protest demonstration in front of the parliament building. The Freedom League came out with the slogan "Moratorium is death to Lithuania's freedom"; Antanas Terleckas called it "a trap for independent Lithuania." On June 18 the Supreme Council Presidium, headed by Landsbergis, decided to oppose the government's proposal, and Vilnius radio predicted that the parliament would follow suit.

On June 19, in Prunskiene's absence, Landsbergis read her call for a moratorium to the parliament without any enthusiasm, and the question went to committees. Speaking on Lithuanian radio the next day,

Landsbergis declared, "The Lithuanian Supreme Council will not discuss the government's proposal in the form in which it was received. It will not vote for or against it either today or this week, or maybe ever." At the same time he called on the people of Lithuania not to think "just in emotional terms" about the idea.

Landsbergis himself favored accepting some sort of moratorium, but he had little space in which to maneuver if he was to maintain his constituency on the Right. He eventually found his way with the help of a newly formed parliamentary faction, the Sajudis Center Fraction, which announced its existence on June 21, presenting itself as an alternative between the Communist Left and the radical Right. Landsbergis actually suggested that the group not announce its existence, but it served as a useful lightning rod for helping him escape the storms on the Right when he publicly accepted the idea of a moratorium.[27]

On June 26, after once again expressing disappointment in the West's inactivity, Landsbergis traveled to Moscow to meet with Gorbachev for an hour and a half and then immediately returned to Vilnius to participate in the Supreme Council's debate on the moratorium. Affirming that Lithuania had only sought to alter "the present collision course," Landsbergis welcomed what he saw as "more goodwill and understanding" on the part of Soviet authorities, and then cautiously, slowly, he spoke in favor of accepting the moratorium. He concluded, however, by complaining that after he had met Gorbachev, the Soviet leader had called Prunskiene. Saying that one could not be sure what was going on in Moscow, Landsbergis directed the deputies to delay their vote for at least two days.

Prunskiene responded by praising Landsbergis's work and quoted Gorbachev as saying that the blockade would be ended automatically when the parliament accepted the moratorium. The Lithuanians, she emphasized, should not add collateral demands, such as a proposal before the parliament demanding that the Soviet Union denounce the 1940 incorporation. Soviet officials added more uncertainty to the situation when the evening Moscow newscast *Vremia*, which was still considered an authoritative source of current government policy, announced that Lithuania must suspend its declaration of independence and that then the talks would take place "in the general context of interrepublican dialogue on the preparation of a new union treaty and on the formation of a union of sovereign socialist states."

The next day, June 27, Landsbergis and Prunskiene returned to Moscow together, meeting with Gorbachev late in the evening at the Soviet leader's villa outside the city. Gorbachev made clear that he would accept the suspension of the implementation of Lithuania's declaration of independence rather than the outright abrogation of the act; the Lithuanians also understood that at the start of negotiations the Soviet government would immediately offer a new treaty of union. When the travelers returned to Vilnius late at night, they told journalists that Gorbachev had agreed to "a moratorium" on the act of March 11 without demanding, as Prunskiene put it, "an unacceptable option that suits only Moscow."

When the two appeared before the Supreme Council the next day, they emphasized different aspects of their meeting with Gorbachev.[28] Prunskiene insisted that Lithuania would risk more by "remaining in the same place" than by proceeding into negotiations. Landsbergis, on the other hand, stressed Lithuania's drive for independence. Opponents of a moratorium challenged both speakers; when asked whether he had confidence in Prunskiene's government, Landsbergis declared that if put to a vote at that moment, he would support the government's proposal.

On June 29 Landsbergis committed himself by presenting a text proclaiming Lithuania's readiness to open talks and its willingness to proclaim "from the beginning of such negotiations a unilateral 100 day moratorium for the act of 11 March 1990 on the restoration of the independent Lithuanian state," meaning that the Lithuanian government "suspends legal actions stemming from it." The moratorium would thereby begin only when the two sides began formal negotiations, and the formal negotiations would themselves start with the acceptance of a special protocol defining their purpose. Landsbergis made clear that he disliked making "concessions to the stronger party," but he warned that if the parliament refused to take this step, it could face "internal anger" and an "internal split."

After heated debate, the Supreme Council accepted the moratorium by a vote of 61 to 35. The nationalist Right wing opposed the idea to the end, while the Center and the Left supported it. The decisive bloc in the vote came from a collection of some twenty-five to thirty deputies who were ready to follow whatever Landsbergis recommended. (This vote, like most in the parliament, was taken by raising identification cards; the votes were not recorded by name.) The crisis seemed temporarily resolved, although, as Landsbergis had made clear, "a lot of time will pass before the beginning of negotiations."[29]

After the announcement of the Lithuanian Supreme Council's decision, Gorbachev immediately lifted the blockade—oil again flowed into the Mažeikiai refinery. The Soviet Union itself had suffered in the blockade as well. As Vladimir Masalov, a Soviet trade specialist explained, "In the first five months of this year consumers in the Soviet Union failed to receive from Lithuania more than 80,000 low-output electric motors for domestic appliances, 565 automatic compressors for KamAZ trucks, and a large quantity of plastic products."[30] The blockade had become an albatross around Gorbachev's neck, and in the end he had demanded only that the Lithuanians accept the word "moratorium." The more quickly the blockade faded into oblivion the less embarrassing it would be for him.

10

GROWING FRUSTRATION

The raising of the blockade relieved only one aspect of the tension between Lithuania and the Soviet government, an artificial one at that. The deeper issues that had evoked the confrontation in March and April remained not only unsolved but untouched and even intensified. Gorbachev had stimulated national tensions in Lithuania and had encouraged neighbors, especially the Belarusians, to raise territorial claims against the Lithuanians. Moscow began developing alternative production sites for those goods for which Lithuania had maintained a monopoly on in the Soviet system; Lithuanian producers and could not regain their markets. As far as many Lithuanians were concerned, the blockade was in fact continuing.

Having done all these things, Gorbachev still had no rewards to offer the Lithuanians for their cooperation; he was further from any settlement with the rebellious republic than he had been before the blockade. The Soviet military was still summoning recruits and demanding that deserters be picked up; the Lithuanians were still resisting conscription and insisting on establishing their own paramilitary and militia forces. Until formal negotiations would begin and the "moratorium" would officially go into effect, the Lithuanian government continued on its journey toward independence.

On July 9 the Soviet government announced the makeup of its delegation for talks with the Lithuanians. Under the chairmanship of Prime Minister Ryzhkov the group included Gosplan director Masliukov, Minister of the Interior Vadim Bakatin, the chairman of the board of the USSR State Bank, and the USSR minister of Foreign Economic Relations as well as other ministers and high-ranking officials. Ryzhkov told journalists that if Lithuania insisted on seceding, it would have to follow a carefully defined procedure; the Soviet government, he went on, would in turn offer several alternatives for Lithuania's continued ties to the Soviet Union.[1]

In contrast, Landsbergis emphasized the need of preparing in stages—forming commissions of experts, establishing a discussion group to prepare the Lithuanian position, and only then actually naming a delegation. Upon hearing that Gorbachev had already named his delegation, Landsbergis commented that perhaps the Soviet Union "begins from the other end, perhaps in this way seeking its political goals at the time of the conference in Houston (a reference to a meeting of the G-7 international economic powers) on the issue of economic aid to the Soviet Union."[2] Although Prunskiene urged action, arguing that "without negotiations we will not resolve a single problem," Landsbergis moved slowly. As Landsbergis's close associate, Virgilius Čepaitis, told me, "there is no reason to hurry" in entering talks with Moscow.[3]

At this point, Landsbergis controlled the direction of Lithuania's policies. Without his support, Prunskiene's proposal for a moratorium would have failed. Landsbergis privately had considered the moratorium inescapable, but by publicly expressing his doubts, he avoided the opprobrium that the Right cast on Prunskiene for having yielded. Nationalists accused the cabinet ministers of having executed Moscow's will rather than Lithuania's, and they praised Landsbergis for having resisted. Delaying the negotiations, moreover, allowed Landsbergis still more opportunity to disassociate himself from the stigma of having supported the moratorium.

Landsbergis had also established his own freedom of movement within the parliament. Leaders of the Center faction thought that they could persuade him to free himself of dependence on the Right wing of the parliament; in the words of one Centrist, the vote on the moratorium "showed that if Vytautas Landsbergis goes with the center, a number of undecided deputies turn with him and the rightist radicals remain in the minority." (The Centrist deputies were pioneers in trying to track the voting of individual members of the parliament.) Instead, Landsbergis dismissed the Centrists as motivated by their own ambitions, and now, aided by the "undecided deputies," he could make his own majority when he so desired.[4]

After the raising of the blockade, the Supreme Council, with Landsbergis's encouragement, assumed control of relations with the Soviet government. Prunskiene's cabinet, of course, argued for its own autonomous authority in its relationship with the legislative branch of government, but Landsbergis came down strongly on the side of the parliament: "The decisions that must be adopted will be adopted by the Supreme Council, an organ enjoying sovereign powers. Therefore this organ must lead this work." The cabinet of ministers, he argued, must yield to the decisions of the council: "The Supreme Council runs everything; that is a constitutional matter…. It is higher than the government, so it is written in the constitution."[5]

Prunskiene countered by arguing that if the parliament wanted to run the negotiations, it should deal with Lukianov and the USSR Congress of People's Deputies. She repeatedly insisted that since Ryzhkov, which whom she was in almost daily telephone contact, would be heading the Soviet delegation, the Lithuanians should organize a comparable delegation, and that definitely did not mean one controlled by the Supreme Council: "I cannot imagine what the Supreme Council's direct control will mean for the talks, and how that will all end." As for the talks, she argued that independence was a process and that therefore the Lithuanians could hardly expect talks to begin with the recognition of their independence.[6]

On July 5, with Landsbergis's blessing, the Supreme Council structured its control of the negotiating team: It would set up a commission to prepare for the talks; the commission in turn would prepare a set of "draft principles" that the council would review. It would also organize working groups of experts and coordinate the work with the cabinet. The parliament would itself choose the members of the delegation to negotiate with the Soviet government.[7] The chairmanship of the council's commission went to Bronius Kuzmickas, Landsbergis's deputy chairman and the man whom Landsbergis considered the person in government closest to his own views.[8]

In this new phase of domestic political struggle, the Right, led by Landsbergis, wanted the Lithuanians to maintain the national unity of the antiblockade spirit; the Sajudis organization, with the help of the media, should mobilize the population to support the state wherever the country's leadership—and that meant Landsbergis and the parliament, not the cabinet—understood that it had to go. (Sajudis policies had taken a strong turn to the Right side of the political spectrum as a result of the movement's reorganization at its Second Congress in April.) They insisted that there were more battles to be fought to overcome negative social behavior left over from the Soviet order. In the summer of 1990 this line of thought advocated "Independence first, then democracy."

Opponents, including Prunskiene and Ozolas, insisted that Sajudis, as a spirit uniting the Lithuanian people, had done its job; Lithuanians now had to develop an orderly new political life tolerating differences of opinion. Both independence and democracy, they emphasized, were processes. As Ozolas argued, "If you want to build a democracy, you have to start today."[9]

By the end of July rumors circulating through Vilnius suggested that the parliament would unseat Prunskiene, replacing her with Gediminas Vagnorius. On July 31, the last scheduled day of the Lithuanian Supreme Council's session, political tension in the Lithuanian capital exploded when *Respublika* published "An appeal to the people of Lithuania," signed by twenty noted intellectuals, five of them members of the Sajudis Initiative Group in 1988. Written to support Prunskiene's position, the declaration warned that democracy would not be served by "bags of money" or "witch hunts" and complained that the Supreme Council had undermined the authority of the executive branch of government and that it was dangerously delaying the talks with Moscow. The appeal concluded by suggesting that the people should think about electing a Constituent Assembly to establish orderly government in the republic.

The political Right attacked the appeal on all fronts, reaching back to one of its most trusted political images by comparing the call for a Constituent Assembly to the Soviet pressure that created the "People's Diet" in 1940. Sajudis leaders forced one signer of the appeal to recant in front of a television camera on the grounds that he had been "deceived." The Lithuanian Christian Democratic Party declared that the "appeal is part of an action coordinated at the international level." The Sajudis Council called the appeal "irresponsible and destructive," showing "clear distrust of the Supreme Council of the Republic of Lithuania" as is usually expressed by "other forces," and it affirmed its confidence in the Supreme Council.[10]

Despite the furor, the declaration's authors subsequently insisted that their action had had positive results. It allegedly blocked a move in parliament that would have given Landsbergis's presidium special powers, it saved Prunskiene's government, and it stirred the Supreme Council to organize its delegation for talks with the Soviet Union. In the spring of

1991 signatories of the "appeal" were prominent in the formation of a left-ist coalition, Forum for the Future of Lithuania, as an opponent to the Sajudis majority in parliament.[11]

On August 21 the council finally named its delegation for negotiations with Moscow, making Landsbergis the chairman. The resolution provided for the inclusion of Estonian and Latvian, as well as émigré, representatives, and there was some debate as to whether Prunskiene, who was then in Greece, should be included or not—she was. In its deliberations, the group ignored the thought of choosing specialists; instead deputies spoke in terms of "Who would best represent Lithuania?" The delegation's eight members included four residents of Vilnius, four of Kaunas.[12]

Probably the major reason for the slow pace of the Lithuanians' preparation for talks lay in the inclination of the Landsbergis administration to bet on Yeltsin in the growing Russian-Soviet power struggle. In mid-July a delegation traveled to Moscow to talk with representatives of Yeltsin's Russian government, and they returned excited, albeit with some reserve. One participant in the delegation predicted that Russia and Lithuania would sign an economic agreement by the end of September, but he saw little prospect of a political agreement because the Russians spoke of restructuring the union of republics. Although "Lithuania will not enter any new union," he declared, the Lithuanians must yet find ways to work with the Russians, who were still "inexperienced."[13]

Some Lithuanians, moreover, saw in Yeltsin's success the possibility that the Soviet Union might in fact collapse. "One could hardly have expected the Soviet Union to crumble from the center," I heard one Lithuanian analyst say in August 1990, "but the process seems to have begun." (At about the same time I heard an American journalist describe the Lithuanian Supreme Council building as the place where the disintegration of the Soviet Union had begun.) The thought that Gorbachev's position would weaken with time undoubtedly slowed the Lithuanians' preparations.

The situation in Moscow actually was changing more rapidly than the Lithuanians understood; Gorbachev's administration was now planning new initiatives toward Lithuania, this time through the party. The process began at the Twenty-eighth Congress of the CPSU, held in the first half of July, where Gorbachev gave the greatest possible exposure to the representatives of the loyalist LCP/CPSU. As *Komsomolskaia pravda* of July 1 reported, Sajudis represented only bureaucratic dictates of the nationalists, and the CPSU, representing the rising forces of democracy, "is winning more and more admirers." Burokevičius proclaimed the Lithuanian CPSU's support of Gorbachev, but then both he and Shved criticized Gorbachev's policies. Shved warned: "The time for ideological disarmament has not yet come....What happened with us was that first the party was ideologically disarmed and then a declaration was made of the republic's withdrawal from the USSR." Both men demanded that Moscow take action, declaring that the CPSU had not met its "obligations" in Lithuania.[14]

Gorbachev used the congress to strengthen his own position. The congress's resolution on the nationalities question recalled Lenin's idea of "a voluntary union of states based on the free self-determination of the peoples,"[15] and Gorbachev gave special recognition to the national question by restructuring the Politburo. He removed close associates such as Iazov and Kriuchkov, both of whom had governmental posts, and packed the Politburo with party secretaries from the republics. Burokevičius thereby became the first Lithuanian to enter that body, but the Politburo had long since lost its place of pride as the leading political organ in the Soviet system. Although some claimed that Gorbachev was now completing the process of shifting the center of decision making over to his presidential office, he was by no means ready to abandon the CPSU and its control mechanisms: He was in fact tightening his control over both party and government while trying to make the party look better to the minority nationalities of the USSR.[16]

Whatever the role of the party in Gorbachev's plans, it now became more active on the Lithuanian front under the leadership of Oleg Shenin, the newly named CPSU CC secretary for organizational questions. Born in the Volgograd region in 1937, Shenin could, in almost the same breath, speak both of "dated dogmas" and also of being "nostalgic for a firm political course." He called himself a supporter of the Soiuz group in the Congress of People's Deputies, and he considered it "undemocratic" for the Center to refuse help to provincial party organizations.[17] This meant that he was ready to respond to the calls issued by Burokevičius and Shved.

On August 17–19, Shenin attended the plenum of the LCP/CPSU Central Committee in Vilnius and also visited party meetings in Kaunas and in Klaipeda. He heard out the complaints of the Moscow loyalists and urged them to intensify their own work. Suggesting that "passions are perhaps a little overheated," he spoke publicly of the party's problems adjusting to a multi-party system, and he announced that he was collecting information on the republic's troubles: "Industrial production is falling, criminality is on the rise, the number of non-Lithuanians wishing to leave their republic is growing."[18]

While in Vilnius, Shenin also witnessed the growing tension in the streets of the city as Lithuanian youths challenged the Soviet authorities. Lithuanian demonstrators were attacking war memorials and commemorative plaques that extolled the Soviet experience, and almost every evening in August Soviet armored troop carriers rolled into the city and discharged soldiers who took up stations protecting the statue of Lenin in front of the KGB building and the statue of Marshal Ivan Chernykhovsky, the Soviet commander who took Vilnius at the end of World War II, in front of the party Central Committee building.

Soviet troops could make demonstrators back away, but they could not control the daily life of the city. They still occupied buildings in Vilnius, but in many cases they looked like prisoners inside, peering through dirty glass doors at the people freely passing outside. Although Soviet forces sat in the Press House in Vilnius, playing cards within sight of Lithuanian militia who were also playing cards, the LCP/CPSU had to publish its own newspapers in Minsk and Königsberg; the press workers in Lithuania would not print their materials.

In the middle of August, the paratroopers pulled out of the Press House and some other buildings, vandalizing them on the way, but they kept control of the Institute of Party History, insisting that it housed valuable materials that should not be made public. When Brazauskas announced that his party was turning over its claim to the building to the Lithuanian government, crowds immediately gathered, challenging the occupiers. (In a conversation with me while standing in front of the building on a quiet Sunday morning, Jermalavičius, the head of the LCP/CPSU's ideological section, vigorously denounced Brazauskas's action as a "provocation.") Looking more and more like an occupation force, the Soviet military could find no respect among the general populace.

Shenin observed all this, and once back in Moscow he called for action by Soviet authorities, warning that the Lithuanian government was aiming at "total dismantling of Soviet power and the renewal of the totalitarian dictatorship of the bourgeoisie in Lithuania."[19] Echoing parts of Varennikov's scenario of March, Shenin insisted that the CPSU CC must direct "the USSR Council of Ministers and other Soviet agencies" to help the Moscow loyalists. He also called for "a new Union treaty draft," the mobilization of "the progressive members of the population of the Lithuanian SSR," and greater control over the central media's reporting on Lithuania. The KGB, he continued, should send a "quick-reaction operations investigation group" to Lithuania, and the CPSU CC should look into ways of fostering conflict between Lithuania and Poland. On August 29 the CPSU CC accepted Shenin's "evaluation and proposals" and declared its readiness to guarantee "the practical realization of the measures described in this report."[20]

Shenin, like others in Moscow, apparently had little faith in the leadership of the LCP/CPSU, and the CPSU transferred General Algimantas Naudžiunas from his military duties at the Soviet space center in Baikonur to Vilnius, where the LCP/CPSU quickly elected him a secretary of its Central Committee. Naudžiunas openly declared that he would have preferred to stay in Baikonur but that duty "to save Lithuania from separatism" dictated that he accept the transfer.[21]

The public instrument of CPSU policy in Lithuania would be the various "Committees of Citizens of the Lithuanian SSR," founded in the demonstrations of March 1990, formally organized April 28, 1990, and headed by Shved.[22] On July 27 this "multinational movement," as the Soviets called it, published a broadsheet, one side in Russian and the other in Lithuanian, denouncing the "demogogic declarations" of the Lithuanian government, denying the existence of any threat from Moscow, and condemning public demonstrations of hostility to the Soviet order in Lithuania. At the end of 1990 representatives of these committees banded together to form the Congress of Democratic Forces, which was later alleged to be the organizer of the Committee for the Salvation of Lithuania.[23]

Against this background of intensified party activity, Gorbachev displayed a growing disinclination to deal seriously with the Lithuanian government.[24] He seemed to have assigned Lithuania a lower priority on his own scale of problems after the CPSU Congress, and when the two sides finally came to the negotiating table in October, he took a tougher stance. Prunskiene reminded him of their discussions in July, but "he declared very resolutely, 'That was another time.'"[25] Meeting on October 11, the Lithuanians offered the Soviets their draft of a protocol affirming Lithuanian independence, and the Soviets countered with a draft speaking of the "links" between the USSR and "the Lithuanian SSR." At the next meeting, in November, the Soviets presented new demands: Lithuania must accept Soviet law and Soviet economic management. The Lithuanians protested, but the signs of a new, tougher position in Moscow were all too clear.[26]

The Soviets carried their battles to control and restrain the Lithuanians across a number of fronts as they sought to make clear that the Lithuanians could reach the outside world only as Moscow permitted. At the Paris Conference of the CSCE, November 19–21, the Soviet delegation blocked efforts to bring the Baltic foreign ministers as "observers" or even "guests." The foreign ministers in turn rejected Shevardnadze's invitation to sit in the meeting as part of the Soviet delegation.[27]

The struggle even spilled over into the sports world. Since the Lithuanians had also declared the independence of their sports organizations from Moscow, Soviet authorities persuaded officials of FIFA, the international soccer federation, to ban Lithuanian soccer teams from international play. Attacking on another front, the Lithuanians tried to send athletes to the Goodwill Games held in Seattle in July, but, as a TBS executive in Atlanta made clear to me, TBS, the sponsor of the games, would not admit athletes of whom Soviet officials disapproved. The Soviets seemed able to block all such maneuvers.

Moscow also mounted a major propaganda offensive aimed at discrediting the Lithuanian government. Appearing on Soviet central television in November, Shved and Naudžiunas declared that the Lithuanian government had made up a list of Communist Party members condemned to execution, but they could not produce an original copy of this document. In December, amid assertions that the Lithuanians were claiming the territory of other republics, a plenum of the Politburo declared that the greatest danger to the Soviet Union lay in "arrant extremist nationalism, the arousal of interethnic discord." Defense Minister Iazov insisted that the army was not bound by law in moments when the cause of preserving the Soviet state demanded action. Conservatives such as Ligachev felt justified by Gorbachev's more assertive stance, but they were nevertheless bitter about having waited for so long.[28]

The Lithuanians resented their isolation. They objected when Germany and the Soviet Union reached a new agreement on the organization of Eastern Europe without mentioning the Baltic republics. They complained when the U.S. government worked to assure itself of Gorbachev's support for the military offensive then being planned against

Iraq. During a night meeting of a congressional conference committee in Washington on October 25–26, for example, David Obey, a representative from Wisconsin, effectively killed a proposal to send aid to the three Baltic nations. Obey and his fellow congressman Lee Hamilton of Indiana subsequently explained that aid could be "delivered only with the acquiescence of the Central Government" and that the Baltic states should not be given special treatment. As Romualdas Ozolas summarized the situation, "Can President Gorbachev be condemned for using force to put down the separatist, the nationalists and the anarchists in general? If so, then as up to now social forces, most likely parties and individual members of parliaments, will do it and not the leaders of governments or states. These will be silent."[29]

Despite the official silence of foreign governments, at home Gorbachev faced growing criticism of his nationalities policy and even political threats from the Right. Particularly prominent among the critics of his Baltic policy was a Latvian, Viktor Alksnis, known as "the Black Colonel" because of his penchant for wearing that color. Alksnis claimed that the U.S. Central Intelligence Agency (CIA) was behind the troubles in Soviet realm, and in November he warned that Gorbachev had just thirty days to restore order: "I don't want this to sound like a threat to you, but this will simply be realized." He demanded that Committees of National Salvation save the Soviet Union as "a united and indivisible state."[30]

Under such pressure, Gorbachev retreated from plans for radical economic reform and demanded still stronger presidential powers. After five years of cutting into the political power of the military, he had now begun to accede to the demands of his unhappy High Command. In the words of one American analyst:

> By the fall of 1990, Gorbachev's political agenda had shifted from advancing *glasnost* and *perestroika* to ensuring his own political survival, preserving the union, creating a new federal system of republics, and maintaining a strong central government that would retain sovereignty over all-Union affairs.... Responding to the conservative agenda, he is attempting to hold the USSR together by emphasizing the maintenance of stability over continued reform."[31]

A series of changes in governmental posts signaled the Soviet leader's new orientation, and the appointment of Boriss Pugo as minister of internal affairs sent a particularly chilling message to the Baltic. In an interview with *Izvestiia* on December 4, Pugo emphasized the growth of organized crime in the Soviet Union, and then he noted, "In addition the President is concerned about the centrifugal tendencies which have appeared recently in the organs of internal affairs." Gorbachev was obviously interested in Pugo's experience as chief of the Latvian KGB and subsequently first secretary of the Latvian Communist Party.[32]

As the end of 1990 approached, the signs that Moscow was planning new action in the Baltic multiplied. Western journalists predicted that the Soviet government would move against any or all of the republics, with possibly Latvia the first target. Alfreds Rubiks, head of the Latvian Communist Party, reportedly told a closed gathering of military and party officials in November that order would be restored "soon, very soon." Moldova backed down from its confrontation with Moscow and rescinded a law making a Romanian dialect the official language of the republic. In a briefing for the staff of *The Washington Post*, CIA chief William Webster predicted that Gorbachev was heading toward a conflict with the Baltic republics.[33] The U.S. administration, concerned with the crisis in the Persian Gulf, continued to support Gorbachev.

On November 24 Landsbergis warned that Lithuania was "in danger" and that Soviet forces were prepared to reestablish the rule of the empire. On December 14, amid news of explosions in Riga and of Soviet troop movements in Lithuania, Romualdas Ozolas warned of the possibility of a Soviet coup on Christmas Eve. Government officials urged the population not to obey the directions of a usurping force, and Lithuanians generally debated the usefulness of armed resistance to Soviet actions. Meeting on Christmas Eve, the Presidium of the Lithuanian Supreme Council reasserted the principle of "passive civil resistance" in opposition to any action by Soviet troops. At the end of December the Lithuanian parliament rescinded its insistence that a protocol be signed before negotiations with Moscow begin.[34]

In the United States, Lithuanian-Americans were organizing aid for Lithuania and angrily calling for action by Congress and by the administration. According to a fund-raising letter dated "Christmas 1990," the Lithuanian-American Community reported that it had sent $268,395 in aid to Lithuania over the past two years. (Of this money, almost $74,000 was used for electronic equipment "for the press and for the Lithuanian government.") Lithuanian-American lobbyists in Washington warned, "Since

Gorbachev returned to the USSR from the Paris summit in November, the Soviet central authorities have been escalating their threats and intimidation tactics against the Baltic States....We expect the atmosphere to grow more tense and consider the threat of a military crackdown to be very real." Administration officials brushed off the arguments and repeated their calls for "dialogue." When Landsbergis visited Washington on December 10, Bush assured him that the United States supported Lithuania's right to self-determination,[35] but the American government at this point clearly had focused its attention on preparing for the Gulf War.

On December 19 a group of prominent Russians, including military figures and intellectuals, decried the spilling of "the people's blood," denounced "separatists," and urged Gorbachev to consider imposing martial law in the rebellious republics. Gorbachev declared that he had no plans to act, and Soviet chief of staff General Mikhail Moiseev, one of the signers of the open letter, asserted, "Not a single additional soldier will be dispatched to the Baltic." Although there had been no bloodshed in Lithuania, the Lithuanians, who knew that Moiseev considered Alksnis's speeches "eloquent," understood that the call for martial law signaled new danger.[36]

On December 20 Eduard Shevardnadze shocked everyone, including Gorbachev, by announcing that he was resigning as foreign minister of the Soviet Union in protest against the threat of dictatorship in the country.[37] Shevardnadze's resignation cast a cloud over the future of U.S.–Soviet relations, and conservatives in Moscow pushed ahead with demands for action in the Baltic. Referring ironically to Shevardnadze's warning, one of Viktor Alksnis's colleagues declared that the "threat of dictatorship" hung "over the Russian-speaking population and those who think differently in the Baltic region."[38] As the New Year of 1991 came to the Baltic, the tension was palpable.

11

THE JANUARY EVENTS

Between January 7 and January 14, 1991, Soviet troops attacked unarmed civilians in Lithuania, a political crisis resulted in Prunskiene's resignation, pro-Moscow forces announced they had taken power, and hundreds of thousands of Lithuanians from all corners of the republic went to Vilnius to show their support of national independence. By January 15, although Soviet troops controlled the streets, the Lithuanians had come out of what they called "the January events" with a renewed sense of national unity, Gorbachev had exposed the bankruptcy of his policies, and the Soviet Union was on the road to collapse.[1]

On Monday, January 7, on orders signed by Defense Minister Iazov on January 5, Soviet paratroopers entered all three Baltic republics, allegedly to look for young men who had fled or were evading service in the Soviet army, but few in the Baltic believed this ruse.[2] Soviet image-makers might have had in mind U.S. vice-president Dan Quayle's acceptance of Soviet actions in Lithuania in March 1990 on the grounds that a government had the right to maintain the integrity of its armed forces, but in fact the troops ignored problems of recruitment. There was no campaign to find delinquent recruits, and local officials received no order from Moscow to do so.[3] Instead, during the night of January 7–8, over 100 Soviet tanks rumbled through the heart of Vilnius in an obvious effort to intimidate the locals.

At the same time the Lithuanians faced a domestic political crisis in the aftermath of the cabinet's announcement of a sharp hike in the price of food. On January 8, after Prime Minister Prunskiene had left for Moscow to discuss the troop movements, demonstrators gathered outside the Supreme Council building to protest the price rise. Supporters of Edinstvo demanded the resignation of the cabinet and the dissolution of parliament, and Terleckas led LFL supporters in demanding Prunskiene's resignation. Seeing that the Russians dominated the square, Terleckas pulled his supporters to one side, but he still demanded Prunskiene's ouster. Edinstvo's forces stormed the parliament building, breaking windows and penetrating into the first floor. Security guards drove them back with the spray from fire hoses.

Inside the building the parliamentary deputies hastily canceled the price rise. In a special radio broadcast, Landsbergis called on Lithuanians to come forward and defend their parliament and the government that "you have chosen." He then appeared at a third-floor window to tell the demonstrators that the parliament had overruled the cabinet's decision to raise prices. In the meantime, Lithuanians poured into Independence Square "to defend the republic," and they shouldered out the Russian demonstrators, who had to retreat to the area in front of the neighboring Mažvydas Republican Library, on the other side of a large fountain from the parliament.

Even before the demonstrations the political Right was accusing Prunskiene of having raised prices deliberately to provoke a crisis. On Monday evening Landsbergis had questioned "the strange coincidence between the threats of the Soviet military and such a sharp price rise." On Tuesday Zigmas Vaišvila, a deputy, suggested that Prunskiene had timed the price rise to coincide with the arrival of the Soviet troops. The Supreme Council, by a vote of 108 in favor, 1 against, and 8 abstentions, voted to change the constitution so that a simple majority of deputies could oust the prime minister—the constitution had previously required a two-thirds majority for a vote of no confidence.

Prunskiene at this time was meeting with Gorbachev, who refused to discuss the troops' actions and instead demanded that Lithuania accept his plan to hold a referendum on the integrity of the Soviet Union. She later characterized Gorbachev as having been "uncommonly passive and unemotional," and his parting words to her had been "Go back and take care of the situation and restore order so that I do not have to do it myself." In the evening, again in Vilnius, Prunskiene, in the face of the parliament's hostility and the certainty of a vote of no confidence, resigned.[4]

Had prices been the true issue of the day, the demonstrations might have ended—the price rise had been rescinded and the government had resigned. Vladyslav Shved, for example, insisted that the crisis was economic, that "the economic situation in Lithuania is deteriorating faster than in Russia." The real issue, however, was political power, not economic policies. Moscow media called the conflicts in Vilnius "social" and "interethnic"; the Soviet authorities had their own program in this crisis.[5]

On January 7 Burokevičius spent three hours in the office of Valery Boldin, head of the General Section of the Central Committee, where he met with Oleg Baklanov (CC secretary for the military-industrial complex), Minister of Internal Affairs Pugo, Defense Minister Iazov, KGB chief Kriuchkov, and Shenin. Burokevičius argued that the time was right for the introduction of presidential rule in Vilnius: The peasantry, the workers, the intelligentsia, and the minority nationalities were all ready to turn on the Landsbergis regime. Moscow must act quickly because the minuscule Lithuanian defense force was planning a coup in conjunction with western intelligence services and émigré centers.[6]

The Soviet leadership immediately but secretly dispatched the deputy minister of defense, Colonel-General Vladyslav Achalov, to Lithuania. The public knew little at the time about Achalov's duties in the Defense Ministry, but Stanislav Tsaplin, deputy chief of the KGB in Lithuania, later called him "Iazov's deputy for emergency situations."[7] Colonel-General P. Grachev, who had just succeeded Achalov as head of airborne troops, later explained that Achalov "was involved in the operational command and control of troops in all the 'hot spots' of the country."[8]

This action was supposed to appear to be a local conflict, but Burokevičius had trouble mobilizing the Lithuanian side. He bluntly asked the Lithuanian KGB chief, Romas Marcinkus, "Who are you with, Chairman?" Marcinkus replied that he operated according to "the orders of the Moscow leadership and my own conscience." He rejected Burokevičius's effort to impose party discipline on him, he told his staff to do nothing unless they received orders directly from Gorbachev, and he resigned. Kriuchkov, however, delayed announcing Marcinkus's resignation and instead told staff in Vilnius that their chief was ill and had gone to Moscow for medical treatment.[9]

The Soviet propaganda machine pictured Lithuania as lapsing into chaos. On Tuesday evening, *Vremia*, the Moscow television news program, reported, "It appears that the Supreme Council is no longer in control of the situation." Edinstvo leaders called for a mass meeting at four o'clock on Wednesday in front of the Mažvydas library; at noon Soviet armored personnel carriers entered the area and parked on the library's north side. Troops helped the demonstrators set up their loudspeakers and other equipment for the rally. During the afternoon a planeload of Soviet paratroopers reportedly arrived at Vilnius airport. (Achalov's forces were already in place.) Just before 4:00 P.M. Soviet tanks surrounded the television tower and silenced Lithuanian television for the next several hours. In Moscow Gorbachev met with "Lithuanian citizens" who demanded the imposition of "presidential rule" in Lithuania. Within the Lithuanian parliament, Shved proposed that the Supreme Council dissolve itself, and the LCP/CPSU called for a general strike.[10]

At 4:00 P.M. armored personnel carriers stood by as Edinstvo's demonstration in front of the library began; Moscow was apparently counting on violence against which it would perforce intervene. Lithuanians had gathered in front of the parliament, and the two groups were separated by a thin line of unarmed Lithuanian militiamen. Landsbergis urged the Lithuanians to remain peaceful; the demonstrators on both sides of the fountain limited themselves to shouting and singing; in the end nothing happened.

When Russian Orthodox archbishop Khrisostom called on the people to avoid violence, the Russians began to disperse. The armored personnel carriers were gone by seven o'clock; the tanks withdrew from the television tower as inexplicably as they had come. I arrived in Vilnius that evening and saw no Russian demonstrators, only Lithuanians still on guard in front the parliament. Moscow news noted that Lithuania was "slightly less tense," and Soviet officials paused to reconsider their course of action now that "interethnic conflict" had failed to take place.

On Thursday afternoon Gorbachev intervened directly, demanding that the Lithuanians cease their efforts to restore "the bourgeois order." (His phraseology closely followed that of Shenin in the latter's report to the Politburo in September 1990.) Moscow, he asserted, was receiving appeals from "public political organizations, industrial collectives, citizens of all nationalities" in Lithuania, for the "introduction of presidential rule." The Lithuanian parliament would be responsible for what happened further if it did not "immediately and completely reestablish the validity of the USSR Constitution and of the Constitution of the Lithuanian SSR, and revoke the anticonstitutional acts adopted earlier."

Gorbachev's telegram arrived in Vilnius at 2:30 P.M., and at 3:00 P.M. Kazimieras Motieka, deputy chairman of the Supreme Council, announced over the radio: "It looks like the hour has come when we all have to decide the most important decision facing Lithuania: Either independence or eternal slavery." Declaring that Russian workers were again on their way to the Supreme Council, he called for additional people to come defend the building. From my vantage point on an upper floor of the Mažvydas library, I saw streams of people coming from all directions, some running, and the square was filled in half an hour. At 4:00 P.M. Landsbergis told a press conference that the Soviets wanted bloodshed so as to justify the establishment of martial law in Lithuania. At 4:30, when no Russian workers had showed up, the crowd in Independence Square began to break up.

Inside the parliament, amid echoes of the people singing in the square, Landsbergis named Albertas Šimenas, an economist, to succeed Prunskiene. Šimenas was a member of the Center faction, but the Right strongly endorsed his candidacy. Virgilijus Čepaitis explained to me that "the Right" was "not strong enough" to form a government by itself and therefore it had to accept "a compromise with the Center," even though the resulting government "might lack determination" in splitting with Moscow. After two hours of debate, the parliament approved Simenas's selection, and Landsbergis proclaimed, "Nobody in the world can say that there is a governmental crisis in Lithuania, that the legitimate government elected by the Lithuanian people is unstable."

On Thursday evening the Soviet forces stepped up their pressure. General Varennikov had now arrived, and Vilnius airport was declared closed by a strike of the Russian workers there. During the night, an estimated 30 Soviet tanks and 1,000 paratroopers roamed through the city, passing by the Press House and the television tower. As news of the troop movement spread, Lithuanians hurried to both sites, but no conflict occurred.

On Friday morning the Soviets moved in earnest. Vilnius awoke to reports that Russian workers would march on the parliament building. At seven in the morning, some 100 Soviet tanks were reportedly running their motors in preparation for moving into the city. Announcements over Lithuanian radio kept calling for calm: "Let us avoid provocations!" When the Russian demonstrators arrived at Independence Square, a large crowd of Lithuanians stood ready, and, in the words of Michael Dobbs (*The Washington Post*, January 12)) "The rival crowds shouted at each other across a thin cordon of Lithuanian policemen.... At one point, some Russian workers started singing 'The Internationale,' the Communist anthem, but were drowned out after a few bars by hoots and jeers from the Lithuanians."

Just before noon the military struck, seizing the Press House and drawing the first blood of the week. Seven people were taken to hospitals; two had been shot, and a truck driver, a veteran of the Soviet army in World War II, had been injured when a tank rolled over his vehicle on the highway. Television cameras recorded the attack on the Press House and showed how a colonel, angered at being doused with water, strafed the side of the Press House with his automatic rifle.[11] Those television pictures, replayed repeatedly over the next thirty-six hours, undoubtedly stimulated Soviet thoughts of silencing the Lithuanian media whatever else they might yet do.

The attack on the Press House changed the nature of the confrontation. The crowd of pro-Moscow demonstrators in Independence Square began to dissolve, and according to Walter Stoessinger (*Die Welt*, January 12–13), by evening "the last Russian" had disappeared. There were no more mass demonstrations against the Lithuanian government. Lithuanians gathered at the Press House to stare at the Soviet tanks parked there and to argue with the soldiers. Others hurried to the television tower, where they parked cars and buses on the access roads; according to Stoessinger's estimate, some 5,000 persons formed a ring surrounding the tower.

The Lithuanians also prepared to resist an attack on parliament. Landsbergis, together with a Catholic priest, presided over a formal ceremony in which volunteers swore an oath on the Lithuanian flag that they would defend the building "to the last drop of blood." During the afternoon Landsbergis tried twice to call Gorbachev on the telephone, but he could not get through—Gorbachev was reportedly dining. The parliament hastily approved the appointment of eleven ministers in Šimenas's cabinet so that a quorum could meet and Lithuania again would have a formal government.

The pro-Moscow forces moved ahead. On Friday afternoon, in a press conference at the LKP CC, Jermalavičius announced the formation of the Committee for the Salvation of Lithuania (CSL), which in turn proclaimed that it was taking "all power in Lithuania." The members of the "committee," however, remained anonymous. That evening Kriuchkov dispatched sixty-five men of his Special Forces unit Alfa, under the command of Colonel M. V. Golovatov, to Lithuania. (Golovatov may have already been in Vilnius on January 6.) The two planes carrying the unit arrived at the Vilnius airport at 11:00 P.M., and the men proceeded to the military base in Vilnius. On Saturday the base established direct radio communications with Moscow.[12]

Although other parts of Lithuania were remarkably quiet, Vilnius now lay under a military blockade. The airport was closed to the public, but Moscow's forces could use it at will. The Soviet army had blocked the highway from Vilnius to the Polish frontier, and it also closed the Vilnius train station, stranding a total of thirty-five trains with some 20,000 passengers. Through the night from Friday to Saturday Soviet armored personnel carriers roamed around Vilnius; at 1:45 A.M. television reported that twenty tanks were driving around the city.

Saturday dawned with attention focused on the meeting in Moscow of Gorbachev's Federation Council, which was expected to pass judgment on the president's proposed treaty of union. The Lithuanians had refused to participate in the council, although Egidijus Bičkauskas, the Lithuanian government representative in Moscow, attended the session as an observer. In Vilnius, as they anxiously waited for news of the gathering, some Lithuanians feared that Gorbachev intended to seat the Committee for the Salvation of Lithuania in the council.

A sampling of opinion with the parliament building on Saturday afternoon illustrated the uncertainties of the day. "They haven't shot us yet," Audrius Siarusevičius, a young journalist, cheerfully called out when he saw me. Čepaitis seemed certain that the parliament would not be attacked: "We are sure that there will be no violence against the legal representatives of government." Rimas Valatka, a deputy and a journalist, declared, "They are squeezing us hard, and it seems that some of our actions are only helping them do it more quickly." Eduardas Vilkas, another deputy and a member of the Academy of Sciences, described the situation as being "without any logic," adding that "if they seize everything, they will have no one to sign an agreement with." That same afternoon Čepaitis told a *Washington Post* reporter, "It's impossible to return this country to the time of Stalin. They may be stupid in Moscow, but they are not complete idiots."

During the afternoon the Lithuanians found hope first in the report that Yeltsin's Russian government had denounced the use of force in the Baltic and then in the news that the Federation Council was dispatching a delegation of three persons to help resolve the conflict in Lithuania by political means.[13] Landsbergis welcomed the report of the delegation's coming but still questioned whether Moscow could be trusted. Moscow nevertheless loosened the blockade, and in a separate press conference in Vilnius, Soviet military officials denied that they were planning to use force.

For reasons that seemed unclear at the time, the presidential delegation did not travel directly to Vilnius. Instead it stopped in Minsk for an overnight stay. Later the Lithuanians were convinced that Gorbachev had deceived them: as Romualdas Ozolas put it, "They released the trains, released the airplanes—go sleep peacefully, and then they struck."[14]

Shortly after 1:00 A.M. tanks were rolling through Vilnius. The Alfa unit had orders to take the communications centers: the radio and television station and the television tower. They preferred not to attack the parliament because of the obvious cost in lives—Iazov had directed the troops to shed as little blood as possible. The paratroopers, under Achalov, were to clear the way to the buildings, and the Alfa unit would move in to capture them.[15] Defenders resisted, but they lacked weapons. Through the foresight of Audrius Butkevičius, the head of the nascent Lithuanian military who had placed cameras in the halls of the television station, viewers were able to see the Soviet troops forcing their way into the building and searching the corridors.

At 1:47 A.M. Landsbergis appeared on television from the parliament building, telling viewers "We have already experienced the value of freedom" and promising that Lithuanians would support the cause of independence. He had again tried to call Gorbachev in Moscow, but he could not get through—Gorbachev was reportedly sleeping. "If blood is spilled," Landsbergis intoned, "it will fall on his head." In conclusion he declared, "Let it be as the Lord wills," but Lithuanians should remember that "a free morning is coming."

By 2:20 A.M. the Soviet troops had taken the radio and television station and the tower. Shots could be heard echoing around the city for another two hours. Loudspeakers on the Soviet tanks played a tape of Jermalavičius's voice, proclaiming the authority of the Committee for the Salvation of Lithuania and telling the people to go home. When the tower was finally quiet, Lithuanian demonstrators returned with portable radios, loudly playing Radio Liberty's Russian-language accounts of the carnage for the benefit of the Soviet troops.[16]

The Lithuanians still expected an attack on the parliament, and many people had rushed to Independence Square at the news that the Soviet tanks were moving. Elderly men and women came dressed in their best clothes, prepared to die rather than submit to the restoration of the old Soviet order—they stood and sang, they knelt and prayed, waiting for the Soviet troops to attack. Although the Soviet military forced the television station to cease programming at 2:09 A.M., the television tower continued broadcasting for another eight minutes, simply showing the crowd in Independence Square as they first recited the Hail Mary in unison and then sang "Lithuania Beloved," the unofficial Lithuanian national anthem during the most difficult years of Soviet rule. The television screen went dead at 2:17 A.M.

The Lithuanian government had no armed forces with which it could resist; words and bodies constituted its only weapons. The cabinet dispatched Algirdas Saudargas, the foreign minister, to Poland, empowering him to form a government-in-exile if necessary. When the parliament gathered at 3:00 A.M., deputies, after debating just what constituted the suppression of government in Lithuania, passed their own resolution empowering Saudargas to act. The deputies issued appeals to the governments and peoples of the world, and they insisted that all local government institutions continue to obey the directives of the established government: "Any other government in Lithuania is illegal and its directives are not binding on the people of Lithuania."[17]

When the citizens of Vilnius—those who had not been standing guard in front of the parliament—arose on Sunday morning, Soviet military vehicles were driving through the streets, and their loudspeakers were proclaiming that the Committee for the Salvation of Lithuania had taken power. (The membership of the committee, however, still remained a secret.) Major General Vladimir Uskhopchik, chief of the Vilnius garrison, was now the commandant of the city, and Lithuanians were to observe a curfew from 10:00 P.M. to 6:00 A.M. Rallies, demonstrations, and processions were banned, as was the use of printing and copying equipment for anti-Soviet purposes. The pro-Moscow forces apparently expected that Gorbachev would announce presidential rule in Lithuania momentarily.

The body count of the Soviet military action stood at 13 dead, with 165 injured, 26 of them seriously. At the parliament defenders were moving construction equipment into place to block access to Independence Square. (On January 23 Moscow television called the barricades "unpeaceful constructions" *[nemirnye konstruktsii].*) In response to the shocking news that Prime Minister Šimenas had disappeared, the parliament named Gediminas

Vagnorius as Lithuania's new prime minister. Although Landsbergis explained that this was a move to protect Šimenas and the Lithuanian government if the prime minister was indeed in hostile hands, when Šimenas reappeared, Vagnorius remained prime minister.

The day turned out to be more peaceful that one might have expected at dawn. The Lithuanians were both encouraged and relieved when they learned that the journalists who had assembled in Vilnius in the course of the week got the news of the violence out to the world. Boris Yeltsin, moreover, flew to Estonia to declare his support for the Baltic republics, and he called on Soviet troops not to carry out orders "to act against legally created state bodies, against the peaceful civilian population that is defending its democratic achievements." He also joined in an appeal by the Baltic presidents to the states of the world and to the United Nations.[18] The Lithuanians—and of course Gorbachev too—discovered that the world was watching the Soviet military's violence.

Once the delegation from Moscow had finally arrived in Vilnius at about noon on Sunday, it played a key role in restoring a semblance of order. The head of the delegation, Vitaly Doguzhiev, apparently was carrying out Gorbachev's orders, but the other two members seemed to have thoughts of their own. Boris Oleinik, a Ukrainian, cryptically declared that the situation "was more difficult than we had expected," and Levon Ter-Petrosian, an Armenian, openly criticized the Soviet government's "unconstitutional" action in Lithuania.

Jermalavičius and other representatives of the Committee for the Salvation of Lithuania met the delegation at the airport and tried to take control of its movements. The delegates, however, insisted on proceeding to the parliament. In the evening, the visitors mediated the conclusion of a truce: The Lithuanian government would ask the demonstrators to withdraw from the parliament, and the military promised to take its patrols off the streets for the night. The night passed quietly, and on Monday Lithuania settled into the routine that was to dominate its life for the next seven months. Vilnius had a divided character: Soviet troops controlled the streets, but the Lithuanians scorned them as occupation forces and went their own way. There was no reconciliation possible.

Moscow made at least one more effort to staff the mysterious CSL. On January 10 Kriuchkov summoned Vytautas Sakalauskas, the former prime minister of Lithuania, from his diplomatic post in Mozambique. When he arrived in Moscow on the January 12, he stayed at a KGB hotel. On

January 13 Kriuchkov, Shenin, and Masliukov asked him to head the new Lithuanian government that would serve under presidential rule. (Iazov had written on his desk pad, "Sakalauskas rather than Burokevičius; Burokevičius will assist.")[19] Sakalauskas then traveled secretly to Vilnius, where he met with Burokevičius, and upon returning to Moscow he spoke again with Kriuchkov, Shenin, and even Doguzhiev. In the end, Sakalauskas saw the situation as hopeless, refused to cooperate, and returned to Mozambique.[20]

The seizure of the television tower was a classic failure. Moscow had succeeded militarily but had failed politically; it had won a little and lost a great deal. Pyrrhus reportedly said after his battle with the Romans, "One more such victory and we are lost," and on the other hand, the poet John Dryden wrote, "Successful crimes alone are justified." As a British commentator put it, "President Gorbachev may win the battle he started by sending paratroops and 'Black Berets' on to the streets of the Baltic states... he has now assuredly lost the war."[21]

A major factor in the Lithuanians' triumph, and probably the reason that the Soviet forces chose not to attack the parliament, was the presence of the horde of foreign correspondents. During that long night, I, like many others, thought that Lithuania was isolated, cut off. In the morning it became clear that the correspondents, who had flocked to the city over the past week, were informing the world. The attack on the television tower was a worldwide public relations disaster for the Soviet government and of course for Gorbachev.

The Lithuanians' tactic of passive resistance thrust on the military, together with its local allies and agents, the responsibility for violence. Military spokespersons in Vilnius and in Moscow objected to correspondents' reference to an "offensive" against the Landsbergis government, but the military and the Edinstvo demonstrators caused all the property damage and all the deaths involved. The Lithuanians had been defending "law and order"; the pro-Moscow forces had attempted a coup d'état and had failed.

Although it refused to give back any buildings its forces had taken in this action, Moscow tried to erase the memories of the violence as quickly as possible. It hastily ceased all references to the CSL—on January 25 a commentator on Moscow radio asked, "Can such a committee which remains anonymous win trust?" The special troops responsible for the mayhem in Lithuania, the Pskov paratrooper division and the Alfa unit, moved on to Riga to carry out their next assignment. Gorbachev, Pugo, and Iazov asserted that they had known nothing about what happened. Even Burokevičius and Jermalavičius denied knowing anything about the CSL. Only the unfortunate commandant of the Vilnius garrison, Major General Vladimir Uskhopchik, had to explain himself, asserting that he had cooperated with the CSL, the members of which still remained anonymous, because it was working closely with the LCP/CPSU.[22]

The LCP/CPSU had won nothing of significance for its efforts. To be sure, it could move its publishing program into Lithuania, and it controlled the official television and radio, but even Gorbachev could now see that its claims of popular support had been unfounded. CPSU representatives berated the incompetence of their comrades in Lithuania. As one party official complained, "The opposition is armed dozens of times better analytically and, so to speak, intellectually.... The Lithuanian population has been abruptly consolidated by blood.... Of course presidential rule should not be introduced now."[23]

The LCP/CPSU in turn sought to affix responsibility elsewhere. The head of pro-Soviet television broadcasting in Vilnius, Colonel Eduardas Kasperavičius—Lithuanians spoke of his program as "Kaspervizija"—complained that Landsbergis had outfoxed Uskhopchik: "The 'stupid' military yielded to provocation and now they are getting it in the neck. The army and the Communists lost, and Landsbergis won. That was a carefully planned, psychologically prepared operation. Landsbergis needed sacrifices, and he found them."[24] Such commentary could not endear the LCP/CPSU leaders to the Soviet military.

The events burned deeply in the minds of officers who resented the blame that the politicians forced upon them, and the experience in Vilnius had a strong effect on the military's behavior in Moscow in August 1991. Grachev later ridiculed the thought that Uskhopchik could have acted on his own responsibility: "They saddle him with all the woes now. This is incorrect in principle. Could you really believe that a garrison commandant is able to send troops to participate in armed action? All commands came from higher up: From the Ministry of Defense and the General Staff." Linking this experience with the military's subsequent refusal to support the August Putsch in Moscow, he added, "As we can see, the army learned a lesson during the Vilnius events as well."[25] In July 1992, Colonel Sergei Goncharov, explaining why his Alfa unit had not attacked the RSFSR parliament building in August 1991, declared, "Vilnius was the last straw and our patience ran out.... Honestly, had it not been for Vilnius we would not have refused to storm the White House."[26]

The defenders of the Russian "White House" in August 1991 also drew lessons from the Vilnius experience. Western correspondents liked to compare the events in Moscow with the violence in Tienanmen Square in 1989, but the leaders resisting the August Putsch rallied their forces in a parliament building, not an open square, and they copied the practices of the Lithuanians on how to provide demonstrators with food and toilet facilities.

For Gorbachev the Vilnius adventure was a fiasco. At the last minute he had backed away from overthrowing the Lithuanian government, and he protested that he had not known what was happening.[27] Although in May 1989 he had told the CPD, "I know everything," during the January events he was supposedly busy eating and sleeping when Landsbergis called and no one else told him anything. He sent the warning telegram to Lithuania on Thursday, January 10; he sat through the Federation Council's discussions on Saturday; and yet he and his press secretary claimed that he knew nothing.[28] Gorbachev also insisted that Kriuchkov and Iazov had known nothing.

The political Right in Russia would not forgive Gorbachev his actions during this crisis, even calling them treasonous. The telegram he sent the Lithuanians on January 10, they argued, was meant to set the stage for the proclamation of presidential rule—the "Hungary 1956 variant": The document was ready but Gorbachev would not sign it. This left the Committee for the Salvation of Lithuania in the awkward position of claiming to replace the legal government of Lithuania but not getting Moscow's endorsement. Feeling that Gorbachev had betrayed them, the organizers of the action in Vilnius subsequently found it easy to believe that "western interests" were directing Gorbachev to be soft toward Landsbergis.[29]

The U.S. government painfully stood by Gorbachev, officially taking him at his word; as Ambassador Matlock reportedly said on January 24, "No one thinks that you yourself gave the order to use force.... Certainly there were provocations from the other side. But nevertheless..."[30] The U.S. government knew what was happening in Vilnius, it expressed concern about the events there, but it left the initiative in Gorbachev's hands. (The bombing of Baghdad was to begin on January 16.) At 11:49 A.M. on Saturday, January 12, Vilnius radio quoted White House Press spokesperson Marlin Fitzwater as saying that it was still premature to speak of the use of force in Lithuania; as one who heard that broadcast, I must say that Washington's calls for "dialogue" appeared ludicrous.

Gorbachev, naturally enough, pictured himself as heroic and victimized at the same time. His critics, he declared in 1992, wanted

> Gorbachev, who was getting out of this dirt and dragging everyone out, to remain in the dirt alone. This will not work. Let them lay these archives on the table for you.... Ten tables like the one here will not suffice for all to see how they pressured me, and demanded that I introduce presidential rule in Lithuania, and so on.... So, we are trying to reduce everything to the position of the president alone.[31]

Such a statement, of course, ignored the significance of his own telegram to the Lithuanians on January 10 and sharpened his image as a lone figure who could not trust the people standing the closest to him.

Gorbachev's action and inaction together with his disingenuous explanations cost him heavily. He proclaimed his democratic intentions for the Soviet Union and closed his eyes as Soviet troops ravaged and looted Lithuania and the Baltic. Only those who desperately wanted to believe believed him, but by such assertions he left himself open to charges of mendacity or incompetence. Even persons sympathetic to him decried the violence: Vytautas Petkevičius, one of the founders of Sajudis but a determined critic of Landsbergis, reportedly upbraided Kasperavičius: "What did you stupid people do! We would have brought down Landsbergis with tractors and you brought tanks!" Gorbachev's critics called for change: Alksnis, calling Gorbachev "essentially indecisive both as a man and as a politician," declared, "[Gorbachev] will have to go.... He knows he is doomed."[32]

While most Lithuanians had lost faith in Gorbachev long before, reformers in Moscow and elsewhere now despaired of him. Levon Ter-Petrosian suggested that while "Gorbachev had decided to let the hard-line centrists crack down in Lithuania with 'an attempted coup,' he at least was smart enough to retreat."[33] Others were not so kind: "Gorbachev has been making fatal mistakes," trumpeted the *Moscow News*: "The criminal orders sent from Moscow's Kremlin against Lithuania hit at the heart of Russia." Another journalist accused the Soviet leadership, including Gorbachev, of a "contemptuous attitude toward law."[34]

Gorbachev had no more options vis-á-vis Lithuania. Whatever his reform sympathies, he could find better organizational support from the conservatives. He could still, of course, count on the support of the U.S. and German governments. President Bush, while condemning the "violence in the Baltics," had recoiled from criticizing Gorbachev personally, explaining "The principle that has guided us is simple: Our objective is to help the Baltic peoples achieve their aspirations, not to punish the Soviet Union."[35] Despite such support, however, Gorbachev's Lithuanian policy was bankrupt.

12

The Road to Ruin

Picking my way among the bonfires in Independence Square on January 13, 1991, I wondered whether, if I got out of this alive, this would be the point at which the book I was planning to write about Gorbachev and Lithuania would conclude. Would Gorbachev follow through and crush Lithuania? Two days later, walking around the parliament with me, Lionginas Šepetys insisted, "We have truth on our side," and he declared that the question was whether this was an isolated action or part of a general offensive in the Baltic. The Soviet forces in fact moved on to Latvia and killed people in Riga the next week; nevertheless, Gorbachev's Baltic adventure soon ended, and in abject failure.

The Soviet propaganda machine blamed both the Lithuanians and foreign influences for the violence, while Gorbachev considered measures to stifle the sections of the media that refused to fall in line. On January 24 the CPSU Politburo declared that rather than "heed the constructive proposals of the USSR president," the Lithuanian government had acted irresponsibly, and it criticized Yeltsin and the Baltic leaders for having made "an open appeal for interference by foreign states in our internal affairs." On April 23 the Moscow television program *Vremia* reported that Americans had provided "newspaper paper, printers, lasers, and videocameras" to help Sajudis take over the media in Lithuania. In Leningrad Aleksandr Nevzorov, a popular television figure, praised the Soviet heroes who had bravely faced "crazed" Lithuanians who had allegedly poured boiling water on them. The Lithuanian government, Nevzorov asserted, consisted of "cowards and scum."

Despite such fiery words, Gorbachev chose to do nothing. Iakovlev reportedly urged him to travel to Vilnius and seek forgiveness, but

Gorbachev refused. He accused the Landsbergis government of having planned to execute Naudžiunas, Shved, and other Communists; he drew parallels to "ideological wars of the past"; he denied that the military action in Vilnius had had anything to do with thoughts of establishing presidential rule; and still coordinating his policy with the discredited LCP/CPSU, he called for "a dialogue" or "negotiations."[1] Iakovlev later wrote, "Ten days after the Vilnius events [Gorbachev] declared that he had had absolutely nothing to do with this. That same day I declared that this constituted a tragedy not just for Lithuania but for our entire people."[2]

The new Soviet foreign minister, Aleksandr Bessmertnykh gave ample testimony to the government's embarrassment when in a press conference he spoke of the "tragic events" in Vilnius where "human lives were lost, and that is the worst thing that can happen in any country.... It is not a reflection of the policy of the leadership.... it is not a method by which the leadership intends to act in relations with its own people and republics."[3] In an attempt at blunt American criticism, Soviet spokespersons argued that Lithuania was more vital to the Soviet Union than Grenada or Panama was to the United States.

Gorbachev had lost Lithuania for any vision he had yet of perestroika, and he left the republic to be ravaged by the military. As the Lithuanian journalist Algimantas Čekuolis put it, "They say that Gorbachev is a good dancer, but when others say 'stamp your feet,' he says 'stamp your feet' a few seconds later. He is a beat slow. He does not know what to do now. He should anticipate events, not follow behind them." In 1988 Gorbachev had stood at the forefront of action, but in 1991 he was lagging behind. Although on paper he had far-reaching power, he was no longer a strong leader.[4]

Juxtaposed to Gorbachev's declining public image was Yeltsin's rising star. Gorbachev repeatedly told his aides that he did not want to preside over the dissolution of the Soviet state—or "empire," as many now called it—but Yeltsin was exploiting just that process. On January 14, having returned to Moscow from Tallinn, Yeltsin again called on Russian soldiers not to move against legally elected governments in the Soviet Union, and in a press conference he sharply criticized Gorbachev's "moving toward the right" and the central government's decision "to turn decisively to the 'iron hand.'" He claimed to have told Gorbachev, "We are going to be shamed in front of the entire world, because this is nothing but the end of democracy."[5]

Gorbachev now put his hope in an all-Union referendum on the question "Do you consider necessary the preservation of the Union of Soviet Socialist Republics as a renewed federation of equal sovereign republics, in which the rights and freedoms of an individual of any nationality will be fully guaranteed?" On January 16, 1991, three days after the bloodshed in Vilnius, the Supreme Soviet set the date of the referendum for March 17, 1991. Also on January 16, Landsbergis announced that on February 9 Lithuanians would answer the question "Should the Lithuanian state be an independent, democratic government?"

The Lithuanians won the battle of referenda, such as it was, reporting that 85 percent of the electorate, some 2.2 million voters, had gone to the polls and 90.5 percent had approved the statement that Lithuania should be independent. (Lithuanians constituted about 80 percent of the population.) A majority of those voting in every region of Lithuania approved the proposition. Gorbachev's referendum drew some 650,000 voters in Lithuania, and it had no significant impact on his Lithuanian policy, or lack thereof.[6]

As the standoff between Moscow and Vilnius dragged on, Soviet leaders began to speak of the possibility of Lithuanian independence under specific conditions. The harshest of these conditions would reduce Lithuania to its boundaries of September 1939—that is, before the Lithuanian state had incorporated Vilnius (but after the Soviet Union had taken the city from Poland) and after the loss of Klaipeda/Memel to Nazi Germany.[7] Under the continued guidance of Oleg Shenin, Moscow loyalists in Lithuania added their voices to the calls for the dismemberment of the republic if its leaders demanded independence. The pro-Moscow forces, Shenin suggested, should now aim at setting up their own Soviet republic in Klaipeda and Vilnius and requesting protection by Soviet troops.[8]

The Moscow loyalists found themselves in an awkward situation. Soviet troops protected them, but they enjoyed almost no support among the people of Lithuania. Despite the military presence, the Lithuanian government could still challenge them, and it even called for the arrest of Jermalavičius for his part in the January events. When the LCP/CPSU succeeded in restarting the presses in the Press House at the beginning of February, the government banned the sale of its Russian and Lithuanian publications at public newsstands. Would-be purchasers had to go to the LCP/CPSU's headquarters on Gediminas Prospect.[9]

The LCP/CPSU continued to insist that the Lithuanians would be better served by remaining a part of the Soviet Union. The LCP/CPSU issued a formal declaration insisting that the economic problems of the day were the fault of the Landsbergis government: The Lithuanian nationalists had willfully destroyed the comfortable life that the Soviet regime had provided in the past. (Such arguments, of course, had little effect on people who knew of the growing economic problems in the Soviet Union.) What was necessary, the Central Committee of the LCP/CPSU declared, was "the active struggle of the toiling masses for the reconstruction of the Soviet constitutional order, the blocking of the totalitarian tendencies of the present political regime in the republic, and the preservation of Soviet citizenship for the residents of Lithuania." The Moscow loyalists went on to demand a law for the recall of parliamentary deputies so as to make possible the restructuring of the legislature and the government.[10]

At the same time, the LCP/CPSU tried to present itself as a partisan of reform. Besides claiming that it was now an "independent" Communist party, it endorsed "a thoughtful transition to market relationships," transferring part of state property into the hands of collectives while at the same time maintaining "socialist domination of the economy and not permitting the exploitation of man by man." Improved productivity, lower tax burdens, and technological progress could all be best realized within the embrace of the Soviet Union's economic system.

The LCP/CPSU denounced the Landsbergis government as carrying out a violent, blindly anti-Communist campaign. The choice, argued Eduardas Kasperavičius, lay between fascism as represented by Landsbergis and democracy as promised by the LCP/CPSU. He blamed the violence of January on Landsbergis, who had effected a "grandiose provocation" directed against the Soviet army and the Lithuanian Communist Party, which, he alleged, were the real victims of those terrible events. Healthy minds, he argued, should understand that the formation of a common front against the fascists was more important than the misguided struggle for independence, although, he and other Communists insisted, the LCP/CPSU naturally supported the idea of *real* sovereignty and independence in union with the Soviet Union.[11]

In its various public appeals, the LCP/CPSU and its supporting agencies remarkably avoided the use of names. Just as the members of the Committee for the Salvation of Lithuania had remained nameless, the Central Committee declaration just quoted bore no signatures, and even when the Communists announced the formation of a Union of Soviet Journalists of Lithuania, the members of the "Coordinating Council" remained anonymous.[12] For the general Lithuanian public it seemed clear that behind the anonymity lay Russian names, and despite its claims that mass discontent was growing in Lithuania, the LCP/CPSU remained a negligible factor in domestic Lithuanian affairs.

Moscow gradually seemed to comprehend the weakness and unreliability of its representatives in Vilnius. In the spring of 1991 speculation arose that even Gorbachev did not like working work with them—Burokevičius, for example, while repeating the slogans of perestroika orthodoxy, was reportedly siding with the conservatives in the CPSU Politburo and in the Central Committee. Accordingly, Gorbachev supporters were reportedly planning a minicoup aimed at providing the LCP/CPSU with new, more progressive leadership. LCP/CPSU Bureau leaders angrily denounced the reports as the work of "Landsbergis's Department of State Security for the purpose of splitting and weakening the Communist Party of Lithuania," but their ineffectiveness was obvious to all who looked.[13]

On June 3, the day Gorbachev left for Norway to receive his Nobel Peace Prize, the USSR Prosecutor's office released its report on the events of January in Lithuania, absolving the army of any blame and insisting that the troops had only responded to the call for help in stopping "provocative" radio and television broadcasts. The troops, the report said, although attacked by drunken demonstrators, had maintained their discipline; the "majority" of the dead had lost their lives not because of the troops' actions but rather had fallen victims to the demonstrators. "It can be said," the report concluded, "that the tragic events of January 13, 1991 in Vilnius were the result of the anticonstitutional activity of the Lithuanian leadership, which had evoked a deep social-political crisis."[14]

New military provocations in Lithuania coincided with the release of the report. Six Soviet armored personnel carriers drove up to the Lithuanian customs post at Medininkai, on the border with Belorussia, and the soldiers jokingly told the Lithuanian guards that they were there to protect them from OMON, Soviet special forces known as the Black Berets. In the evening Soviet troops took positions at the Vilnius airport and stationed forces at several bridges and on the approaches to the Supreme Council. At about 11:00 P.M. Landsbergis called on the people once again to rally at the parliament. The television suddenly went off the air for some fifteen minutes, while Lithuanians once more poured into

Independence Square. The Soviet forces then withdrew without explanation, and at 1:00 A.M. Virgilius Čepaitis appeared on television to announce that the city was again quiet.

At a press conference in Oslo on June 5, when asked about such goings-on, Gorbachev criticized the western press, not the Soviet troops. He spoke passionately of the "thousands, hundreds of thousands of refugees" said to be fleeing ethnic conflicts in the Soviet Union, and then he attacked the question: "I will never agree to the fact that the moment some tension arises in the Baltic republics, the entire Western press kicks up a fuss and shouts: Help, they want to stage a coup again." He finished with a series of disconnected thoughts that suggested that he, in fact, suspected an effort to embarrass him: "I do not think that someone organized anything. But perhaps someone wanted, as it were, to play this trick, bearing in mind that Gorbachev is travelling to the Nordic countries." A short time later, June 17, he had to beat back a challenge to his authority in the USSR Supreme Soviet.[15]

Lithuania and Moscow were stalemated, and at times the Soviet actions in Lithuania approached the level of comic opera, albeit bloody comic opera. Speaking in Moscow on May 29, Pugo specifically denied that OMON, a Soviet special forces group, was attacking Lithuanian customs posts. Television reporters then showed him footage put together by Nevzorov, OMON's troubadour, and Pugo had to admit that those were indeed his forces. He could not, however, explain where their orders were coming from. In any case, the Soviets insisted that there was nothing sinister about this activity. According to *Pravda* of July 1, the Ministry of Internal Affairs informed OMON leaders from Lithuania of the necessity of "observing legality" and "avoiding excesses."

The Lithuanian customs posts, it might be noted, were essentially a symbolic gesture aimed at showing that the Lithuanian government controlled the territory of the republic. They were makeshift structures occupied by unarmed men, and Soviet forces, usually from OMON, attacked such posts eighteen times in the course of 1991—the first time on January 27, two weeks after "Bloody Sunday." The bloodiest attack was at Medininkai at the end of July.[16] It is as yet unclear who ordered the raids, but Moscow did little if anything to stop them.

The LCP/CPSU demanded stronger measures than just raids on customs posts to help it achieve some semblance of authority in Lithuania. At a CPSU CC plenum in July, Burokevičius called national separatism "a very dangerous phenomenon" and warned that the supporters of Soviet rule in Lithuania were "losing confidence in the ability of union institutions to properly resolve even one question concerning Lithuania."[17] The LCP/CPSU leaders could not have been more open about their dependence on Moscow's support and their resentment that they were not receiving more.

In Lithuania the old debate about dealing with Moscow continued. Questioned about his tactics and strategy, Landsbergis suggested, "Confrontation is also interaction," while Prunskiene argued that "a declaration.... cannot produce results." Landsbergis's adviser Čepaitis argued that Moscow should consider how better to deal with Lithuania: "The problem of our relations with Moscow is one of self-control. M. Gorbachev is one of the world's most realistic politicians." Brazauskas insisted that serious negotiations with the Soviet Union were necessary for Lithuania's economic life.[18]

Through the summer of 1991 most attention tended to focus on Gorbachev's determined efforts to forge a new treaty of union and on George Bush's planned visit to Moscow; the Lithuanians had the dual role of objects and observers in both processes. Lithuania remained a factor in U.S.-Soviet relations, but both sides were trying to minimize it. After the January events, Bush had postponed his trip but had refused to cancel it, thereby again signaling his concern for Gorbachev. As for Gorbachev's new treaty, the Lithuanians wanted no part of it, and they refused to participate in the discussion. Soviet authorities in turn made grandiose statements about how the Lithuanians would suffer if they insisted on staying out of the new union. In this complex of considerations, neither Moscow nor Vilnius showed much interest in trying to resolve their mutual problems quickly.

The Lithuanians expected little of the United States at this point. In May, when Landsbergis was in Washington, Bush had told a press conference that "we have a strong and I think a good relationship with President Gorbachev" and that he would urge "a peaceful resolution" of all problems. Despite Soviet misgivings, Bush spoke with Landsbergis. The Lithuanian, on the other hand, told a congressional committee, "We could advise the Congress and the government of the USA from our own experience: Do not trust a government of thieves." In California, he spoke more sarcastically, suggesting that the Lithuanians and the Georgians are considered "true egotists, who think that their freedom is important and do not realize that this creates problems for others." In Prunskiene's more cautiously phrased opinion, "The present participation of the USA is in fact nonparticipation."[19]

On the eve of Bush's visit to the USSR, Gorbachev embarked on a new spasm of positive activity. He claimed to have made positive steps toward the new treaty of union, and on July 25 and 26 the CPSU CC approved his proposals for a new party program that would convert the CPSU into a Social Democratic organization, dropping its revolutionary rhetoric and finding a place in a multiparty system. On the other hand, despite speculation to the contrary, Gorbachev gave no sign of withdrawing from his post as general secretary of the party. As he met Bush, Gorbachev seemed to have achieved a certain degree of stability in both party and government.[20]

In an obviously calculated effort to win publicity at this Great Power love feast, Yeltsin and Landsbergis, who had met during Gorbachev's visit to the United States in 1990, again provided a surprise for the two presidents. In June Yeltsin had won election as the president of the Russian republic, and he thereby could claim a popular mandate such as Gorbachev never could. Now, almost simultaneously with Bush's arrival, a Lithuanian delegation headed by Landsbergis flew into Moscow and drove to the Russian Supreme Soviet Building. There the two sides signed agreements on establishing formal relations between their governments, on cultural and economic relations, and on questions relating to Kaliningrad. "Bush is in Moscow, but the journalists are following B. Yeltsin," wrote one commentator,[21] as the Russian leader disrupted Gorbachev's carefully planned schedule.

Bush determinedly supported Gorbachev. When news came that attackers had killed guards at a Lithuanian customs post, Gorbachev promised that he would direct KGB chief Kriuchkov to seek out the truth, and Bush seemingly approved. (Gorbachev apparently learned of the matter from his American visitors and then turned to Kriuchkov for an explanation.) Kriuchkov never seemed to get around to seeking out the truth, however, and LCP/CPSU spokespersons, arguing that only Bush and Landsbergis stood to gain by the killings, suggested that the U.S. government may have played a role in the incident.[22] In fact, it was OMON forces in Riga who for as-yet unexplained reasons had gone to Lithuania to do the job. But the Americans seemed satisfied with Gorbachev's response to the killings.

Addressing the Ukrainian parliament on August 1 in what the columnist William Safire skewered as his "Chicken Kiev" speech, Bush sounded as if he were reading a text prepared by Gorbachev. Although he privately advised Gorbachev to let the Baltic republics go, the U.S. president publicly praised the Russian's "astonishing" achievements and warned the republics not to expect help from the U.S. against the center. The U.S. president accepted Moscow's view of secession as his own, declaring "freedom cannot survive if we let despots flourish or permit seemingly minor restrictions to multiply until they form chains, until they form shackles.... Americans will not support those who seek to replace a far-off tyranny with a local despotism. They will not aid those who promote a suicidal nationalism based upon ethnic hatred." For good measure, he criticized those who might pursue "the hopeless course of isolation,"[23] here accepting a mantra that Gorbachev frequently used to characterize the policy of the Lithuanians.

After Bush's departure, Gorbachev continued his campaign for the signing of a new union treaty, but on August 19 his entire program, such as it was, collapsed, when Moscow awoke to the news that a conservative junta, an "Emergency Committee," had taken power. The would-be coup failed in a matter of days, but the damage done to the Soviet system, already weakened by the struggles of perestroika, was irreparable. Rather than saving the Soviet system, the plotters had struck the final blows in its collapse.

Gorbachev himself did not understand what had happened. The coup plotters—who included Iazov, Kriuchkov, Pugo, and Shenin—came from the men he himself had raised to power, yet when he returned to Moscow on Thursday, August 22, his first moves were to reach into the same barrel for replacements. (An old Soviet saying spoke of the Communist Party leadership as a bucket of crabs; you could just reach in and it would make no difference which one you pulled out, they were all the same.) Only gradually did he realize that his political stage had disintegrated. He had hesitated too long in moving power from the party to the government, and now Boris Yeltsin, the man of the moment, banned the Communist Party. By the end of the year of 1991, the Soviet Union no longer existed, and Gorbachev was out of power.

Gorbachev's administrative structure in the Baltic, which had responded with enthusiasm to the Putsch, collapsed in the immediate aftermath of its failure. In the first days of the coup, August 19 to 21, Soviet troops and tanks moved through Vilnius. At Landsbergis's urging, the Lithuanians hastily ratified the treaty that he had signed with Yeltsin. Knowing from bitter experience the penchant of Soviet troops for looting and vandalizing buildings they had occupied, Lithuanian authorities hurriedly moved computers and documents out of the parliament building.[24] A new offensive seemed imminent, and Lithuanians again collected in front of the parliament to defend the republic's institutions with their bodies.

When news came on Wednesday afternoon, August 21, that the coup in Moscow was disintegrating, the atmosphere in Vilnius changed dramatically. Soviet troops drew back and on Thursday abandoned the television tower that they had held since that fateful morning in January. The Supreme Council banned the Communist Party, and it announced the seizure of party property. When Lithuanian officials approached Communist Party headquarters, however, Soviet troops warned them away. On Friday the military finally pulled out of the building, taking the LCP/CPSU leaders with them. Rushing into the building, the Lithuanians claimed to smell smoke from burning papers, and they found a warm cup of coffee on Naudžiunas's desk.

Friday, August 23, was the fifty-second anniversary of the Molotov-Ribbentrop pact. The Lithuanian government called for the arrests of Burokevičius, Naudžiunas, and Jermalavičius, and crowds attacked the last symbols of Soviet rule. When the statue of Lenin was lifted from the square in front of the KGB building, its hollow legs snapped, thereby becoming the photographic symbol of these hectic days throughout the territory of the Soviet Union. Two days later the Lithuanians were able to take over the KGB building itself.[25]

Burokevičius and his colleagues were reduced to taking refuge in Russia, reportedly hiding at a Soviet military base in order to avoid extradition. From his seclusion, Burokevičius occasionally issued statements and sent letters to the Russian press, asserting that the LCP/CPSU had wished only the best for Lithuania and denying any responsibility for the January violence there.[26] In January 1994 Lithuanian security officers arrested Burokevičius and Jermalavičius in Minsk, Belarus, and brought them back to Lithuania for trial.

In the aftermath of the August Putsch, the Lithuanian government could finally bask in the glow of diplomatic recognition. Individual governments, the United Nations, the International Olympic Committee, one after another recognized the independence of all three Baltic states. To be sure, the United States held back until Gorbachev's lame-duck administration in Moscow had made clear its readiness to acknowledge this development. Bush insisted, "When history is written, nobody is going to remember that we took 48 hours more than Iceland, or whoever else it is,"[27] but the Lithuanians have refused to forget.

Who lost Gorbachev? Sitting among the ruins of the Soviet system, Gorbachev insisted that the West had failed him, and many people in the West agreed. As *The European* reported in late August, "Almost half the voters of western Europe believe that the West created the climate for this week's coup against Pres. Gorbachev by failing to give his reforms adequate support." Gorbachev stated his case very simply to the American business magazine *Forbes*: "If [the West] had acted quicker during my visit to London last year [i.e. 1991], you could have avoided the putsch."[28]

In fact, Gorbachev "lost" Gorbachev. In the late 1980s he had advocated the establishment of "a state ruled by law," but one might question whether he himself knew what he meant. When the Lithuanians moved to replace arbitrary party rule with a multiparty political order, Gorbachev objected, either because he saw himself losing or because he simply did not want to let go of party "diktat." He escalated his response—words, then blockade, and ultimately force—making a shambles of his grand vision of "a state ruled by law," but all to no avail. He lost Lithuania, and then his own structure turned against him and collapsed.

Gorbachev argued that the Lithuanians had not dealt with him in good faith, that they had betrayed him. He had expected the Lithuanians to accept his promises on faith when they had already been hearing Moscow's vainglorious promises for half a century. Gorbachev's promissory notes had no more backing than those of his predecessors; he produced little. Even people close to him complained of his equivocations: "Do nothing until there is nothing to be done."

Most important, Gorbachev was not willing to decentralize the Soviet system. He made promises and then withdrew them, insisting that the center knew best; and he staffed his administrative center with people who turned on him. The August Putsch had disrupted his new plan to sign a new treaty of union between the republics, but significantly, when the

Putsch failed, the treaty was forgotten. He had weakened the centralized institutions of the old Soviet order, and he had not created stable replacements.

The turning point in his Lithuanian policy came in the Central Committee plenum in February 1990. Brazauskas was still looking for ways to cooperate with Gorbachev, who, the Lithuanian kept saying, seemed to "understand." The very fact that Gorbachev turned to a person like Burokevičius would suggest that the Soviet leader never understood the national question in the Soviet Union in general and the situation in Lithuania in particular.

In view of Gorbachev's announced efforts to establish a multiparty civil society, it is ironic but nevertheless informative that this turning point came in a party meeting. Brazauskas made the transition into the political world of the constitutional structure, and Gorbachev did not. The repressive forces of the Soviet state, the military and the KGB, of course played a significant role in the drama, but as weapons of Gorbachev and the party. The Soviet prime minister, Nikolai Ryzhkov, admitted that he did not understand the anger of the Lithuanians, and his memoirs indicate that he had little to do with the Lithuanian question.[29]

After the February 1990 CC Plenum, Gorbachev lost the party connection for dealing with Lithuania through Brazauskas. The CPSU leadership's decision to back Burokevičius undermined Brazauskas's position as the mediator between Moscow and Vilnius and severely compromised the possibility of Gorbachev's finding a sympathetic ear in the mainstream of Lithuanian politics. In March 1990 and again in January 1991, Brazauskas had publicly tried to communicate directly with Moscow to save the situation in Vilnius, but he seemingly had no effect on Gorbachev's determination to crush the Lithuanians' resistance.

This in turn opened the way for Landsbergis to carry Lithuania's colors into a confrontation with Moscow. Landsbergis's strength in fact lay in confrontation, while Gorbachev did not have the determination to see a confrontation through to the end. Even if Moscow had overthrown Landsbergis, however, Gorbachev could rule Lithuania only through a military dictatorship, a situation that at the very least would doom thoughts of reform in other parts of the Soviet Union.

On the Lithuanian side of the equation, Brazauskas brought Lithuania to the verge of independence and then lost his position as leader of the nation. He had kept saying that Gorbachev "understood," he had convinced himself that it was possible to achieve "independence" through negotiations, and then he had suddenly found himself on the sidelines, watching others do battle. He kept his party together, renaming it the Lithuanian Democratic Labor Party (LDLP or LDDP), and then he returned to the top of the political hill with his party's startling victory in the parliamentary election of 1992 and his own election as president in February 1992. The story of Brazauskas's further political fortunes, however, lies outside the framework of this study.

After March 1990 Kazimiera Prunskiene sought some sort of negotiated settlement with Gorbachev, but although she won considerable international sympathy, she too was unsuccessful. She thought she saw an opportunity in the summer of 1990, but since Gorbachev frequently used bait-and-switch tactics, holding open alluring possibilities that he subsequently backed away from, it is difficult to say that a realistic settlement was possible at that time. Eventually Prunskiene paid the ultimate political price for having tried to negotiate with Moscow, and the nationalists forced her out of office during the January events of 1991.

Landsbergis's policy of confrontation emerged from the conflict as victorious and successful; in the tangle of Soviet, American, and Lithuanian interests in 1990 and 1991, he occupied the moral high ground. Probably his greatest achievement was to cast the question of Lithuania's independence as a moral issue, which was therefore not negotiable, and then to persuade so many other people to accept that view. When Gorbachev raised the stakes of confrontation, Landsbergis won mass support from Lithuanians, many of whom had reservations about him personally but nevertheless felt they had no choice. (As I passed through the parliament building on January 15, 1991, Antanas Terleckas stopped me to insist that Landsbergis was "irreplaceable.") Once independence was established and recognized, however, confrontation basically ended, Landsbergis's position as leader deteriorated quickly, and his camp suffered a devastating defeat in the parliamentary elections of 1992.

Behind these political leaders, one should also recognize the determination and dedication of the Lithuanians who responded to Moscow's military and paramilitary forces without resorting to mass violence. The only people who died in the Soviet actions against the Lithuanians were killed by the Soviet forces. I for one believe that if the Lithuanians had shot back during the "January events," the Soviet troops would not have stopped after taking the television tower; and Gorbachev would surely have proclaimed "presidential rule" in the republic. As it was, the Soviet forces branded themselves as occupiers who were in fact not sure what they were supposed to do.

The United States government played the role of anguished spectator to all these goings-on. Its traditional policy of not recognizing the incorporation of the Baltic republics into the Soviet state fell to a low priority when it perceived the major issue as being Gorbachev's survival. Although conservatives in the Soviet Union kept suggesting that nefarious western agencies were behind the country's troubles, the White House did not favor the breakup of the Soviet Union. It welcomed the Soviet withdrawal from Afghanistan and Eastern Europe, but it seemed to prefer keeping the Soviet Union intact rather than facing fifteen or more different sovereign states.

There were, to be sure, reasons for not recognizing the Lithuanian government even apart from the White House's sympathy for Gorbachev. In its refusal to acknowledge Lithuania's incorporation into the Soviet Union, the US government had insisted on the existence of a Lithuanian state without a government. The question became whether this government was the legitimate representative of that state, but the White House chose to respond to other considerations.

The Lithuanian parliament's declaration of independence ranks as something of an act of Socialist Realism in itself. "Independence" was more an idea than a fact at a time when Soviet troops controlled the republic and even the leaders of Lithuania were traveling with Soviet passports. Lithuanians themselves understood that there was a gap between their idealistic conception of the essence of independence and the physical accidents of the Soviet presence in the republic. In July 1994 a well-known writer whose patriotism could not be doubted declared that, in the spring of 1990, "there was no independent Lithuanian state,"[30] but he would still argue that the United States should have recognized Lithuania at that time.

The U.S. administration, however, delayed taking a public stance on the question of whether it would support the Lithuanians or back Gorbachev. Instead it kept the question open, telling the Lithuanians that there were standards to be met, but not realizing that the Lithuanian leaders, convinced of the moral justice of their cause, would interpret this as setting some sort of objective examination that they had to meet. When President Bush finally made his position clear, Landsbergis complained about American betrayal, and in turn American officials resented his harsh words.

In any event, the U.S. government was not ready to handle the explosion of the nationalities question in the Soviet Union any more than Gorbachev was. American specialists on Soviet affairs had paid little attention to the issue in the early 1980s. Telling national leaders to believe in Moscow's promises only emphasized what limited understanding western leaders had of the historic processes that had molded the non-Russian regions of the Soviet empire.

The triangle of Moscow-Vilnius-Washington has evoked a number of permutations of conspiracy theories. There are those who claim that "Washington" directed the actions of the Lithuanians so as to destroy the Soviet Union, and those who claim Gorbachev took directions from "Washington" and deliberately led the Soviet Union to ruin. There are also those who still insist that Sajudis was Moscow's creation. There are even those who argue that Bush and Gorbachev, at Malta, together with leaders of Great Britain and France (who were not there), tried to carve up Eastern Europe a la Molotov-Ribbentrop and Yalta.[31] Inevitably these theories will gain some supporters, but they hardly stand up against the evidence.

Ultimately Gorbachev failed in the style of a Greek tragedy, the victim of his own shortcomings. In an interview on Chicago television on May 14, 1991, Landsbergis called the Soviet leader "a double man of very different possibilities, good and bad." Gorbachev tried to reform the Soviet system of which he himself was a product, and he did not understand the new forces that emerged through the cracks that he opened. He shied away from unrestrained use of force, perhaps for personal reasons, perhaps for fear of strengthening the reactionary forces that he did not want to see return. In the end he abandoned his vision of the future in an effort to keep himself in power.

Evaluating Gorbachev's work, Kazimiera Prunskiene wrote:

> I could have recognized Gorbachev's style of work, his constantly new efforts to balance political forces in order to control the constantly changing situation, as the meaningful talent of a creative politician if I would have found a positive answer to one decisive question: Did he really plan to reform the communist empire, to free nations and peoples, to build a state of laws, and to introduce justice and democracy?

She concluded that he did not. She saw him as having freed processes that he wanted to control but could not. For lack of clear decisions, he let "the political strings slip from his hand."[32]

NOTES

Abbreviations used in notes

EIB   *ELTA Information Bulletin*, Brooklyn, monthly, 1988-1991.
FBIS Foreign Information Broadcast Service, Daily Report, Washington, D.C.
LIC   Lithuanian Information Center, Brooklyn, press releases.
LRAT *Lietuvos Respublikos Aukščiausiosios Tarybos (pirmojo šaukimo), Stenogramos.* Vilnius (Lithuanian Supreme Council, Stenograms).
RFE   Radio Free Europe, Munich.
USNA United States State Department Decimal File, Washington, D.C.

Introduction: Uncharted Paths

1. Michael Mandelbaum in *The Rise of Nations in the Soviet Union: American Foreign Policy and the Disintegration of the USSR*, ed. Michael Mandelbaum (New York: Council on Foreign Relations, 1991), p. 5. See also the assertion by Ian Bremmer and Ray Taras that "the central question concerns less why the Soviet Union fell apart than how it managed to remain together in the first place," in *Nations & Politics in the Soviet Successor States*, ed. Ian Bremmer and Ray Taras (New York: Cambridge Univ. Press, 1993), p. xxii.

2. See Hedrick Smith, *The New Russians* (New York: Random House, 1990), p. 352; Egor Ligachev, *Zagadka Gorbacheva* (Novosibirsk: Interbuk, 1992), p. 218; Valery Legostaev, *Tekhnologiia izmeny* (Moscow: Paleia, 1993), p. 148.

3. Elizabeth Drew, "Letter from Washington," *The New Yorker*, May 14, 1990, p. 94.

4. Article 6 read: "The leading and guiding force of Soviet society and the nucleus of its political system, of all state organizations and public organizations, is the Communist Party of the Soviet Union." *Constitution (Fundamental Law) of the Union of Soviet Socialist Republics* (Moscow: Novosti, 1977), p. 21.

5. *Komsomol'skaia pravda*, April 20, 1991.

6. See "The Annual Meeting of the American Committee on US-Soviet Relations," in *New Outlook* 1 (Winter 1990-1991): 64-68; Peter Reddaway, "The End of the

Empire," *New York Review*, November 7, 1991; Jerry Hough, "Gorbachev's Endgame," *World Policy Journal* 4 (Fall 1990): 642. For another sanguine picture of Gorbachev's reform program, see the comments by Stephen F. Cohen, *New Outlook* 1: 70-74.

7. See Barrington Moore, Jr., *Liberal Prospects under Soviet Socialism: A Comparative Historical Perspective*, The First Annual W. Averell Harriman Lecture, Columbia University (New York: Columbia University, 1989). David Remnick's characterization of Andrei Sakharov as "a one-man loyal opposition" does not fill this gap. See Remnick's *Lenin's Tomb: The Last Days of the Soviet Empire* (New York: Vintage, 1994), p. 164.

8. The statement on assimilation appears in Helene Carrère d'Encausse, *L'empire éclate: La revolte des nations en U.R.S.S.* (Paris: Flammarion, 1978), p. 273; Viktor Chebrikov's KGB report on "anti-Soviet, nationalist, and politically dangerous" materials, dated March 21, 1988, was part of "Revelations from the Russian Archives," an exhibition at the Library of Congress, Washington, D.C., Summer 1992; see also Anatol Lieven, *The Baltic Revolution* (New Haven, CT: Yale Univ. Press, 1993), p. 221.

9. See Alexander Motyl, *Sovietology, Rationality, Nationality* (New York: Columbia Univ. Press, 1990), pp. 156, 184; Geoffrey Hoskings, *The Awakening of the Soviet Union* (Cambridge, MA: Harvard Univ. Press, 1990), pp. 87-88; Graham Smith, "The State, Nationalism and the Nationalities Question in the Soviet Republics," in *Perestroika: The Historical Perspective*, ed. Catherine Merridale and Chris Ward (London: Edward Arnold, 1991), p. 202; Donald L. Horowitz, "How to Begin Thinking Comparatively About Soviet Ethnic Problems," in *Thinking Theoretically About Soviet Nationalities*, ed. Alexander Motyl (New York: Columbia Univ. Press, 1992), pp. 15-17.

10. See John Armstrong, "The Ethnic Scene in the Soviet Union: The View of the Dictatorship" (first printed in 1968), *Journal of Soviet Nationalities* 1 (1990): 37-40.

11. Motyl, *Sovietology*, p. 95; Graham Smith, "The State, Nationalism and the Nationalities Question," p. 204; Liah Greenfield, *Nationalism: Five Roads to Modernity* (Cambridge, MA: Harvard Univ. Press, 1992). p. 488.

12. Motyl paid tribute to the role of émigrés in keeping alive national ideals in his *Sovietology*, pp. 132-145. For an example of the way in which such contacts worked, see Liutas Mockunas, "The Dynamics of Lithuanian Emigre-Homeland Relations," *Baltic Forum* 1 (1985): 50-69, and his "Knygų keliai į Lietuvą," *Metai* (Vilnius) 12 (1992): 96-107; also the commentary by Vytautas Kaltenis, "Tamsi troba be knygos," *Tiesa*, May 7, 1993.

13. Graham Smith, "The State, Nationalism and the Nationalities Question," p. 204.

14. Hedrick Smith, *The New Russians*, 196.

15. Drew, "Letter from Washington," p. 94.

16. On the "nonrecognition" policy, see Robert Vitas, *The United States and Lithuania: The Stimson Doctrine of Nonrecognition* (New York: Praeger, 1990).

17. See A. A. Berle's memorandum of a conversation with Povilas Žadeikis, July 28, 1942, USNA, 860M.01/274, and Elbridge Durbrow's memorandum of a conversation with Žadeikis on August 28, 1942, USNA, 860m.001 sm/8-2842

18. See "Anti-Communist Resistance Potential in the Baltic Republics," in *Selected Estimates on the Soviet Union, 1950-1959*, ed. Scott A. Koch (Washington, D.C.: CIA, 1993), p. 240.

19. See EIB 3 (1985).

20. EIB 2 (1987).

21. EIB 8 (1987).

22. EIB 11 (1987). Michael Beschloss and Strobe Talbott dismissed such calls as having "a quaint, quixotic ring"; see their *At the Highest Levels: The Inside Story of the End of the Cold War* (Boston: Little, Brown and Company, 1993), p. 8.

23. In 1984 the Soviet government demonstrated its sensitivity about the Baltic by boycotting the Olympic Games in Los Angeles. See Alfred Erich Senn, "The Soviet Boycott of the 1984 Olympics: The Baltic Dimension," *Baltic Forum* 2 (1985): 88-104.

24. Viz. the campaign that nationalist émigrés conducted against the linking of Vilnius and Madison, Wisconsin, as "sister cities," described in my articles, "Apie Vilniaus-Madisono susigiminiavimą," *Akiračiai* 7 (1987): 2-3; "Vilnius ir Madisonas susigiminiavas," *Akiračiai* 4 (1989): 1; and "Vilnius-Medisonas: Liko pasirašyti sutartį," *Komjaunimo tiesa* (Vilnius), May 1, 1989.

25. Robert Blackwell, as cited in *Congressional Roundtable on U.S.-Soviet Relations. 1984 Report* (Washington, D.C.: Peace Through Law Education Fund, 1984), p. 22.

26. Some commentators have me doing things I did not do. Anatol Lieven, for example, placed me at the meeting that organized Sajudis; Vytautas Landsbergis credited me with attending "all" the meetings of the Sajudis Initiative Group and the Sajudis Council; and another author called me "a member" of the Founding Congress of Sajudis. See Lieven, *The Baltic Revolution*, p. 225; Landsbergis's interview with *Tiesa*, March 18, 1993; *The Baltic States: Estonia, Latvia, Lithuania*, World Bibliographical Series, vol. 161, ed. Inese A. Smith and Marita V. Grunts (Santa Barbara, CA: Clio, 1993), p. 44.

1. Inside Perestroika

1. Egor Ligachev, *Zagadka Gorbacheva* (Novosibirsk: Interbuk, 1992), p. 6.

2. Tariq Ali, *Revolution from Above* (London: Hutchinson, 1988), p. 171. See also S. Frederick Starr, "The Road to Reform," in *Chronicle of a Revolution*, ed. Abraham Brumberg (New York: Pantheon, 1990), p. 19; Hedrick Smith's picture of Tatiana Zaslavskaia, *The New Russians* (New York: Random House, 1990), pp. 12-16.

3. Egor Ligachev's comment in *Argumenty i fakty* 4 (1991).

4. Iu. V. Andropov, *Izbrannye rechi i stat'i*, 2d edition (Moscow: Izd. polit. lit, 1983), p. 294.

5. Ligachev, *Zagadka Gorbacheva*, p. 23.

6. See Ligachev's account of the intrigues, in his *Zagadka Gorbacheva*, pp. 45-67, and Hedrick Smith's speculation about the timing for the removal of "Chernenko's life support," *The New Russians*, p. 77.

7. Valery Legostaev, "Demokrat s radikal'nymi vzgliadami," *Den'* 13 (1992). Legostaev later reworked his essays, critical of Gorbachev, in his book *Tekhnologiia izmeny* (Moscow: Paleia, 1993).

8. Muscovite critics later suggested that Gorbachev systematically exploited the sincerity and the political naïveté of "provincial" officials. See Nikolai Anisin's comments in *Den'* 23 (1991).

9. Mikhail Gorbachev, *Perestroika: New Thinking for Our Country and the World* (New York: Harper & Row 1987), pp. 120-122. On Gorbachev's qualifications, see also Alexander Motyl, "The Sobering of Gorbachev: Nationality, Restructuring, and

the West," in *The Soviet Nationality Reader,* ed. Rachel Denber (Boulder, CO: Westview, 1992), pp. 573-596.

10. Ilia Zemtsov and John Ferrar, *Gorbachev: Chelovek i sistema 70 let posle oktiabria* (London: Overseas Publications, 1987), p. 33.

11. Roy Medvedev and Giulietto Chiesa, *Time of Change: An Insider's View of Russia's Transformation* (New York: Pantheon, 1989), pp. 3-4.

12. Ibid., p. 22; Hedrick Smith, *The New Russians,* p. 18.

13. See Brazauskas's statement in *Materialy plenuma Tsentral'nogo komiteta KPSS 19-20 sentiabria 1989 goda* (Moscow: Politizdat, 1989), p. 103.

14. Medvedev and Chiesa, *Time of Change,* pp. 7, 23.

15. *Berlinske tidende Sondag,* July 26, 1992.

16. Medvedev and Chiesa, *Time of Change,* pp. 79-80; cf. Ligachev's misgivings, *Zagadka Gorbacheva,* p. 272.

17. Medvedev and Chiesa, *Time of Change,* p. 82.

18. Legostaev, "God 1987-i—peremena logiki," *Den'* 14 (1991); Ligachev, *Zagadka Gorbacheva,* pp. 82-83.

19. Legostaev, in *Den'* 14 (1991).

20. Ligachev, *Zagadka Gorbacheva,* p. 85.

21. See Aleksandr Iakovlev, *Predislovie. Obval. Posleslovie* (Moscow: Novosti, 1992), pp. 127-29; *Zaria vostoka* (Tbilisi), February 28, 1989; David Remnick, "The Trial of the Old Regime," *The New Yorker,* November 30, 1992, p. 120. According to Hedrick Smith, Iakovlev ducked a question as to whether in 1983 he had been more critical of the existing order than Gorbachev. Smith, *The New Russians,* pp. 73-74.

22. *La Stampa* (Turin), Aug 23, 1991; *Berlinske tidende Sondag,* July 26, 1992. On the maneuvering to name editors and influence the mass media, see Ligachev, *Zagadka Gorbacheva,* pp. 80-92. Ligachev, who accused Iakovlev of working *neglasno* and *kabinetno* (i.e., secretly), dated the fundamental break between the two as coming in the fall of 1987. Eduard Shevardnadze, Gorbachev's foreign minister, would seem to have followed the same practice of the fait accompli. Cf. Michael Beschloss and Strobe Talbott, *At the Highest Levels* (Boston: Little, Brown and Company, 1993), especially p. 118.

23. Medvedev and Chiesa, *Time of Change,* pp. 82-83.

24. Ibid., p. 112.

25. Valerii Legostaev, "Proba sil v oktiabre," *Den'* 15 (1991).

26. Ibid.

27. Medvedev and Chiesa, *Time of Change,* pp. 181-82.

28. On pravovoe gosudarstvo, see William F. Butler, "Toward a Rule of Law?" in *Chronicle of a Revolution,* pp. 72-89.

29. Cf. Neil Robinson, "The Party is Sacred to Me: Gorbachev and the Place of the Party in Social Reform, 1985-1990," Discussion Paper Series 10, Russian and Soviet Studies Center, University of Essex, June 1991.

30. Medvedev and Chiesa, *Time of Change,* p. 224.

31. See the essay by Eduard Bagramov, "Kak delalas' natsional'naia politika," *Nezavisimaia gazeta,* January 24, 1992. Bagramov urged Gorbachev to intervene on the side of the Armenians.

32. See *Zhurnalist,* 1988/8.

33. Valerii Legostaev, "Nina Andreeva—izgoi pliuralizma," *Den'* 16 (1991). See the history of the letter offered in Medvedev and Chiesa, *Time of Change,* pp. 191-195. For

a more cautious interpretation of Ligachev, see Jonathan Harris, *Ligachev on Glasnost and Perestroika*, Carl Beck Papers, No. 706, University of Pittsburgh, Pittsburgh, 1989. See also Ligachev's version, comparing Andreeva to Bukharin, in his *Zagadka Gorbacheva*, pp. 126-137. On Andreeva herself, see Hedrick Smith, *The New Russians*, pp. 135-140. Andreeva's letter and Iakovlev's response are translated in *Gorbachev and Glasnost: Viewpoints from the Soviet Press*, ed. Isaac J. Tarasulo (Wilmington, DE: SR Books, 1989), pp. 277-302.

34. *Zhurnalist*, 1988/8.

35. See Ligachev, *Zagadka Gorbacheva*, p. 107.

36. Boris Kagarlitsky, *Farewell Perestroika: A Soviet Chronicle* (London: Verso, 1990), p. 2.

2. The Lithuanian Tangle

1. See Aleksandras Shtromas's discussion of this question in his *Politine samone Lietuvoje* (London: Nida, 1980), pp. 43-74. As early as 1961 the Soviet KGB expressed fears that former resistance fighters were interested in joining the party; *Pravda*, April 21, 1990, complained about a hidden opposition in Lithuania that served as the link between the postwar resistance and the national revival of 1988. The statement on party membership is from Romuald J. Misiunas, "The Baltic Republics," in *The Nationalities Factor in Soviet Politics and Society*, ed. Lubomyr Hajda and Mark Beissinger (Boulder, CO: Westview, 1990), p. 209. Western analysts often focused on the party as a monolithic unit and missed the question of erosion from below. Viz. Emmett George, "Party Response in Lithuanian Unrest," in *The Soviet West: Interplay between Nationality and Social Organization*, ed. Ralph S. Clem (New York: Praeger, 1975), pp. 90-105.

2. V. Stanley Vardys, "Lithuanians," in *The Nationalities Question in the Soviet Union* (London: Longman, 1990), p. 77; Shtromas, *Politine samone Lietuvoje*, pp. 43-74; Vytautas Skuodis, "Lietuvių tautos diferenciacija pavergtoje Lietuvoje," *Į Laisvę* 102 (1988): 13-14. Very few Lithuanians entered the CPSU apparatus in Moscow. In September 1989 Sigitas Renčas noted that he was then the only one, but "a few years ago there were four of us." *Tiesa*, September 19, 1989. See also Vytautas Tininis, *Sovietine Lietuva ir jos veikejai* (Vilnius: Enciklopedija, 1994).

3. Georgii Efremov, *My liudi drug drugu. Litva: budni svobody 1988-1989* (Moscow: Progress, 1990), p. 17.

4. *Pravda*, February 6, 1988. Gorbachev was at this point carrying the same sort of message to the Latvians and the Estonians.

5. See Felicity Berringer in *The New York Times*, February 17, 1988, and her comments to Georgii Efremov, *My liudi*, pp. 32-33. On the party's campaign to discredit the observance of February 16, see also *Diena*, August 23, 1994.

6. Efremov, *My liudi*, p. 23.

7. *Sovetskaia kultura*, September 1, 1988.

8. See Alfred Erich Senn, *Lithuania Awakening* (Berkeley: Univ. of California Press, 1990), pp. 40-44. On the events generally in Lithuania in 1988-1989, see also V. Stanley Vardys, "Lithuanian National Politics," *Problems of Communism* (July-August 1989): 53-76.

9. On Mitkin, see Tininis, *Sovietine Lietuva*, pp. 203-205. On Moscow's control of

the LCP, see: Algirdas Brazauskas, *Lietuviškos skyrybos* (Vilnius: Politika, 1992), pp. 14, 115-116; Thomas Remeikis, "The Communist Party of Lithuania: A Historical and Political Study," Ph.D. diss. University of Illinois, 1963, pp. 494-500

10. See *Gimtasis kraštas*, October 14, 1988; also, Jermalavičius's retrospective interview in *Lietuvos rytas*, January 17, 1990.

11. Vardys, in *The Nationalities Question in the Soviet Union*, p. 80. See also Senn, *Lithuania Awakening*, pp. 39-40.

12. Roy Medvedev's statement about the conference that "Large sectors of the public participated in the preceding phase, including people who had remained outside the events in the first phases of perestroika," has relevance to Lithuania in a starkly different way from how Medvedev conceived of it for Moscow. See Roy Medvedev and Giulietto Chiesa, *Time of Change: An Insider's View of Russia's Transformation* (New York: Pantheon, 1989), p. 238. According to Brazauskas, the party Central Committee received too many nominations and simply chose to make its own decision. *Lietuviškos skyrybos*, p. 11.

13. Interview, *Lietuvos rytas*, April 9, 1993.

14. The risks taken by the intellectuals of Sajudis refute assertions that "nationalists" seek power and privilege and avoid "uncompromising politics of principle." Cf. Ernest Gellner, "Nationalism in the Vacuum," in *Thinking Theoretically About Soviet Nationalities*, ed. Alexander Motyl (New York: Columbia Univ. Press, 1992), p. 254.

15. The LFL announced its existence in May; see LIC, press release, May 9, 1988; RFE, *Situation Report: Baltic Area* 11 (1988): 34-35.

16. In its news release of June 14, 1988, LIC referred to Sajudis as "a newly founded club of Lithuanian intellectuals promoting Gorbachev's policy of perestroika" and on August 19 called it "an officially tolerated group." On September 29, on the other hand, it suggested that the LFL was "reformist" rather than "revolutionary" by referring to it as a "major nongovernmental group pressing for reform."

17. Šepetys in *RVL* (Vilnius), March 6, 1992; Ligachev, *Zagadka Gorbacheva*, (Novosibirsk: Interbuk, 1992), p. 85.

18. Ligachev later argued that "nationalism and separatism" were the "tragedy of perestroika" and that Gorbachev had no right to include him in the "we" who had underestimated the dangers of national feeling. *Zagadka Gorbacheva*, pp. 218, 220, 241,

19. *Zhurnalist*, 1988/8.

20. See Senn, *Lithuania Awakening*, pp. 102-103; Efremov, *My liudi*, pp. 118-119.

21. *TarybŲLietuva*, no. 33, November 26, 1990.

22. As a sign of his own misunderstanding of the situation in Moscow, Mitkin complained that Sajudis leaders sympathized with *Moscow News*, which was in fact one of Iakovlev's favorite periodicals. Author's interview with Šepetys, June 29, 1993.

23. See Šepetys's account in *RVL*, March 6, 1992.

24. See Ligachev, *Zagadka Gorbacheva*, pp. 100, 219; Valerii Legostaev, *Tekhnologiia izmeny* (Moscow: Paleia, 1993), pp. 146-148.

25. Efremov, *My liudi*, p. 118.

3. Defining the Problems: Second Introduction

1. Kazimiera Prunskiene, *Leben für Litauen* (Berlin: Ullstein, 1992), p. 181.

2. See Alfred Erich Senn, *Lithuania Awakening* (Berkeley: Univ. of California Press,

1990), p. 113.

3. *Tarybų Lietuva* 33 (1990).

4. See commentary by E. Tadevosian in *Politicheksoe obrazovanie* 13 (August 1988): 84-92; *Materialy plenuma tsentral'nogo komiteta KPSS, 19-20 sentiabria 1989 goda* (Moscow: Politizdat, 1989), p. 23.

5. See Anatoly Khazanov, "The Ethnic Situation in the Soviet Union as Reflected in Soviet Anthropology," *Cahiers du Monde russe et soviétique* 31 (1993): 213-222; Gregory Gleason, "Nationalism and its Discontents," *Russian Review* 52 (January 1993): 79-90.

6. See *Konstitutsiia (osnovnoi zakon) Litovskoi Sovetskoi Sotsialisticheskoi Respubliki* (Vilnius: Mintis, 1987); *Konstitutsiia SSSR. Politiko-pravovoi kommentarii* (Moskva: Izd. polit. lit., 1982), pp. 205-206, 213; Senn, *Lithuania Awakening*, p. 162. The chief editor of the authoritative commentary on the Soviet constitution was Anatoly Lukianov, who had been in law school with Gorbachev but who eventually aligned himself with the conservatives in the events of August 1991.

7. See Julian V. Bromlei, "Ethnic Relations and Perestroika," in *Perestroika Annual: Two*, ed. Abel G. Aganbegyan (Washington, D.C.: Brassey's [US], 1989), pp. 104, 118-119; and also the statement by a KGB defector, "...to talk of there being antagonistic relations between the Russians and the other peoples of the USSR is deliberately to misinform world public opinion and the Western world," in Ilya Dzhirkvelov, *Secret Servant: My Life with the KGB and the Soviet Elite* (New York: Harper & Row, 1987), p. 187. As Bremmer and Taras wrote in their criticism of western writings on the topic, "Sovietology as a field of inquiry was therefore well equipped to study the Soviet nation, which in fact did not exist, and yet ill-equipped to handle the nations of the USSR, which did." *Nations & Politics in the Soviet Successor States*, ed. Ian Bremmer and Ray Taras (New York: Cambridge Univ. Press, 1993) p. xxii.

8. M. V. Iordan, in *Natsional'nye protsessy v SSSR v usloviiakh perestroiki: Voprosy teorii i praktiki* (Moscow: Akademiia nauk, institut filosofii, 1990), p. 22. Gorbachev's advisor on the national question, E. A. Bagramov, later declared of party statements, "What was valued in an advisor was not the ability to bring out new ideas in principled fashion but rather the ability to invest old positions with a new form." See *Nezavisimaia gazeta*, January 24, 1992. On Soviet understanding of the national question, see also Uwe Halbach, "Die Nationalitätenfrage: Kontinuität und Explosivität," in *Die Umwertung der sowjetischen Geschichte*, ed. Dietrich Geyer (Göttingen: Vandenhoeck & Ruprecht, 1991), pp. 210-237.

9. Comments of A. S. Kopto, in *Natsional'nye protsessy*, pp. 6-7. The discussion here focuses on works published in 1988 and 1989, but even such a work as *Mezhnatsional'nye otnosheniia v SSSR. Istoriia i sovremennost'* (Moscow: Akademiia nauk, 1991) illustrates the persistence of old clichés for the study of the national question.

10. G. L. Smirnov and E. A. Bagramov, in *Natsional'nye protsessy*, pp. 38, 77-78.

11. Ibid., p. 79

12. Dmitrii Likhachev, "Patriotizm protiv natsionalizma," in *Govoria otkrovenno: zametki pisatelei o mezhnatsional'nykh otnosheniiakh* (Moscow: Khudozh. lit-ra, 1989), p. 98.

13. Cf. *Natsional'nye protsessy*, p. 5.

14. Françoise Thom, *The Gorbachev Phenomenon: A History of Perestroika* (London: Pinter, 1989), p. 77.

15. *Washington Times*, undated clipping, 1988.

16. See the views expressed in *Russia and the World. New Views on Russian Foreign Policy*, ed. Boris D. Pyadyshev (New York: Carol Publishing Co., 1991), p. 20, and A. S. Cherniaev, *Shest' let s Gorbachevym. Po dnevnikovym zapisiam* (Moscow: Progress-Kul'tura, 1993), p. 325.

17. *Sotsial'no-politicheskie problemy mezhnatsional'nykh otnoshenii v SSSR: teoriia i praktika* (Moscow: Institute of Marxism-Leninism, 1989), p. 23.

18. Ibid., p. 30.

19. Ibid., pp. 417-446. See also Julian V. Bromlei, "Ethnic Relations and Perestroika," in *Perestroika Annual: Two*, ed. Abel G. Aganbegyan (Washington, D.C.: Brassey's [US], 1989), pp. 111-114.

20. See also: Iu. V. Bromlei, in *Natsional'nye protsessy v SSSR v poiskakh novykh podkhodov* (Moscow, 1988); *Chto delat'. V poiskakh idei sovershenstvovanii mezhnatsional'nykh otnoshenii v SSSR* (Moscow, 1990), pp. 23, 38, 41-46; R. G. Abulatinov, "Perestroika i mezhnatsional'nye otnosheniia," *Voprosy istorii* KPSS 2 (1989).

21. Bagramov and Smirnov, in *Natsional'nye protsessy* (1990), pp. 69, 126.

22. See Vadim Bakatin, *Izbavlenie ot KGB* (Moscow: Novosti, 1992), p. 49.

23. See Hedrick Smith, *The New Russians* (New York: Random House, 1990), p. 161.

24. See Senn, *Lithuania Awakening*, p. 114.

25. Cf. Molotov's denial of the existence of a secret protocol in F. Chuev, *Sto sorok besed s Molotovym: Iz dnevnika F. Chueva* (Moscow: Terra, 1991), pp. 19-21. In 1940 the Soviet authorities, then on good terms with the Germans, charged the Baltic governments with being pro-British; after hostilities with Germany had begun, Soviet historians claimed that the Baltic governments had been pro-German.

26. Commenting on what he called Gorbachev's "democratic authoritarianism," Charles Krauthammer declared, "Gorbachevism is government by oxymoron." See his essay "With Russians Like These... " *The Washington Post*, April 20, 1990.

27. Hedrick Smith, *The New Russians*, p. 11.

28. As examples of the use of the materials, see the series "Voratinklis," published in *Lietuvos aidas* in the course of 1992, and Kazimiera Prunskiene's books on the topic: *Užkulisiai* (Vilnius: Politika, 1992), *Leben für Litauen*, and *Iššukis drakonui* (Kaunas: Europa, 1992). For an official account of Lithuanian KGB operations before 1985, see G. K. Vaigauskas, *Lietuvių nacionalistų kenkejiška veikla ir kova su ja* (Kaunas, 1992), a translation of a KGB handbook first published in Moscow in 1986. See also Romuald J. Misiunas, *The Archives of the Lithuanian KGB* (Köln: Berichte des Bundesinstituts für ostwissenschaftliche und internationale Studien, 1994).

4. The Battle Is Joined

1. Moscow TASS, August 23, 1988.

2. See Ligachev, *Zagadka Gorbacheva* (Novosibirsk: Interbuk, 1992), pp. 217-224. The perception that this was indeed a dangerous situation may well have developed only later. At this time, the press release on the Politburo's meeting apparently subsumed the Lithuanian question under "several other questions of the internal and foreign policy of the Communist Party." See *Spravochnik partiinogo rabotnika 23* (Moscow: Izd. polit. lit., 1989): 148-149.

3. Alexander Motyl, *Sovietology, Rationality, Nationality* (New York: Columbia Univ. Press, 1990), p. 178.

4. Hedrick Smith, *The New Russians* (New York: Random House, 1990), pp. 489-490. Robert Kaiser asserted that "he was firmly in the driver's seat," in his *Why Gorbachev Happened* (New York: Simon and Schuster, 1992), p. 244.

5. Roy Medvedev and Giulietto Chiesa, *Times of Change: An Insider's View of Russia's Transformation* (New York: Pantheon, 1989), pp. 280-281. Iakovlev reportedly complained about the lack of support that Gorbachev showed him in this transfer. See A. S. Cherniaev, *Shest' let s Gorbachevym* (Moscow: Progress-Kul'tura, 1993), pp. 317-318. In an interview with a Lithuanian newspaper in 1994, Iakovlev criticized Ligachev and others for their misunderstanding of the situation in Lithuania. See *Respublika*, August 19, 1994.

6. See Ligachev, *Zagadka Gorbacheva*, pp. 86, 88, 95, 101, 188.

7. Cf. Paul Quinn-Judge, in *The Christian Science Monitor*, November 14, 1988. Gorbachev's foreign policy advisor, A. S. Cherniaev, also viewed Medvedev as one of the liberal members of the Politburo; see his *Shest' let s Gorbachevym*, passim.

8. Dmitry Mikheyev, *The Rise and Fall of Gorbachev* (Indianapolis, IN: The Hudson Institute, 1992), p. 111. Boris Yeltsin said of Medvedev, "His chief virtues, for which Gorbachev appointed him, are obedience and a total lack of new ideas." See Yeltsin's *Against the Grain* (New York: Summit, 1990), p. 152. For Medvedev's own denunciation of "political extremism of the nationalistic kind," see his essay "The Ideology of Perestroika," in *Perestroika Annual: Two*, ed. Abel G. Aganbegyan (Washington, D.C.: Brassey's [US], 1989), pp. 28-29.

9. See Alfred Erich Senn, *Lithuania Awakening* (Berkeley: Univ. of California Press, 1990), pp. 112, 238.

10. See *Der Spiegel*, January 16, 1989; *Zaria vostoka* (Tbilisi), February 28, 1989. He eventually identified Moscow's problems with Lithuania as arising from "social masochism," which was "expressed in the regurgitation ad infinitum of specific real or fictitious facts and problems. Around these problems passions are fomented." *Komsomol'skaia pravda*, April 20, 1991

11. See Mitkin's account in *Tarybų Lietuva* 33 (1990).

12. Senn, *Lithuania Awakening*, pp. 171-172. As a witness to this decision on the part of Sajudis to go ahead, I felt at the time that this was a key moment in Sajudis's development.

13. Georgii Efremov, *My liudi drug drugu* (Moscow: Progress, 1990), p. 130.

14. See Chapter 10, "Removal of the Party Secretaries," in Senn, *Lithuania Awakening*, pp. 198-216.

15. Resolution no. 22, the Constituent Congress of the Lithuanian Reform Movement "Sajudis," *Draft Resolutions* (Vilnius, 1988). The Sajudis Initiative Group's formal program, dated October 12, appears in *Perestroika in the Soviet Republics: Documents on the National Question*, ed. Charles F. Furtado, Jr. and Andrea Chandler (Boulder, CO: Westview, 1992), pp. 147-157.

16. See his memoir in *Tarybų Lietuva* 33 (1990).

17. See Mitkin's account, ibid.

18. See Brazauskas, *Lietuviškos skyrybos* (Vilnius: Politika, 1992), pp. 30-33. In *Lithuania Awakening*, pp. 207-208, I declared that the choice was between Brazauskas and Šepetys, but this was apparently just for show. A high party official later informed

me that the real contest was between Giedraitis and Brazauskas. At the end of November Moscow TASS quoted Giedraitis as suggesting foreign influences at play in Lithuania, saying that "some Sajudis leaders do not dissociate themselves from alien persons." Press release (in English), December 1, 1988.

19. Hedrick Smith, *The New Russians*, p. 380; author's interview with Brazauskas, January 11, 1993.

20. In a last-ditch effort to save his own position, Mitkin even agreed to an interview, but in writing, with *Tiesa*, the party newspaper. Russian text in *Sovetskaia Litva*, October 18, 1988. In his memoirs, Mitkin argued that Sajudis had exploited "Brazauskas's weak character traits" and had used him as a Trojan horse. See *Tarybų Lietuva* 33 (1990).

21. Saulius Girnius, in RFE, *Situation Report: Baltic Area* 12 (October 28, 1988): 21.

22. *Steigiamojo Suvažiavimo Stenogramos* (Vilnius: Lietuvos Persitvarkymo Sajudis, 1988), p. 12; Russian text in *Moskovskie novosti* 44 (1988). For a more detailed discussion of the congress, see Senn, *Lithuania Awakening*, pp. 217-236.

23. Saulius Girnius declared that Sajudis leaders are "being forced into taking more radical measures by the actions of the Lithuanian Freedom League." RFE, *Situation Report: Baltic Area* 12 (November 14, 1988): 14.

24. TASS press release, November 13, 1988.

25. See Brazauskas, *Lietuviškos skyrybos*, pp. 66-68.

26. Kestutis Girnius, in RFE, *Situation Report: Baltic Area* 13 (November 22, 1988).

27. Brazauskas's speech was printed in *Sovetskaia Litva*, November 20, 1988; Sepetys's version of the events appeared in *Tiesa*, April 9, 1992. See also Vytautas Landsbergis's speech, *Komjaunimo tiesa*, November 29, 1988; Brazauskas later claimed that Landsbergis had deceived him, see *Lietuviškos skyrybos*, pp. 28-30. Saulius Girnius, RFE, *Situation Report: Baltic Area* 13, wrote, "Moscow exerted great pressure." See also Anatol Lieven's criticism of Brazauskas's stand in his *The Baltic Revolution* (New Haven, CT: Yale Univ. Press, 1993), p. 227. Lieven mistakenly dated the confrontation as having taken place in October.

28. Viz. *Tiesa*, November 20, 1988.

29. Interview, January 11, 1993. Brazauskas's explanations closely parallel Wojciech Jaruzelski's explanations for his own actions in Poland in 1981. Cf. John Darnton's interview with Jaruzelski in *The New York Times*, March 4, 1993.

30. *Tiesa*, July 10, 1992.

31. Moscow radio, November 29, 1988.

32. *The New York Times*, December 2 and 3, 1988, declared that the Soviet authorities had given the Baltic deputies a "fair hearing."

33. "Solving Urgent Problems of Harmonizing Inter-ethnic Relations by Joint Effort and Perestroika," supplement to *Moscow News* 49 (1988), reprinted in *Perestroika in the Soviet Republics*, pp. 72-74.

34. *Izvestiia*, November 24, 1988. Kapelushny polemicized with his Lithuanian critics in *Izvestiia* of December 14, 1988, and February 27, 1989.

35. *Pravda*, December 20, 1988.

36. See "Sajudis vybiraet kurs," *Sovetskaia Latviia*, November 2, 1988.

37. Stories arose of a Russian group called "Soiuz," calling for resistance to Lithuanian rule. See *Sovetskaia Litva*, November 1, 1988.

38. See Vadim Bakatin, *Izbavlenie ot KGB* (Moscow: Novosti, 1992), p. 49; Senn,

Lithuania Awakening, pp. 240-241. Text of group's proclamation, *Komjaunimo tiesa,* November 12, 1988; see also *Krasnaia zvezda,* November 30, 1988. Moscow made no secret of the military's support of the group, see *Izvestiia CK KPSS* 3 (1991): 100. Although the group's proclamation was dated November 4, *Stroitel'naia gazeta* (Moscow) reported its formation on November 2.

39. See Armstrong, "The Ethnic Scene in the Soviet Union," *Journal of Soviet Nationalities* 1: pp. 38-39.

40. Discussion in Saulius Girnius and Abba Sabbat-Swidlicka, "Current Issues in Polish-Lithuanian Relations," RFE, *Report on Eastern Europe,* January 12, 1990, pp. 39-50.

41. Ibid., p. 48. See also Lieven's discussion of the Poles in Lithuania in his *Baltic Revolution,* pp. 158-173.

5. Sovereignty or Independence?

1. As Landsbergis told a Polish journalist, "We are accused of wanting too much and too quickly. That is not true. We want even more, and we want it even more quickly." *Tygodnik powszechny,* February 5, 1989.

2. Algirdas Brazauskas, *Lietuviškos skyrybos* (Vilnius: Politika, 1992), pp. 31, 36.

3. Interview with the author, January 11, 1993.

4. *Tiesa,* April 25, 1992.

5. Testifying to the vagueness of the term, Landsbergis told a Polish journalist in December 1988, "The most important goal is to achieve Lithuania's sovereignty, which does not mean an automatic break with the Soviet Union." *Tygodnik Powszechny,* February 5, 1989.

6. Algirdas Brazauskas, *Interviu Lietuvos radijui* (Vilnius: LKP CK Leidykla, 1990), p. 15. He called for a "free" Lithuania in a "free," restructured Soviet Union. For the text of the LCP initiative on the national question, see *Perestroika in the Soviet Republics,* ed. Charles F. Furtado, Jr. and Andrea Chandler (Boulder, CO: Westview, 1992), pp. 153-157.

7. See *Sovetskaia Litva,* January 27, 1989; text of interview on Voice of America, January 27, 1989, in Sajudžioinfo archive, the records of the Sajudis information office in Chicago that are now in my possession. In his *Lietuviškos skyrybos,* p. 36, Brazauskas dated the meeting January 22.

8. Brazauskas, *Interviu Lietuvos radijui,* pp. 15-16; Astrauskas's statement in *Tiesa,* July 19, 1992.

9. *Pravda,* January 8, 1989.

10. Politburo report published in *Rossisskie vesti* 16 (June 1992).

11. Report in *Vozrozhdenie* (Vilnius), February 10, 1989.

12. Brazauskas, *Lietuviškos skyrybos,* pp. 49-56. He recounted that at one point Chebrikov "smashed his fist into the table in front of me and shouted that Lithuania will never be independent and will never leave the Soviet Union." Ibid., p. 54.

13. Interview of February 11, in *Interviu Lietuvos radijui,* pp. 19-20.

14. Brazauskas, *Lietuviškos skyrybos,* pp. 40-42; text of the Lithuanians' draft constitution, dated February 28, in *Perestroika in the Soviet Republics,* pp. 157-63.

15. *Pravda,* February 16, 1989.

16. Quoted by Ruta Grinevičiute in *Lietuvos rytas,* March 5, 1992. The account here of the meeting itself is based on documents in the archive of Sajudžioinfo. See

also the account published in *Sovetskaia Litva*, February 17, 1988.

17. On Klimaitis, see *Atgimimas* 2 and 7 (1989). In 1992 the Landsbergis administration imprisoned Klimaitis on suspicion of having served the KGB, but it never
brought him to trial. See Virginijus Gaivenis, "Istoriia shpionazha A. Klimaitisa: bez
prava byt' osuzhdennym," originally printed in *Respublika* and republished in *Golos
Litvy* 27-31 (1993).

18. LIC, press release, February 16, 1989. The official press in Vilnius emphasized
the government-sponsored demonstration in the capital rather than Sajudis's celebration in Kaunas. See *Komjaunimo tiesa* and *Tiesa*, February 17, 1989.

19. Interview of February 18, 1989, *Interviu Lietuvos radijui*, pp. 29-30.

20. Brazauskas, *Lietuviškos skyrybos*, p. 43.

21. Resolution in *Sovetskaia Litva*, February 26, 1989; see also Vladislav Shved's
demand for stronger action against Sajudis, in *Tiesa*, February 24, 1989. See *Pravda's*
concern, February 22, 1989, about the party's loss of grassroots control; also,
Sakalauskas's comments on the way he was being spoken to in Moscow at this time,
Tiesa, March 2, 1989. Edinstvo enthusiastically supported the decisions of the plenum
and even praised Brazauskas's talk. *Sovetskaia Litva*, March 17, 1989. Šepetys left office
with some resentment over his colleagues' failure to defend him against Moscow's
attacks. Interview with the author, June 29, 1993.

22. Brazauskas, *Interviu Lietuvos radijui*, pp. 32-33. Sajudis spokespersons were very
critical of his behavior and his explanations. LIC, press release, February 22, 1989.

23. *The New York Times*, March 4, 1989; *The Washington Post*, March 3, 1989; *The
Independent* (London), February 8, 1989. On the other hand, Juozaitis told a Voice of
American correspondent that the Sajudis Council recognized "that we cannot rely on
Brazauskas and save him at just any cost, that this would be impractical and undemo-
cratic."

24. Brazauskas, *Interviu Lietuvos radijui*, pp. 51-55. Brazauskas told a Lithuanian
reporter, "I am favorably impressed by how well the General Secretary is informed
about Lithuania—he even knows the names of a large number of people." *Literatura
ir menas*, March 25, 1989. At a CPSU plenum in the middle of March, Gorbachev lav-
ishly praised the accomplishments of Lithuanian agriculture. *Pravda*, March 18, 1989.

25. Steve Crawshaw, in *The Independent*, March 22, 1989.

26. FBIS media analysis, "Sajudis's election concession lowers tension in
Lithuania," March 22, 1989. Some commentators speculated that Gorbachev looked
on Brazauskas as possibly "a Lithuanian Shevardnadze."

27. In the words of Vytautas Radžvilas, "Sajudis had rightly expected a favorable
outcome of the election but its results have surpassed all its expectations.... The
Lithuanian Communist Party came to the elections handicapped by the legacy of the
period of stagnation and its moral responsibility in the eyes of the public for all the
mistakes and crimes committed in the past." *Savaitės žinios* 1 (1989): 2 (original in
English).

28. See *Komjaunimo tiesa*, March 30, 1989; *Sovetskaia Litva*, March 30, April 12,
1989; Brazauskas, *Interviu Lietuvos radijui*, p. 61. As Arvydas Juozaitis sarcastically
summarized Brazauskas's position, the party secretary "said he was sorry for good dear
Lithuania, which now will not be represented in Moscow by people who deserve it."
Savaitės žinios 2 (1989): 10.

29. See Radžvilas's comments in *Savaitės žinios* 1 (1989): 3.

30. *Musų žinios* (Taurage) 4 (March 30, 1989).

31. Interview in *Excelsior* (Mexico City), March 29, 1989.

32. LIC, press release, April 4, 1989.

33. See Ozolas's account of the meeting in *Atgimimas* 15 (1989); *Savaites žinios* 2 (1989).

34. See text in *Perestroika in the Soviet Republics*, pp. 163-64. These were the very thoughts that he had maneuvered to table in November 1988.

35. See Brazauskas, *Lietuviškos skyrybos*, pp. 53, 64.

36. On the question of the KGB's watching him, Brazauskas wrote, "I do not know when they began to follow me." *Lietuviškos skyrybos*, pp. 57-59.

37. *Savaitės žinios* 5 (1992): 7.

38. A. S. Cherniaev, *Shest' let s Gorbachevym* (Moscow: Progress-Kul'tura, 1993), pp. 297-298.

6. The Baltic Way

1. See *Pravda*, May 26, 1989. Quotations from the work of the congress can be found in *Pervyi s"ezd narodnykh deputatov SSSR. Stenograficheskii otchet* (Moscow: Verkhovnyi Sovet SSSR, 1989).

2. Brazauskas, *Lietuviškos skyrybos* (Vilnius: Politika, 1992), p. 62.

3. See Ozolas's interview in *Moskovskie novosti* 22 (1989); Brazauskas, *Lietuviškos skyrybos*, p. 120; interview with Kazimieras Motieka, reported in *Tiesa*, June 1, 1989. The Lithuanians met privately with Iakovlev on June 1. Brazauskas, *Interviu Lietuvos radijui* (Vilnius: LKP CK Leidykla, 1990), p. 93.

4. *Pervyi s"ezd Narodnykh Deputatov SSSR. Stenograficheskii otchet*, 1, p. 167. Landsbergis returned a little while later to say, "We regret that my earlier words were wrongly understood" (ibid., p. 174,) In an interview on Lithuanian radio that evening, Brazauskas dissociated himself from Landsbergis's "ultimatum."

5. Brazauskas's talk in *Tiesa*, June 2, 1989; Landsbergis's in Vytautas Landsbergis, *Atgave viltį* (n.p., n.d.), pp. 56-59; Prunskiene's in her *Leben für Litauen* (Berlin: Ullstein, 1992), pp. 226-232.

6. The Lithuanians had discussed the possibility of a walkout as a means of winning attention even before the opening of the congress. Cf. Algimantas Čekuolis's interview in *Vakarines naujienos*, May 23, 1989.

7. Prunskiene, *Leben für Litauen*, p. 192, Brazauskas, *Interviu Lietuvos radijui*, pp. 96-97. In May Gorbachev had told members of the Politburo, "think, think how actually to restructure our federation. Otherwise everything will indeed fall apart." A. S. Cherniaev, *Shest' let s Gorbachevym* (Moscow: Progress-Kul'tura, 1993), p. 295.

8. Tomkus's statement in *Komjaunimo tiesa*, May 28, 1989; Landsbergis's in *Komjaunimo tiesa*, June 9, 1989, and *Tiesa*, June 13, 1989.

9. See Lev Bezymenskii, "Tainy pakta. Kak rabotala komissiia Iakovleva," *Sovershenno sekretno* 12 (1991): 4-8.

10. See Prunskiene, *Leben für Litauen*, pp. 178, 183; Nikolai Medvedev's interview in *Tiesa*, June 1, 1989.

11. See Prunskiene, *Leben für Litauen*, p. 65; *Sovetskaia Litva*, June 1, 1989; Laurinkus's statement on Vilnius radio, June 28, 1989.

12. See Iakovlev's extensive interview in *Pravda*, August 18, 1989; Brazauskas's crit-

icism of the interview, in his *Interviu Lietuvos radijui*, pp. 127-128.

13. LIC, press release, July 29, 1989.

14. Vilnius radio to North America, July 1, 1989.

15. N. Mikhaleva in *Pravda*, July 12, 1989.

16. See *Krasnaia zvezda*, July 13 and 19, 1989; *Sovetskaia Litva*, August 10, 1989.

17. See Genzelis's account in *Tiesa*, April 25, 1992, and also Ozolas's "Partiia i per-estroika," *Soglasie* 7 (April 30, 1989); Brazauskas's interview of June 23 in *Interviu Lietuvos radijui*, pp. 110-111, also 116.

18. Ibid., p. 126; interview on Lithuanian radio, August 18, 1989.

19. Talk in Gotland, August 1989, reported in *Akiračiai* 9 (1989). Before the meeting Brazauskas announced that he had created a "council of advisors," some twenty-five persons, "even though this was not provided for in any documents." *Interviu Lietuvos radijui*, pp. 109-110.

20. Brazauskas told me of the Politburo's action in our interview, January 11, 1993; on his assurances of Gorbachev's understanding, see *Interviu Lietuvos radijui*, pp. 120-121.

21. Brazauskas, *Lietuviškos skyrybos*, p. 59.

22. Text in EIB 8 (1989). Paleckis explained himself in an interview in *Sovetskaia Rossiia*, September 6, 1989. When party conservatives attacked his action, he received support from both Brazauskas and Iakovlev. See *Diena* (Vilnius) and *Lietuvos rytas*, August 5, 1994, the fourth anniversary of the declaration.

23. Brazauskas, *Lietuviškos skyrybos*, p. 72.

24. Texts of both resolutions reprinted in *Perestroika in the Soviet Republics*, ed. Charles F. Furtado, Jr. and Andrea Chandler (Boulder, CO: Westview, 1992), pp. 165-169.

25. Rita Dapkus, at the Sajudzioinfo office in Chicago, sent the statement and the appeal to the United Nations on September 5, 1989. Sajudžioinfo archive.

26. The declaration was published in both *Pravda* and *Tiesa*, August 27, 1989. English text in *Perestroika in the Soviet Republics*, pp. 201-205.

27. Ligachev, *Zagadka Gorbacheva* (Novosibirsk: Interbuk, 1992), p. 243. See also Brazauskas's awkward defense of Baltrunas in *Interviu Lietuvos radijui*, pp. 140-141.

28. Moscow World Service, August 30, 1989.

29. See *Tiesa*, August 29, 1989; *Izvestiia*, August 31, 1989; *Sobytiia i vremia* 18 (1989); text of Supreme Council's resolution in *Perestroika in the Soviet Republics*, pp. 169-170.

30. Brazauskas had a chance to explain himself in *Pravda*, September 9, and *Izvestiia*, September 15, 1989.

31. On the speculation concerning Gorbachev's role, see Walter C. Clemens, Jr., *Baltic Independence and Russian Empire* (New York: St. Martin's Press, 1991), pp. 233-234.

32. See *Pravda*, September 2, 1989; *Sovetskaia Rossiia*, September 10, 1939.

33. Published in *Rodina* 5 (1992), reprinted in *Tiesa*, August 29. 1992.

34. See Brazauskas, *Lietuviškos skyrybos*, p. 51.

35. *Sovetskaia Litva*, September 6, 1989.

36. Arbatov spoke on Helsinki radio, August 28, 1989, FBIS, August 29, 1989, p. 23; see also Cherniaev, *Shest' let s Gorbachevym*, p. 297, and Brazauskas, *Lietuviškos skyrybos*, p. 51.

37. Interview on Lithuanian radio, September 15, 1989; Brazauskas, *Interviu Lietuvos radijui*, pp. 144-145.

38. *Materialy plenuma Tsentral'nogo Komiteta KPSS, 19-20 sentiabria 1989 goda*, pp. 212-235.

39. Ibid., pp. 99-103. During Brazauskas's talk there was absolute silence—no shouts, no applause. Brazauskas, *Interviu Lietuvos radijui*, pp. 147-148.

40. Brazauskas, *Interviu Lietuvos radijui*, pp. 151, 153.

41. *La Vanguardia* (Barcelona), September 3, 1989.

42. Memorandum by Lozoraitis, November 13, 1989, and émigré letters in Sajudžioinfo archive.

43. Brazauskas, *Lietuviškos skyrybos*, p. 65; *Interviu Lietuvos radijui*, pp. 190-196.

44. Text in *USSR Documents Annual. 1990: Restructuring Perestroika* (Gulf Breeze, FL: Academic International Press, 1991), pp. 256-257.

45. See stenogram of gathering, *Pravda, Izvestiia, Tiesa*, December 1-5, 1989.

46. Brazauskas, *Lietuviškos skyrybos*, p. 66.

7. At the Crossroads

1. See Michael R. Beschloss and Strobe Talbott, *At the Highest Levels* (Boston: Little, Brown and Company, 1993), p. 102; and Vernon Walters, in *The Washington Post*, November 21, 1989.

2. Ambassador Matlock presented his views in a paper at the annual conference of the American Association for the Advancement of Slavic Studies, Philadelphia, PA, November 19, 1994. See also Beschloss and Talbott, *At the Highest Levels*, pp. 52, 141-143, 163-164; A. S. Cherniaev, *Shest' let s Gorbachevym* (Moscow: Progress-Kul'tura, 1993), pp. 302-303.

3. See Šepetys's account of the parliamentary maneuvering necessary to win approval of the amendment, *Tiesa*, April 9, 1992; also Vytautas Tininis, *Sovietine Lietuva ir jos veikejai* (Vilnius: Enciklopedija, 1994), pp. 280-287.

4. See Brazauskas, *Lietuviškos skyrybos* (Vilnius: Politika, 1992), pp. 75-78; resolutions in *Lietuvos Komunistų Partijos XX Suvažiavimo dokumentai* (Vilnius: LKP CK, 1990); *Dokumenty XX s"ezda Kompartii Litvy* (Vilnius: LKP CC, 1990).

5. Soviet account in *Pravda*, April 21, 1990.

6. See *Sovetskaia Litva*, December 1, 1989; See Mykolas Burokevičius, *Lietuvos KP ideologinis darbas su inteligentija 1940-1965 m.* (Vilnius: Mintis, 1972), p. 89.

7. On Shved and the pro-Moscow forces, see *Komjaunimo tiesa*, September 13, 1989; also *The Los Angeles Times*, April 8, 1990.

8. Brazauskas, *Lietuviškos skyrybos*, p. 78.

9. See Lev Bezymenskii, "Tainy pakta. Kak rabotala komissiia Iakovleva," *Sovershenno sekretno* 12 (1991): 4-8; author's interview with Kazimieras Motieka, January 10, 1990. See also Nina Andreeva's comments in *Voenno-istoricheskii zhurnal* 6 (1990); *Edinstvo. Informatsionnyi biulleten* 6 (1990). Landsbergis's comments on the decision in Alfred Erich Senn, "Su Akiračių veliava. Įspudžiai iš Lietuvos," *Akiračiai* 3 (1990).

10. Description of the meeting based on "Vneocherednoi plenum TsK KPSS— 25-26 dekabria 1989 goda. Stenograficheskii otchet," *Izvestiia TsK KPSS* 6 (1990): 40-141.

11. See Cherniaev, *Shest' let s Gorbachevym*, pp. 321-322.

12. As he did in most discussions of Gorbachev's attitudes, Brazauskas characterized Gorbachev as sympathetic in these talks too. *Lietuviškos skyrybos*, p. 9.

13. See *Sovetskaia kultura*, 1990/3.

14. *Materialy plenuma tsentral'nogo komiteta KPSS. 5–7 fevralia 1990 g.* (Moscow: Politizdat, 1990), p. 299.

15. The description of Gorbachev's visit is based on my own observations. See my reports, "Gorbačiovas reklamuoja Lietuva" and "Su *Akiračių* veliava," in *Akiračiai* 2 and 3 (1990). A. S. Cherniaev called this trip to Lithuania "one of the most intellectually rich of his 'meetings with the country,'" *Shest' let s Gorbachevym*, p. 323.

16. Interview with the author, January 14, 1990.

17. Beschloss and Talbott, *At the Highest Levels*, p. 176.

18. Details of the debate taken from *Materialy plenuma tsentral'nogo komiteta KPSS. 5–7 fevralia 1990 g.* See also Ligachev, *Zagadka Gorbacheva* (Novosibirsk: Interbuk, 1992), pp. 221-223.

19. Speaking on Vilnius radio, February 9, Brazauskas said, "I had not expected such a hostile attitude, especially from those persons who visited us with Comrade Gorbachev, or from those who had come before him."

20. Author's interview with Justas Paleckis, June 22, 1993.

8. Reconstituting the Lithuanian State

1. See Brazauskas, *Lietuviškos skyrybos* (Vilnis: Politika, 1992), pp. 96-98. Brazauskas told *Der Spiegel*, January 29, 1990, "We do not think we are separatists. We only intend to implement perestroika within the party."

2. Brazauskas, *Lietuviškos skyrybos*, p. 99.

3. Soviet writers vied with each other in picturing the trouble that secession would bring Lithuania. One wrote, "A sudden separation of Lithuania will be like the separation of the parachutist from a plane, who only in the air remembers that he left his parachute in the cabin." B. Korolev, in *Sovetskaia Belorussia*, February 2, 1990.

4. See *The New York Times*, March 8, 1990.

5. See *Laikos ir įvykiai* 11 (1990); *Tiesa*, April 14, 1990; Saliomonas Vaintraubas's essay in *Lietuvos rytas*, March 12, 1990. After March 11, 1990, *Komjaunimo tiesa* changed its name to *Lietuvos rytas*, and *Sovetskaia Litva* became *Ekho Litvy*. *Tiesa* waited until July 1, 1994, to become *Diena*.

6. Prunskiene, *Leben für Litauen* (Berlin: Ullstein, 1992), p. 80.

7. On Čepaitis's organization of the Sajudis Deputies Club, see my interview with him in *Akiračiai* 10 (1990).

8. Quoted in Ruta Grinevičiute, "Kovo 11-oji: priešaušrio vizijos," *Lietuvos rytas*, March 6, 1992.

9. Michael Beschloss and Strobe Talbott, *At the Highest Levels* (Boston: Little, Brown and Company, 1993), p. 194.

10. Ruta Grinevičiute recounted the debates in her series, "Kovo 11-oji: priešaušrio vizijos," in *Lietuvos rytas*, March 5 to 11, 1992. Her account of the meeting with Matlock, which Vilnius radio reported on March 9, 1990, appeared on March 6, 1992. See also Romualdas Ozolas, *Pirmieji atkurtosios nepriklausomybes metai* (Vilnius: Valstybinis leidybos centras, 1992), pp. 6-7. I have discussed the American position

with several State Department officials, and Ambassador Matlock gave me his version of the meeting with Landsbergis and Ozolas on November 19, 1994.

11. Author's interview with Lozoraitis, Washington, D.C., May 27, 1992.

12. Printed in EIB 3 (1990): 5-6.

13. Ibid., p. 6.

14. See *Lithuanian Independence: The U.S. Government Response 1990–1991*, ed. Algirdas J. Silas (Chicago: Ethnic Community Services, 1991), p. 4.

15. See Vytautas Landsbergis, *Atgave vilti* (n.p., n.d.), p. 98; Grinevičiute in *Lietuvos rytas*, March 6, 1992.

16. A. Bendinskas, cited in *Gimtasis kraštas* 17 (1990).

17. See LRAT, *Stenogramos*, vol. 1.

18. *The Road to Negotiations with the U.S.S.R.*, 2d, revised ed. (Vilnius: State Publishing Center, 1991). p. 71.

19. See Abraham Brumberg's comments in *The Washington Post*, April 17, 1990.

20. Hedrick Smith, *The New Russians* (New York: Random House, 1990), p. 378; Anatol Lieven, *The Baltic Revolution* (New Haven, CT: Yale Univ. Press), pp. 230-239.

21. Iu. D. Masliukov told *Izvestiia*, March 10, 1990, "The government has not declared a boycott against anyone and does not intend to."

22. Landsbergis, *Atgavė viltij*, p. 83.

23. See Grinevičiute's account in *Lietuvos rytas*, March 10, 1992.

24. See *The New York Times*, March 13, 14, 21, 1990. Writing in *New Times* 42 (1990), Leonid Mlechin declared, "The first days and weeks after the declaration of Lithuanian independence were critical in the life of our country.... Who knows in what abyss the country would have found itself if the 'hawks' had secured an order to act."

25. *Vtoroi S"ezd Narodnykh Deputatov SSSR. Stenograficheskii otchet*, 6 vols. (Moscow: Verkhovnyi Sovet SSSR, 1990), 3: 129-177, 213-214; *The Road to Negotiations*, pp. 72-73.

26. *The New York Times*, March 16, credited Medvedev with a "brief eloquent defense." After declaring Lithuania's independence, the Supreme Council in Vilnius had recalled the Lithuanian deputies to the USSR Supreme Soviet, leaving only Medvedev as a representative of their interests. While in Moscow Medvedev worked with Yeltsin's camp. Interview with the author, June 28, 1993.

27. See *The Los Angeles Times* NewsFax, Moscow Edition, April 4, 1990; "Lithuania Alone," *Soviet Analyst*, April 25, 1990; the analysis of the secession law by Lowry Wyman in *Lithuanian Independence: The Re-establishment of the Rule of Law*, ed. S. Paul Zumbakis (Chicago: Lithuanian Independence Series, 1990), pp. 4-13, 127-133; also Helene Carrère d'Encausse's analysis of the law as both error and failure, in her *The End of the Soviet Empire* (New York: BasicBooks, 1993), pp. 211-216.

28. See A. S. Cherniaev, *Shest' let s Gorbachevym* (Moscow: Progress-Kul'tura, 1993), pp. 337-339.

29. See Beschloss and Talbott, *At the Highest Levels*, pp. 195-201; *Eastern Europe Newsletter*, April 2, 1990. Iazov favored arresting Landsbergis and Prunskiene; apparently frustrated, he wrote on his desk pad, "What is presidential rule!" *Literaturnaia gazeta*, July 15, 1992.

30. Igor Sedykh, Novosti press release, April 16, 1990.

31. I have assembled much of this account of events in Vilnius from materials in the

archive of Prof. Ellen Gordon, who was in Lithuania at this time.

32. See Hedrick Smith, *The New Russians*, pp. 362-367; Algirdas Kumža, "Vytautas Landsbergis," *Politika* 34 (1991): 60-61; Michael Dobbs's portrait of "Lithuania's Pedantic Revolutionary," *The Washington Post*, May 7, 1990. On Dr. Stockman, see Martha Brill Olcott, "The Lithuanian Crisis," *Foreign Affairs* (Summer 1990): 38, and Richard Nixon, *Seize the Moment* (New York: Simon and Schuster, 1992), pp. 58-59. Landsbergis's taste in political cartoons apparently ran toward seeing himself as St. George fighting the dragon.

33. As an example of the collective memory of Soviet rule that the Lithuanians shared, see Onute Garbštiene, *Hell in Ice* (Vilnius: Ethnos '91, 1992), a diary of exile life in Siberia, 1941-1957.

34. Vadim Bakatin, *Izbavlenie ot KGB* (Moscow: Novosti, 1992), p. 45. The groups also reinforced each other's reports. See Baltinas's report on the work of the Lithuanian KGB, *Sovetskaia Litva*, February 28, 1990. According to *Krasnaia zvezda*, March 4, 1990, the military had expected better living conditions in Lithuania; see also *Krasnaia zvezda*'s report of demonstrations in Lithuania, March 20, 1990. In *Pravda*, April 10, 1990, Shved declared that Lithuania was becoming "a neo-Stalinist society." Iakovlev told the Lithuanians that of all Gorbachev's sources of information on Lithuania, Burokevičius was the least reliable. Author's interview with Justas Paleckis, June 22, 1993.

35. *The Road to Negotiations*, pp. 83-85.

36. Egor Ligachev, *Zagadka Gorbacheva* (Novosibirsk: Interbuk, 1992), p. 98.

37. See Nikolai Medvedev's criticism of the action in *Pasaulis* 10 (1991): 3.

38. *Atmoda*, no. 13, September 2, 1990; documentation in the Gordon archive.

39. Cf. Bill Keller's report of Lithuania's isolation in his "For Lithuania, Few Allies in Moscow," *The New York Times*, March 27, 1990; Ann Cooper gave the same sort of report to NPR's "All Things Considered." See also Craig R. Whitney, "The News of Lithuania, but with Kremlin Spin," *The New York Times*, April 11, 1990.

40. Elizabeth Drew, "Letter from Washington," *The New Yorker*, May 14, 1990, pp. 96-99. Several U.S. government officials referred me to this article as an accurate picture of the agony of U.S. foreign policy at this point.

41. *Vremia*, April 11. Moscow radio, April 14 and 17, emphasized stories of refugees fleeing persecution in Lithuania.

42. *The Road to Negotiations*, pp. 97-98.

43. See his speech of April 23, 1990, in Vytautas Landsbergis, *Laisves byla* (Vilnius: Lietuvos aidas, 1992), pp. 75-76. Cf. Anatol Lieven's characterization of Landsbergis's penchant for referring to dark, unnameable forces, in his *Baltic Revolution*, p. 29.

9. The Blockade: Lessons and Costs

1. The Lithuanian government actually had two antiblockade commissions, one set up by the parliament, one by the government. Although members of the Sajudis majority in parliament criticized Brazauskas for not having a plan ready to meet a blockade, the parliamentary commission would seem to have done little itself. Brazauskas discussed the blockade with me on August 28, 1990.

2. Documentation of the economic crisis can be found in the Gordon archive. In an APN dispatch on April 24, Igor Sedykh reported that the economy was paralyzed and

that mass unemployment threatened the workforce, and yet the population was turning against Moscow and supporting independence.

3. Brazauskas, *Lietuviškos skyrybos* (Vilnius: Politika, 1992), p. 107.

4. Vytautas Landsbergis, *Laisves byla* (Vilnius: Lietuvos aidas, 1992), p. 48; Lithuanian press release, April 24, 1990.

5. For examples of the American debate, see: "The Bush Message to Vilnius: Talk," editorial in *The New York Times*, April 25, 1990; R. T. Davies, "Recognize Lithuania," *The Washington Post*, April 8, 1990; George P. Shultz, "What I'd Tell Mikhail Sergeyevich," *The Wall Street Journal*, April 9, 1990; Irving Kristol, "Bush is Right About Lithuania," *The Wall Street Journal*, April 11, 1990; Charles Krauthammer, "Why Lithuania is Not Like South Carolina, *Time*, April 16, 1990; Abraham Brumberg, "Lithuania—A Case for Compromise," *The Washington Post*, April 17, 1990; Victor Danilenko, "Vilnius: Its Own Worst Enemy," *The New York Times*, April 17, 1990; William Safire, "World to Vilnius: Suffer," *The New York Times*, April 23, 1990.

6. Ilia Baranikas, APN press release, April 27, 1990

7. Elizabeth Drew, "Letter from Washington," *The New Yorker*, May 14, 1990, pp. 94, 96.

8. Ibid., pp. 96-97; *Lithuanian Independence: The U.S. Government Response 1990–1991*, ed. Algirdas J. Silas (Chicago: Ethnic Community Services, 1991), pp. 2-3, 7; *The Washington Times*, March 29, 1990; *The Washington Post*, March 30, 1990.

9. Michael Dobbs, in *The Washington Post*, April 9, 1990, speculated that Shevardnadze was more ready to seek a negotiated solution while Gorbachev wanted the Lithuanians to surrender.

10. *Lithuanian Independence: The U.S. Government Response*, p. 4; Drew, "Letter from Washington," p. 97.

11. Drew, "Letter from Washington," p. 101.

12. *Lithuanian Independence: The U.S. Government Response*, p. 14.

13. See Michael Beschloss and Strobe Talbott, *At the Highest Levels* (Boston: Little, Brown and Company, 1993), p. 203; *The Washington Post*, April 24 and May 22, 1990.

14. Despite Safire's columns, *The New York Times*, in view of the op-ed pieces by Danilenko and Scheaffer (in January), would not seem to have deserved the criticism it received from the Soviets for having allegedly "encouraged" the Lithuanians. See *The New York Times*, March 28, 1990. In *The Los Angeles Times* of April 8, 1990, Esther Schrader criticized Lithuania's "amateur government" and complained that western journalists had "overhyped" the entire conflict.

15. *The Road to Negotiations with the U.S.S.R.*, 2d, revised ed. (Vilnius: State Publishing Center, 1991), p. 68; Landsbergis, *Laisves byla*, pp. 80-82; Beschloss and Talbott, *At the Highest Levels*, p. 206.

16. See Kazimiera Prunskiene, *Gintarines ledi išpažintis* (Vilnius: Politika, 1990), pp. 44-47; Beschloss and Talbott, *At the Highest Levels*, pp. 206-207.

17. See *The New York Times*, May 25, 1990; Aleksandr Iakovlev, *Muki prochteniia bytiia* (Moscow: Novosti, 1991), pp. 172, 237; Iakovlev's interview in *Moskovskii komsomolets*, April 27, 1990. The Lithuanians rejected calls for a referendum, on the one hand saying that the result would be obvious and on the other not wanting to create a precedent for similar calls against Latvia and Estonia, both of which had larger Russian majorities.

18. LRAT, *Stenogramos*, 8: 5-8. The text was drafted in Russian so that there would be no ambiguities in translation.

19. Kazimiera Prunskiene, *Leben für Litauen*, (Berlin: Ullstein, 1992), pp. 188-191. In January 1993, when I asked Mme. Prunskiene about her attitudes toward Gorbachev, she referred me specifically to this book. See also Beschloss and Talbott, *At the Highest Levels*, pp. 211-212.

20. Beschloss and Talbott, *At the Highest Levels*, pp. 219-230.

21. Report by Helen Somack in *The Independent*, June 2, 1990.

22. *Pravda*, July 11, 1992.

23. Egor Ligachev, *Zagadka Gorbacheva* (Novosibirsk: Interbuk, 1992), pp. 244-247.

24. Beschloss and Talbott, *At the Highest Levels*, p. 226; Hedrick Smith, *The New Russians* (New York: Random House, 1990), p. 412.

25. Prunskiene, *Gintarines ledi išpažintis*, p. 80.

26. For Prunskiene's view, see ibid., pp. 59-66.

27. The account of the role of the Sajudis Center Faction is based on a memorandum written at my request by Rimvydas Valatka, a member of the faction, in April 1991.

28. A British correspondent suggested, "The most plausible explanation is that the Soviet president, a master exponent of the art of divide and rule, has been playing games." Imre Karacs, in *The Independent*, June 28, 1990.

29. The debate is recorded in LRAT, *Stenogramos*, vol. 8.

30. *Izvestiia*, July 4, 1990.

10. Growing Frustration

1. Moscow World Service, July 7, 1990.

2. See Landsbergis's speech to the Lithuanian Supreme Council, July 10, 1990.

3. On Čepaitis's views at this time, see my interview with him, "Ar reikalinga Kovo 11-tos Partija? Pokalbis su Virgilijum Čepaičiu," *Akiračiai* 10 (1990): 5.

4. Memorandum by Rimvydas Valatka, April 1991; Landsbergis expressed his own negative view of the Center Faction's motives at a meeting of Sajudis leadership, July 25, 1990, at which I was present.

5. LRAT, *Stenogramos*, 11: 294.

6. Prunskiene's speech in parliament, July 5, 1990, ibid., 11: 295; public speech in Vilnius, July 26. 1990.

7. LRAT, *Stenogramos*, 11: 513.

8. Statement in Chicago to representatives of *Akiračiai*, May 18, 1991.

9. Ozolas made the statement on July 25, 1990, at the same meeting of the Sajudis leadership at which Landsbergis spoke.

10. *Lietuvos aidas*, August 7, 1990; declaration dated, July 31, 1990. The signer who recanted was Juozas Urbšys, independent Lithuania's foreign minister in 1939–1940; Justinas Marcinkevičius, a writer and another signer, announced that he was withdrawing from public life.

11. See Arvydas Juozaitis, "Ateities forumas: dar ne praeitis," *Respublika*, January 7, 1994; author's interview with Juozaitis, "Ko siekė 'kreipimasis'? Pokalbis su Arvydu Juozaičiu," *Akiračiai* 4 (1990): 4. See also Anatol Lieven, *The Baltic Revolution* (New Haven, CT: Yale Univ. Press, 1973), pp. 256 and 413.

12. Debates in LRAT, *Stenogramos,* vol. 14.

13. Three of the travelers— Čepaitis, Česlovas Stankevičius, and Valdemaras Katkus—came late to the meeting of July 25 mentioned above in notes 4 and 9, to report on their Moscow experiences.

14. *Pravda,* July 7, 1990. Iakovlev told the congress that the Baltics had taken "an irrational path" that "I categorically do not support." See *Current Soviet Policies XI: Documents from the 28th Congress of the Communist Party of the Soviet Union* (Columbus, OH: Current Digest of the Soviet Press, 1991), p. 62.

15. *Pravda,* July 15, 1990.

16. Ligachev, who himself left the Politburo at this time, saw this as marking the party's relinquishing of power. See Katrina Vanden Heuvel, "Comrade Ligachev tells his side," *The Nation,* December 2, 1991. This does not contradict the thought that Gorbachev was trying to control the party and undermine his opposition. It could also be argued that Gorbachev's restructuring of the Politburo pushed the CPSU toward becoming a federation of Union Communist Parties; this could be considered another step on the path blazed by the Lithuanians. Cf. Valery Legostaev's chapter entitled "The Congress of Destroyers," in his *Tekhnologiia izmeny* (Moscow: Paleia, 1993), pp. 162-184.

17. On Shenin, see *Sovetskaia kultura* 30 (1990); *Pravda,* July 31, 1990; his speech to the Twenty-first Congress of LCP/CPSU, as reported in *Vakarines naujienos,* October 1, 1990; also *Den'* 23 (1991). Soiuz, the strongest and best-organized group in the CPD, was formed in the late winter of 1990. One of its first moves had been to call for suspension of the Lithuanian declaration of independence, the dissolution of the Lithuanian parliament, and the introduction of presidential rule in the republic. See Elizabeth Teague, "The Soiuz Group," *Report on the USSR* 20 (1990): 16-21

18. See *Nezavisimaia gazeta,* January 29, 1991. Shenin gave interviews on Moscow radio and television, August 18 and 21, 1990.

19. See Burokevičius's warnings about "bourgeois totalitarianism" in *Pravitel'stvennyi vestnik* 37 (1990): 5.

20. *Nezavisimaia gazeta,* January 29, 1991. In an interview with *Pravda,* June 17, 1991, Shenin declared that the government must defend the interests of Communists.

21. See *Vakarines naujienos,* October 29, 1990; *Komsomol'skaia pravda,* February 8, 1991; *Pravda,* January 13, 1992. In an interview on January 11, 1993, Brazauskas told me that he had earlier requested Naudžiunas's transfer to Lithuania, and he insisted that Naudžiunas was not a major player in LCP/CPSU policies, but other people have assured me that he indeed was. See also Naudžiunas's interview in *Vakarines naujienos,* October 29, 1990.

22. See *Krasnaia zvezda,* March 20, 1990.

23. See Peter Gumbel's picture of the interplay of the pro-Moscow groups in *The Wall Street Journal,* January 17, 1991; also *Izvestiia CK* 3 (1991): 102; *Izvestiia,* October 2, 1991.

24. Gorbachev was now planning a new union treaty. Writing in *New Times* 42 (1990), Leonid Mlechin suggested that it was in Moscow's interest to drag out the talks because the Soviet government was itself not sure what it wanted to do.

25. Kazimiera Prunskiene, *Leben für Litauen* (Berlin: Ullstein, 1992), p. 191.

26. See *The Road to Negotiations,* 2d, revised ed. (Vilnius: State Publishing Center, 1991). pp. 160-163, 171-172, 182-183.

27. EIB 12 (1990): 14-15.

28. Egor Ligachev, *Zagadka Gorbacheva* (Novosibirsk: Interbuk, 1992), p. 247; Iazov's interview in Kermovo *Nasha gazeta*, January 1, 1991. Lithuanian nationalists had themselves provided material for propaganda attacks. On January 20, 1990, for example, the Sajudis Seimas had declared, "A large part of ethnic Lithuania's territory is outside the borders of the Lithuanian SSR." See Lithuanian Reform Movement Sajudis, *Lithuanian Way* 1 (Vilnius 1990): 79-80.

29. Romualdas Ozolas, *Pirmieji atkurtosios nepriklausomybes metai* (Vilnius: Valstybinis leidimo centras, 1992), p. 87. On the work of Lee Hamilton and David Obey, see their explanation, "Congress and the Baltics," *The Indianapolis Star,* December 12, 1990; A.M. Rosenthal's criticism of the action in *The New York Times,* November 6, 1990. Ironically, Soviet conservatives argued that the West was putting greater emphasis on "links with individual Soviet republics." See *Russia and the World. New Views on Russian Foreign Policy,* ed. Boris D. Pyadyshev (New York: Carol Publishing Co., 1991), p. 84.

30. See *Krasnaia zvezda*, November 18 and 27, 1990; *Komsomol'skaia Pravda*, November 20, 1990; *Literaturnaia Rossiia*, December 11, 1990; *Literaturnaia gazeta*, December 19, 1990; *Den'* 13 (1991); *The New York Times*, December 24, 1990; *Sovetskaia Rossiia*, October 1, 1989.

31. Bruce D. Slawter, "The Crisis in the Baltics and the Kremlin's Drift Toward Autocracy," *Strategic Review* 2 (Spring 1991): 71, 73-74.

32. Gorbachev's apologists have pictured his political shifting as a tactical maneuver: "That's why he made a very dangerous political move and took position right of the centre in order to keep the grip on the country at the difficult historical turning point." *New Times* 12 (1992): 19. For an account of Pugo's early career, see Sergei Zamascikov, "The Ascent of Boriss Pugo or Voss's Long Road to Moscow," *Baltic Forum* 1 (1984): 67-73.

33. *The Washington Post*, December 15, 1990.

34. Landsbergis explained the action, taken at his initiative, as an effort to move the talks off their "point of stagnation" and to make clear whether the Soviet government wanted to negotiate at all. LRAT, *Stenogramos*, 23: 58.

35. EIB 1 (1991): 9; circular to Lithuanian-American Community signed by Asta Banionis and Tomas Remeikis, December 18, 1990; U.S. government briefing for Baltic-American leaders, December 1990. An editorial in *The New York Times* of December 10 once again endorsed the principle of dialogue.

36. See *The New York Times*, December 20 and 24, 1990; *Newsweek*, January 14, 1991.

37. Speech reprinted in *The New York Times*, December 21, 1990. See also his interesting comments in an interview published in *Russia and the World*, pp. x-xi.

38. Moscow radio, December 20, 1990.

11. The January Events

1. I was in Vilnius from January 9 to 16; see my account, *Crisis in Lithuania, January 1991* (Chicago: Akiračiai, 1991).

2. One of Gorbachev's advisors later insisted that Gorbachev was deceived by it. See Vitalii Ignatenko's account in *New Times* 12 (1992): 20.

3. See *Izvestiia*, October 1, 1991.

4. Many western commentators seem to accept the argument that Prunskiene did not have to resign but chose to do so for as yet obscure reasons. Viz. Anatol Lieven, *The Baltic Revolution* (New Haven: Yale Univ. Press, 1993), p. 247: "...Prunskiene may not have been averse to provoking a crisis." Such arguments, however, ignore the action of the parliament in changing the constitution, thereby virtually guaranteeing the vote of no confidence that the Right had been yearning for since the summer of 1990.

5. Viz. the newsreporting on *Vremia* during the week. In Vilnius on Sunday, January 13, I spoke with a foreign diplomat who wondered why all this violence had ensued over a price hike. See also Brazauskas's explanation of the government's price policy in his *Lietuviškos skyrybos* (Vilnius: Politika, 1992), pp. 110-112. Latvia and Estonia also raised prices about this time but without the internal turmoil that the Lithuanians experienced.

6. See Leonid Mlechin, "Sud'ba Gorbacheva byla reshena v Vil'niuse," *Novoe vremia* 5 (1992): 17-19. Burokevičius later declared that this three-hour meeting did not discuss Lithuania at all, but his insistence that the "Gorbachevites" organized the January days and that Landsbergis provoked the crisis has no documentary base whatsoever. See his interview, "As dar sugrišiu Lietuvon..." *Lietuvos rytas*, May 3, 1993; also his letter to *Pravda*, July 9, 1992.

7. *Izvestiia*, October 18, 1991. Achalov had also been responsible for troop movements in Lithuania in March 1990.

8. Grachev, who was in Central Asia from January 3 to 8, later claimed not to know what his paratroopers were doing in Vilnius. *Izvestiia*, October 15, 1991.

9. Marcinkus later claimed that Moscow had communicated more with his deputy Tsaplin than with him. Interview in *Lietuvos rytas*, August 18, 1992. Cf. Tsaplin's insistence that he should not be considered a "Lithuanian Pinochet" and that he knew nothing about military action. *Izvestiia*, October 18, 1991. Tsaplin, however, confirmed that the LCP/CPSU was dissatisfied with the work of the Lithuanian KGB. During the violence, I noticed that the KGB building in the center of Vilnius was dark; the action seemed to be elsewhere, probably centered in Šiaures miestelis, the large Soviet military base in the center of the city.

10. Iazov's notes to himself, "Everything will be ready by 17:00 hours" and "A large rally—at 16.00 hours!" may well have referred to the events of this day. See *Literaturnaia gazeta*, July 15, 1992.

11. I was in the Press House about an hour before the attack; the defenders were expecting Russian workers, not Soviet tanks. Fire hoses, unfurled through the lobby of the building, were their only weapons.

12. *Izvestiia*, October 1, 1991. On the "creation" of the CSL, see the interview with Oktiabris Burdenka, *Respublika*, January 16, 1991.

13. Gorbachev was reportedly surprised by the support shown for Lithuania by other republican representatives in the council. See *The Christian Science Monitor*, January 14, 1991.

14. *Atgimimas* 11 (1992).

15. See *Izvestiia*, October 1, 1991; *Gimtasis kraštas* 14 (1991).

16. On military details, see *Izvestiia*, October 1, 1991.

17. The text of the parliamentary debate appears in LRAT, *Stenogramos*, vol. 24. On January 19 in Bonn, Germany, Saudargas told me that he had taken no steps to form

a government-in-exile because the government in Vilnius was still functioning.

18. See Michael Beschloss and Strobe Talbott, *At the Highest Levels* (Boston: Little, Brown and Company, 1993), p. 387.

19. *Literaturnaia gazeta*, July 15, 1992.

20. Boris Piliatskin, "Zagovor protiv Litvy," *Izvestiia*, October 4, 1991.

21. "The Evil Empire Strikes Back," *Soviet Analyst*, January 23, 1991.

22. See *Izvestiia*, October 1, 1991. See also Uskhopchik's earlier interview in *Sovetskaia kultura*, September 1, 1990. Pugo and Varennikov publicly supported him; see *Moscow News* 4 (1991). Two years later, Egidijus Bičkauskas, who in 1991 was the Lithuanian representative in Moscow, stated that during the night of January 13-14 one of Iazov's aides had insisted "The Minister knows everything" and had refused to call him to the phone to talk with Bičkauskas. *Lietuvos rytas*, January 13, 1993.

23. The speaker was probably Evgeny Trofimov. See *Literaturnaia gazeta*, July 14, 1992.

24. Interview, *Lietuvos rytas*, July 25, 1991.

25. *Izvestiia*, October 15, 1991.

26. *Rossiiskaia gazeta*, July 11, 1992. As one KGB officer later described the experience, "...if the authorities had to oppose nationalism and centrifugal forces, they should not have done so as ineptly as in Vilnius in January 1991, when, in addition, there was no one willing to assume responsibility for the mess." Interview with V. M. Kozhemiakin, *Nezavisimaia gazeta*, December 11, 1993. Achalov, on the other hand, was one of the defenders of the parliament against Yeltsin's attacks in September and October 1993.

27. Press conference, February 6, 1991.

28. See Ignatenko's account in *New Times* 12 (1992): 19-22. Cf. David Remnick, *Lenin's Tomb: The Last Days of the Soviet Empire* (New York: Vintage, 1994), p. 395: "Later, when I asked Gorbachev's former economic adviser, Nikolai Petrakov, whether Gorbachev truly 'slept through' the Vilnius events in ignorance, he said, simply, 'Don't be naive'." See also A. S. Cherniaev's bitter picture of Gorbachev's behavior in his *Shest' let s Gorbachevym* (Moscow: Progress-Kul'tura, 1993), pp. 405-419.

29. See "Pažyma," *Opozicija* 3 (1994), which was said to be an unedited transcript from an audio tape recording of a conversation with the chief of USSR military intelligence in Lithuania, January 18, 1991; also: Egor Ligachev, *Zagadka Gorbacheva* (Novosibirsk: Interbuk, 1992), p. 149: Valerii Legostaev, *Tekhnologiia izmeny* (Moscow: Paleia, 1993), passim; Valentin Varennikov's comments from prison, in *Den'* 28 (1001). When a Russian court dismissed charges against him for having participated in the August Putsch, *The Washington Post* of August 12, 1994, wrote, "In January 1991 Varennikov led the Soviet forces that put down nationalist protests in Vilnius." Varennikov himself denied having played any part in the January events; see *Respublika*, August 19, 1994.

30. See Cherniaev, *Shest' let s Gorbachevym*, pp. 416-417. In a conversation on November 19, 1994, Ambassador Matlock confirmed Cherniaev's account of the conversation, adding only that Gorbachev began his explanation by saying that the Soviet Union was "on the brink of civil war." Matlock said of his own statement that he "feared" that he may have overstepped normal "diplomatic bounds" in confronting Gorbachev.

31. Interview published in *Literaturnaia gazeta*, July 8, 1992.

32. See *Moscow News* 6 (1991); Petkevičius quoted in *Lietuvos rytas*, April 5, 1991.

33. *The New York Times*, April 15, 1991.

34. See *Moscow News* 3 (1991); *Komsomol'skaia pravda*, January 31, 1991. On the reactions in Moscow to the news from Vilnius, see also Remnick, *Lenin's Tomb*, pp. 387-394, and Cherniaev, *Shest' let s Gorbachevym*, pp. 405-407.

35. *Lithuanian Independence: The U.S. Government Response*, ed. Algirdas J. Silas (Chicago: Ethnic Community Services, 1991), pp. 21-22.

12. The Road to Ruin

1. Press conference, January 22, 1991. On the proposal that Gorbachev go to Lithuania, see *New Times* 12 (1992): 22; A. S. Cherniaev, *Shest' let s Gorbachevym* (Moscow: Progress-Kul'tura, 1993), p. 407.

2. Aleksandr Iakovlev, *Muki prochteniia bytiia* (Moscow: Novosti, 1991), p. 349.

3. See *The New York Times*, January 16 and 26, 1991.

4. See the critical accounts of Gorbachev's behavior in the spring and summer of 1991, from different points on the political spectrum, in Boris Yeltsin, *The Struggle for Russia* (New York: New York Times Books, 1994), and Valery Boldin, *Ten Years that Shook the World* (New York: BasicBooks, 1994); Čekuolis's comments in *Pasaulis* 8 (1991): 5.

5. See Leon Aron, "Moscow Diary: January 12–17, 1991," *Global Affairs* 2 (6): 44-61. A week later, however, Yeltsin failed in an effort to persuade the Russian parliament to condemn the action in Lithuania. Andrei Kozyrev, later Russia's foreign minister, declared that Soviet leaders cannot use "force to hold together the 'Unbreakable Union.'" *Russia and the World*, ed. Boris D. Pyadyshev (New York: Carol Publishing Co., 1991), pp. 318-319.

6. The Lithuanian results in *Lietuvos aidas*, February 12 and 14, 1991. The Lithuanian vote was originally called a "poll" (*apklausa*); Landsbergis then referred to it as a "plebiscite" (*Lietuvos aidas*, February 12, 1991); and thereafter the Lithuanians regularly used the term "referendum." At any rate, the referenda quickly faded into the debris of Gorbachev's abandoned programs and proposals. See also *Referendum in the Soviet Union. A Compendium of Reports on the March 17, 1991, Referendum on the Future of the USSR* (Washington: Commission on Security and Cooperation in Europe, April 1991).

7. Cf. Yuri Prokofiev's statement reported in *Izvestiia*, February 25, 1991.

8. Shenin interview in *Pravda*, February 19, 1991; see also *Literaturnaia gazeta*, July 15, 1992.

9. The party printed 40,000 copies of its Russian newspaper, *Litva Sovetskaia*, and 18,000 of its Lithuanian newspaper, *Tarybu Lietuva*. In July 1991, *Tiesa*, the newspaper of the independent LCP, appeared in just over 100,000 copies.

10. See *Litva Sovetskaia*, June 14, 1991. For other statements by the LCP/CPSU, see *Podborka documentov otpechatannykh v gazete "Litva Sovetskaia" v ianvare 1991g.* (Vilnius: Info, 1991).

11. See interview, *Litva Sovetskaia*, July 10, 1991.

12. Ibid., June 7, 1991.

13. See Vedas Rechlavičius's study of the intrigue in the LCP/CPSU, in *Lietuvos rytas*, June 13, 1991, and Burokevičius's interview in *Rakurs* (Tomsk), reprinted in *Lietuvos aidas*, June 28, 1991. The party's response in *Litva Sovetskaia*, June 30, 1991.

14. Text in *Tarybu Lietuva*, June 12, 1991. Anatol Lieven, *The Baltic Revolution* (New Haven, CT: Yale Univ. Press), p. 202, called this report "one of the most disgraceful single episodes of Gorbachev's presidency."

15. See FBIS, 1991, no. 109, pp. 11-13. Some future psychological study of Gorbachev should consider his penchant for referring to himself in the third person as well as his practice of addressing the people with whom he had to deal as "ty," the familiar form of "you" in Russian. On the power struggle in Moscow, see Dawn Mann, "The Circumstances Surrounding the Conservative Putsch," *Report on the USSR* 36 (1991): 1-5.

16. See the account of the posts' work by Tomas Šernas, the lone survivor of the massacre at Medininkai, in *Lietuvos rytas*, July 30, 1994.

17. *Pravda*, July 29, 1991.

18. Landsbergis in *Pasaulis* 10 (1991): 6; Prunskiene in *Pasaulis* 15-16 (1991): 18; Brazauskas in *Pasaulis* 13-14 (1991): 2-6; Čepaitis in *Ekho Litvy*, June 12, 1991.

19. Bush's statement in *The New York Times*, May 9, 1991; Landsbergis's in *Laisves byla*, (Vilnius: pp. 231, 239; Prunskiene's in *Pasaulis* 15-16 (1991): 17, 19.

20. Nevertheless Nikolai Mitkin argued that the problem of party unity was the key to the future of the Soviet system, and he attacked Iakovlev as a "neoliquidator." *Litva Sovetskaia*, August 11, 1991.

21. Igor Sedych, in *Respublika*, July 31, 1991.

22. P. Čiulinas, in *Litva Sovetskaia*, August 11, 1991.

23. *The New York Times*, August 2, 1991. In a presentation to the annual meeting of the American Association for the Advancement of Slavic Studies, on November 19, 1994, U.S. ambassador Jack Matlock argued that except for "two unfortunate sentences," Bush had actually paid considerable tribute to Ukrainian national feeling. For a Soviet version of what Bush said in private, see Cherniaev, *Shest' let s Gorbachevym*, p. 463. There were also Russians who thought the state might be better off if Gorbachev just let Lithuania go. Cf. L. V. Chebarshin, *Iz zhizni nachal'nika razvedki* (Moscow: Mezhdunarodnye otnosheniia, 1994), p. 118.

24. *Respublika*, August 20, 1991.

25. See Saulius Girnius, "Dismantling Soviet Armed Detachments in Lithuania," *Report on the USSR*, October 11, 1991, p. 30-31.

26. See *Pravda*, November 13, 1991, and July 9, 1992.

27. *Washington Times*, September 4, 1991. Iceland had actually recognized Lithuania in February.

28. *The European*, August 23-29, 1991; *Forbes*, June 8, 1992.

29. See Nikolai Ryzhkov, *Perestroika: Istoriia predatel'stv* (Moscow: Novosti, 1992), pp. 208-210.

30. Saulius Šaltenis, in a conversations with Romas Sakadolskis of the Voice of America, *Lietuvos aidas*, July 19, 1994.

31. See, for example, Phillip Bonosky, "Nurturing Baltic Reaction," *Covert Action Information Bulletin* 35 (Fall 1990): 17-20; Bonosky, *Devils in Amber* (New York: International Publishers, 1992); Valerii Legostaev, *Tekhnologiia izmeny* (Moscow: Paleia, 1993); Kriuchkov's speech to the USSR Supreme Soviet in the summer of 1991, published in *Den'* 27 (1991). For the fanciful image of a Great Power summit in Malta that divided up Eastern Europe, see the editorial by Arminas Norkus, "Kakta i NATO duris," *Lietuvos aidas*, February 1, 1994.

32. Kazimiera Prunskiene, *Leben für Litauen* (Berlin: Ullstein, 1992), pp. 191-193.

INDEX